Model Aircraft Precision Aerobatics

A Guide for Beginners and Improvers

By Peter J Jenkins

Second Edition

Edition 2 - Published – January 2022

Edition 1 - First Published – April 2021

Text copyright © 2022 Peter J Jenkins

All rights reserved

Table of Contents

Preface 9

Chapter 1.   Introduction 11

Chapter 2.   Aerobatics For Beginners 15

    Starting Off 15

    Basic Trimming and Setup 15

    Pitch, Roll and Yaw 19

    Starting Aerobatic Manoeuvres 20

        The Line 20

        Flying a Loop 20

        Flying a Roll 21

    Some Guidance on How to Improve 22

        Half Loop Half Roll – The Immelmann Turn 22

        Half Roll Half Loop - Split S 23

    What Next? 24

Chapter 3.   Some Basic Concepts 25

    Introduction 25

    The Aerobatic Box 26

    Flying the Line 27

    Flying Manoeuvres 28

    Plan your Flight 31

    Some Current Aerobatic Conventions 32

    The Effect of Gravity 33

    Airspeed and Groundspeed 35

    Correcting for the Wind 35

        Effect of Headwind 36

        Effect of a Crosswind 37

    The Effect of the Wind Gradient 39

The Canalyser 40

Chapter 4. Setup and Trimming 43

Introduction 43

Servo Setup 44

Servo Centring 45

Control Throws 45

Hinges 45

Initial Setting of Centre of Gravity (CG). 46

One Change at a Time 46

Trimming for Straight and Level Flight and Fine Trimming the CG 46

Engine/Motor Thrust Line 50

Lateral Balance 50

Vertical Downline 51

Vertical Upline 52

Wing Incidence 52

Geometric Accuracy 53

Knife Edge Trimming 53

Aileron Differential 53

Good to go? 54

Chapter 5. The Basics Of Aerobatic Manoeuvres 55

Introduction 55

Top, Bottom and Middle Lines 56

Loops 57

Use of the Throttle 64

Use of Rudder 66

You Need to Use All the Controls – (almost all the time) 67

Rolls 67

    Normal Roll 67

    Slow Roll 71

    Point Roll 71

    Rolls in Opposite Directions 71

    Flick or Snap Roll 71

    Effect of Crosswind on a Roll 72

Stall Turn (aka Hammerhead) 72

Stalling 75

Spinning 76

The Issue of Weathercocking 78

Inverted flying 79

Hand held or Tray mounted Transmitter 81

Transmitter Functions 82

Chapter 6. Some Practice Routines 85

Introduction 85

Flying a Rectangular Circuit 85

Flying the Line 86

Inverted Flying 86

1st Mini Schedule 87

2nd Mini Schedule 88

3rd Mini Schedule 89

4th Mini Schedule 90

5th Mini-Schedule 91

6th Mini Schedule 91

Building up to your First Full Schedule 93

Chapter 7. Flying the Clubman Schedule 95

C-01 Racetrack Take Off Sequence (K=1) 97

C-02 Inside Loop (K = 2) 98

C-03 Half Reverse Cuban Eight (K=2) 99

C-04 Slow Roll (K=3) 101

C-0-5 Half Cuban Eight (K=2) 103

C-06 Immelmann Turn, Split S Combination (K = 3) 104

C-07 Humpty Bump (Pull, Half Roll, Pull, Pull) (K = 2) 107

C-08 Half Roll, Inverted Flight, Half Roll (K = 2) 110

C-09 Stall Turn (K = 3) 111

C-10 Half Roll, Outside Loop, Half Roll (K = 3) 112

C-11 Humpty Bump – (Pull, Pull, Half Roll, Pull) 114

C-12 Cuban Eight – With Half Roll, Half Roll 115

C-13 Half Square Loop, Half Roll on Upline 117

C-14 Three Turn Spin 119

C-15 Racetrack Landing sequence 120

The role of the Caller 122

Judging 123

Chapter 8.   How to Start Flying in Competitions 125

Introduction to Aerobatics Events 125

New Pilot Open Days (NPOD) 125

What to Expect at Your First Competition 127

Chapter 9.   Aerobatic Aircraft Characteristics 129

What Sort of Model Makes a Good Aerobatic Steed? 129

Specific Design Features of F3A Aerobatic Models 130

Examples of Aerobatic Airframes 131

IC or Electric Power 136

Advice on Purchasing F3A Equipment 136

Chapter 10.   Conclusions 139

Annex A.   More details on Setup and Trimming 141

Introduction 141

Servo Setup 141

- Twin Servo Setup 143
- Servo Centring 144
- Control Throws 144
- Hinges 146
- Condition Switches 147
- Trimming for Straight and Level Flight and Fine Trimming the CG 148
- Other Trimming Methods 149
  - "Zero Gravity" Trimming 149
  - Triangulation Trimming 150

Annex B. Some Aerodynamic issues 152
- Canalyser 152
- Monoplane vs Biplane 152
- The Issue of Weathercocking 153

Annex C. Explanation of Aresti Symbols 155

Annex D. Mini Schedule Calling Cards 157
- 1st Mini Schedule 157
- 2nd Mini Schedule 157
- 3rd Mini Schedule 158
- 4th Mini Schedule 158
- 5th Mini Schedule 159
- 6th Mini Schedule 159

Annex E. GBRCAA Intermediate Schedule 161
- Introduction 161
- I-01 Racetrack Take-off Sequence (K=1) 162
- I-02 Triangular Loop (Base at the bottom) (K=3) 163
- I-03 Stall Turn, Full Roll Up (K=3) 165
- I-04 Four Point Roll (K=3) 166
- I-05 Immelmann Turn with Half Roll (K=2) 168

I-06 Square Loop with 1⁄2 Rolls in Legs 1 and 3 (K=4) 169

I-07 Split S Full Roll, Exit Inverted (K=2) 170

I-08 Cuban Eight with Half Rolls, Exit Inverted (K=3) 171

I-09 Humpty Bump Push, Pull, Pull (K=2) 173

I-10 Figure S (K=4) 174

I-11 Figure 6, Half Roll Down (K=3) 175

I-12 Knife Edge, Exit Inverted (K=4) 176

I-13 Half Outside Loop (K=1) 177

I-14 Three Turn Spin (K=4) 178

I-15 Racetrack Landing Sequence (K=1) 180

Index **183**

PREFACE

This book covers a range of topics all designed to help the newcomer to Precision Aerobatics to understand how they can get started and improve. This is the book I would have loved to have had when I first started trying to fly Precision Aerobatics. So, this book is based on my own experience of teaching myself through analysing the aircraft's behaviour and also what I gained by entering competition aerobatics and getting help from more experienced pilots. The more "technical" areas of the explanation are based on my background in aeronautical engineering.

I have also drawn on feedback from the many taster events I have run to introduce newcomers to flying aerobatics using the GBRCAA[1] Clubman Schedule. Many of these pilots expressed some concern before the event but to a man, and woman (yes, it is a sport in which there is equality), feedback at the end of the day was of bubbling enthusiasm. That is not to say they all went on to fly in full competition but a good many did and still do. What's clear is that ordinary Club pilots can take up precision aerobatics and improve sufficiently to compete in national competitions particularly given the support within the GBRCAA community.

I had always wanted to progress to flying "proper" aerobatics but time pressures had meant that my flying was limited to a relatively few occasions during the year. It wasn't until I retired that I was able to devote the time required to improve my flying. As I fly in the UK, my first step was to take my BMFA[2] B Certificate test as this is a good route into flying aerobatics. The BMFA B provides a good grounding for aspiring aerobatic pilots and, at the time, was a requirement for flying in competition.

Just after gaining my BMFA B Certificate, I was enticed by an advert for a "competition" for pilots who had not flown in competition. This introduced me to the concept that most of the time in competition you are competing against yourself to see if you can improve your scores from the last flight or last competition. Of course, it's always nice to win as well! Suffice to say that I ended up 7th out of 10 contestants and was bitten by the precision aerobatics bug, or to give it the FAI[3] classification, "F3A" bug. I was flying a Wot 4 (see cover photo), a typically rugged sports model with aerobatic capabilities but not something that can be described as a pure aerobatic aircraft! Properly trimmed though, airframes like Wot 4s are an excellent and cheap way into precision aerobatics.

This beginners' competition was flown alongside an FAI World Cup event with some of Europe's top F3A pilots flying. This was the first occasion that I had seen a proper F3A model and electrically powered ones as well! I was

---

[1] Great Britain Radio Control Aerobatic Association – a specialist body of the BMFA responsible for selecting the GB team for international competitions
[2] British Model Flying Association – the largest model flying body in GB and recognised by the FAI for conducting selecting British model flying teams to compete in international competitions.
[3] Fédération Aéronautique Internationale – World governing body for Air Sports

in awe of the flying ability of these top pilots. Their performance just blew me away and helped to nurture the F3A bug. But where could I find a book or article to help me in my journey?

In the end, the only useful book I could find that was still available was on full size aerobatics – called "Aerobatics" by the late Neil Williams. Much of what Neil Williams has written is applicable to model aerobatics but not all. That was what prompted me to write this book and give those interested in taking up aerobatics useful guidance and explanations of the art of model aircraft aerobatics.

By the way, don't be put off by the age thing. I entered my first proper aerobatic competition when I was almost 61!

Finally, I'd like to thank Al Williams, Mike Rieder, Jim Smetherham and Kevin Caton for reading through the manuscript, suggesting better ways of presenting the information and picking up errors of omission and commission. Their input has helped me to see the wood from the trees when trying to present the information in a logical and understandable way. As ever, there are many ways of dealing with such a wide subject so it is entirely up to me to have interpreted their input to arrive at what I hope will be an interesting and informative publication.

Preface to Edition 2

I have made some changes in this Edition that have been suggested by reviewers and readers. The major ones are:

- The GBRCAA Clubman Schedule was completely restructured for 2022 onwards and increased the number of manoeuvres so I have re-written Chapter 7, Flying the Clubman Schedule.

- As a result of the new Clubman Schedule, I have re-written Chapter 6, Some Practice Routines.

- I have added a new Annex D that contains Calling Cards for the six Mini Schedules in Chapter 6.

- The FAI published the next edition of their Sporting Code for F3A and there have been a number of changes. The most important is the replacement of judging the "Smoothness and Gracefulness of the Manoeuvre" by "Constant Flying Speed".

- In the UK, the GBRCAA Intermediate Schedule is sometimes used as the entry level schedule by pilots who have some experience in aerobatics gained outside the Association. Consequently, I have decided to include a description of how to fly the Intermediate Schedule in Annex E to help these pilots.

I would also like to thank Andrew Palmer, Chris Meynell, Professor Ian Poll, Alan Williams and Mike Rieder (as well as from a number of readers) for their feedback on the text for both Edition 1 and Edition 2. I have taken these forward where I think incorporating them would help to improve the book.

CHAPTER 1. INTRODUCTION

1. I hope that this book encourages you to dip your toe into the fascinating world of precision aerobatics whether you wish to compete or just to fly the manoeuvres for your own satisfaction. Whilst it may look daunting at first, I've approached the topic in a logical way and presented it in bite size chunks. The chapter that follows is intended for pilots who have recently got their BMFA A Certificate, essentially demonstrating their ability to fly safely and legally. You can, of course, cut straight to the chapters that describe flying the manoeuvres but I cannot stress enough the importance of setting up and trimming your aircraft to extract its best capabilities and make it easier to fly. The aim is to fly manoeuvres not just the aircraft!

2. Aerobatics in the model flying world is generally divided into three disciplines: precision aerobatics/pattern flying (F3A in the FAI[4] designation), IMAC (scale aerobatics) and 3D flying. When I searched the web for information on aerobatics, most of the information was on how to fly 3D with little on precision or pattern flying.

3. The International Model Aerobatic Club[5] (IMAC) that runs competitions that include both precision and 3D or a combination of the two as free style. IMAC requires the use of scale aerobatic aircraft whereas F3A flying does not. IMAC is a separate organisation from the FAI.

4. The lack of an available and up-to-date "How to Fly F3A" book was what triggered me to write this book. The topics I cover are:

- Getting started if you are a beginner to precision aerobatics

- Some basic concepts in aerobatics including the effect of gravity and wind

- Setting up and trimming the aircraft

- Flying the basic aerobatic manoeuvres

- Some practice routines for beginners

- Flying the GBRCAA Clubman Schedule

- How to start flying in competitions

---

[4] International Aeronautical Federation (FAI) Aeromodelling Commission https://www.fai.org/commission/ciam
[5] International Miniature Aerobatic Club (IMAC UK) https://imacuk.org/

- Aerobatic aircraft characteristics

- In the Annexes, I cover:

  - More detail on Trimming

  - More detail on some Aerodynamic Issues

  - A description of the Aresti notation for aerobatics

  - Six Mini Schedule Calling Card

  - The GBRCAA Intermediate Schedule

5. So, what is precision or pattern or F3A aerobatics? Well, it's been described as aerial ballet by some and figure skating by others! Essentially though, it is flying manoeuvres whose shapes are precisely defined and need to be flown with accuracy, constant speed, positioning and size. Size in this context is a consistent size between different manoeuvres that uses the Aerobatic Box[6] (the 3-dimensional space you have to fly within when performing aerobatics) to best advantage and so gains higher points than manoeuvres of varying size. While judging rules are Objective, their application tends to be Subjective. Constant speed in this context is within the manoeuvre being flown and is subjective, of course, and in that respect, there is some similarity with figure skating where the same basics apply and where the performance is judged subjectively as well.

6. In this book, I am catering for the complete beginner to aerobatics e.g., a pilot who has recently gone solo, as well as the pilot who has a lot of experience of flying model aeroplanes and aerobatics but not necessarily precision aerobatics. As such, the early chapters for the newcomers and the later ones for more experienced pilots. Topics get covered at basic level and then in increasing detail and complexity. The idea is to give you some basic settings to get you going with a limited range of manoeuvres. Then, as you decide you want to get into aerobatics a bit more, you move up to a more capable aircraft and this will need some more complex setting up so I provide more detail for that. The most detail is found in the Annexes although you may find some information is repeated for consistency.

7. Work through this book and, as your flying improves, **keep coming back to it to research more elements of flying**. You will find you get far more enjoyment out of flying and you will increase the chance of taking your pride and joy home at the end of every session. Sometimes, even a 5-year-old hard used specialist F3A airframe

---

[6] See Chapter 2 for a fuller description of the Aerobatic Box and a diagram.

can look like new! You may also find that your club mates sit up and take notice when you fly and will come and ask you for your help on how to get their aircraft to perform better and how they can improve their flying.

8. In Great Britain, the vast majority of model flyers belong to the British Model Flying Association[7] (BMFA). The BMFA has a number of specialist bodies responsible for administering and running the various competitions. The Federation Aeronautic Internationale (FAI), an international body, administers all forms of air sports and categorises Model Aircraft Aerobatics as F3A. The "bible" for F3A Aerobatics is published by the FAI regularly and is called the Sporting Code[8].

9. The Great Britain Radio Controlled Aerobatic Association (GBRCAA) is the specialist body in the BMFA that organises F3A flying in Great Britain (GB) and selects the team to represent GB in international competitions organised by the FAI. The GBRCAA website[9] contains a wealth of data as well as all the aerobatic schedules currently flown in GB. There is also a very informative and friendly forum[10] covering a diverse range of topics as well as an excellent "For Sale and Wanted" section which is worth keeping an eye on at the end of every aerobatic season (usually September/October). You will need to register on the forum in order either to post any comments or to reply to adverts.

10. There will be the equivalent of the BMFA in most other countries so you should be able to make contact with your own national body to get advice on how to get involved in precision aerobatics.

11. The biggest single impact on your flying is you! Practice often and practice the right things and you will improve out of all expectations. Incidentally, you learn more from flying in one competition than hours of practicing on your own – plus it's much more fun and you meet likeminded individuals who are always keen to help you with whatever problems you have.

12. As with any competitive sport, it is possible to spend a great deal of money on the latest, greatest thing whether it is the airframe, engine/motor or radio gear. Quite often though, new pilots make use of second-hand models, motors/engines and other equipment to start with. As I mentioned earlier, the skills built up in flying F3A means that an airframe can have performed hundreds of flights but most still look like new. This represents a cost-effective way of entering the sport. Depending on who the previous owner was, the aircraft might also be fully trimmed, especially if you buy it as a ready to fly package. Often this will include the transmitter setup details as well. Trimming in the widest context is far more than the transmitter setup though. At this stage, a well set up older design coupled even with a fairly basic computer radio will help you more than buying new and having to set

---

[7] BMFA – www.bmfa.org
[8] FAI Sporting Code - https://www.fai.org/page/ciam-code
[9] GBRCAA website – www.gbrcaa.org/
[10] GBRCAA Forum www.gbrcaa.org/smf/

it up yourself, as well as being more cost effective. A brand-new aircraft doesn't make you a better pilot on its own!

13. Today, all competition aerobatics are flown as turnaround schedules where one manoeuvre flows into another. So, you start with a centre manoeuvre and then fly one at the edge of the Aerobatic Box so that you turn the aircraft round to come back to centre for another manoeuvre and so on. This takes some getting used to as performing one manoeuvre poorly will impact on the entry to the next manoeuvre. It's a bit like snooker. Good snooker players plan several shots ahead and aim to get the cue ball correctly positioned for the next shot while pocketing the target ball.

14. Finally, it is very important to realise that when people say "he/she is a natural pilot" that there may be a grain of truth in that, but the major reason is the amount of time and effort the pilot has put in, not just in practice, but practising the right thing. In addition, they will have put in much effort to trim their aircraft to extract maximum performance and regularly revisit and tweak that trim. The idea is to make the aircraft as undemanding as possible to fly so you can expend your time and energy on flying the schedule.

15. The biggest difference you will notice in your flying, once you have put all this advice into action, is that you are now much more aware of the importance of discipline in your flying, you will be able to fly on a line while flying manoeuvres, you will be able to fly in much more difficult flying conditions than you thought possible and you will still be able to take you aeroplane home in one piece time after time.

16. There is no substitute for practising the right thing – natural ability will only take you so far. It's worth reflecting on the words of one of England's Women's International Soccer players, Alex Scott:

"Hard work always beats talent when talent doesn't work hard"

CHAPTER 2. AEROBATICS FOR BEGINNERS

STARTING OFF

17. If you have just graduated to flying solo with your trainer aircraft, you will be able to fly some basic aerobatic manoeuvres with it. However, as you improve, you will find the designed in stability features, e.g. dihedral, will make flying aerobatics harder and so you might want to consider getting a low wing and more aerobatic aircraft, although the high wing models like the Wot 4, shown on the cover photo, (the wood version not the foamy) is a reasonable starting point.

18. If the aircraft that you use is a light foamy type, then you will be restricted to flying in low wind conditions since you will yet to have developed the skill required to fly aerobatics in windy conditions. Foamies are also less able to retain their shape and so trimming them becomes almost every flight activity. As a rule, an aircraft that weighs in at around 3½ to 4 lbs (1.5 to 1.8 Kg) will be easier to fly in typical British weather conditions.

19. It matters not whether your aircraft is IC or electric powered. For IC powered aircraft, you must be confident with the tune of your engine so that it starts easily and keeps running whatever you do with your aircraft.

20. I have written this Chapter for those you are not using specialist aerobatic designs but ordinary club models. I have greatly simplified the set up procedures since many aircraft that will be used by readers will not have the adjustability that more specialised designs do. If you are lucky enough to be starting off with such a specialist aerobatic aircraft then give this Chapter a miss!

BASIC TRIMMING AND SETUP

21. The first thing you must do is to have your aircraft fly straight and level (S&L) hands off. This requires the aircraft to be stable and in trim. Yes, I know you have done that but with your hands/thumbs off the sticks, see if it really does go S&L from horizon to horizon. Correct the Tx trims until it does fly S&L hands off.

22. Most basic club aircraft only have a few things you can adjust easily for trimming and that's the position of the CG, ensuring the aircraft flies in a straight line and engine/motor thrust alignment. Trainer aircraft with a lot of dihedral and flat-bottomed wing sections are not very suitable for aerobatics! If you are already flying your chosen aerobatic aircraft, it is worth spending a little time to get the CG position optimised.

23. For a given CG, in order to fly S&L hands off you will have had to adjust the down force generated by the tail plane. We use the elevator trimmer to achieve this. This applies to a set speed and throttle setting. Fly faster and the aircraft will climb as more lift is generated by the increased speed. Fly slower and the aircraft will descend

as less lift is generate by the decreased airspeed. So, the aircraft is trimmed to fly hands-off at one speed only. The next issue is that with a forward CG, you will need a greater down force on the tail to balance this. Think of a see-saw with a heavier person than you at one end. You need someone else at your end to balance the weight or else you need a longer bit of see-saw at your end so you can sit further out to balance the heavy person.

24. Back to our aircraft with a forward CG. All is fine till you roll the aircraft inverted and you suddenly find that the aircraft is now apparently nose heavy and the nose is dropping towards the ground very quickly. This is because the tailplane is still providing the down force you trimmed but as the aircraft is inverted gravity is acting in a different way – it's still downwards but the aircraft is upside down. So, **with reference to the outside world**, while the weight is still acting downwards but the tail force is now acting upwards! Hence, the aircraft quickly pitches its nose towards the ground.

25. Moving the CG rearwards, is like having the heavy person edge towards the middle of the see-saw and now you need less weight at your end of the see-saw to balance their weight. It's the same with an aircraft so that moving the CG rearwards means you need less downforce on the tail and we see that by reducing the up-elevator trim. Now when we roll the aircraft inverted, the force pushing the tail down (up as it looks to you standing upright on the ground) the aircraft's nose pitches towards the ground more slowly

26. You can test out how far forward the CG is for your aircraft by just rolling inverted but it is less of a shock to give your aircraft a bit more room to react without scaring you! We do this by pulling the aircraft into a 45° climb and applying sufficient additional power so that the aircraft's speed remains the same as it was when flying S&L. In other words, the aircraft remains at the trimmed speed. Then, roll the aircraft inverted and let go of the elevator stick. For most sport aerobatic models, we are looking for a small tendency for the nose to drop in the direction of the ground.

27. If the model's nose drops quickly towards the ground, the CG is too far forward. Establish where your CG is and move the battery pack backwards till you can see the CG has moved back by about 1/8 inch (3 mm). Repeat the procedure until the model just starts to drop its nose, then the CG is in a good starting position.

28. You should always remember that the position of the CG on the plan should be a safe one but not necessarily the optimum one. This test allows you to find the optimum position for your aircraft. In fact, you don't even need to measure where the CG is (assuming you have a forward CG) but just use the aircraft's behaviour to changes in the CG position to trim the aircraft to make it easier to fly when inverted.

29. Other techniques you can use to help when flying inverted is to increase the amount of control movement i.e. down elevator and/or decrease the amount of Expo so that pushing the elevator stick forwards produces more movement than pulling the elevator stick backwards by the same amount. Experiment, till you feel that you have reached a position with which you feel comfortable flying inverted.

30.   The next adjustment is to help us to fly a true vertical downline without the aircraft pitching towards the canopy or yawing left or right. This is achieved by climbing to height and then closing the throttle and diving vertically. Look to see if the aircraft yaws left, right or goes down in a straight line. Adjust the rudder trim so that the flight path remains straight. We'll leave using a mix on the elevator to get a vertical dive hands-off till later (see para 151).

31.   The next two adjustments are to the engine/motor thrust line. What we are looking for is the aircraft's immediate reaction to changes in thrust as once the aircraft speed increases other aerodynamic forces come into play. What we are trying to achieve is to get a balance between the engine's/motor's thrust line and the three-dimensional position of the CG and centre of drag so that there is minimal to no interaction as power is increased and decreased. Remember, we are aiming to fly the aircraft at a constant speed or as near constant as we can manage. In other words, at its trimmed speed so that we have the least need to adjust the other three flying controls to counter any effect of power on and power off.

32.   If it is possible to reach the engine/motor mounting bolts, the adjustments are as follows:

- Trim the aircraft so that it flies straight and level (S&L) with about 2/3 power[11]. Then apply full power quickly but smoothly and don't touch the elevator   If the aircraft climbs immediately, you need to tilt the motor downwards slightly. If the aircraft descends immediately, you need to tilt the motor upwards slightly. The easiest way to do this is to put washers between the motor and its mount to tilt the motor up or down. (NB: You should remember that as power is added, the aircraft's speed will increase and so will the lift generated by the increase in speed. The aircraft will then climb but there will be a finite time while the extra power accelerates the weight of the aircraft. The same holds true in the opposite sense for decreasing power.)

- From level flight, pull the nose up to vertical and apply sufficient power smoothly to maintain the S&L speed as you do so. Any deviation from the vertical will be due to the engine/motor side thrust being incorrect. If the aircraft pulls to the left, then you need to increase the tilt of the engine to the right and vice versa. Again, placing a washer between the motor mount and the bulkhead will provide that adjustment.

---

[11] Specialist aerobatic aircraft usually have a greater than 1:1 power to weight ratio. We set those to ½ power for our cruise speed. Typical club aerobatic aircraft do not have such powerful engines/motors so we use 2/3 power for our cruise speed and we apply full power smoothly before we start the looping part of any manoeuvre in order to get the speed up first and then to try not to lose too much speed while flying the vertical part of a manoeuvre e.g. a loop.

Washer here for more right thrust

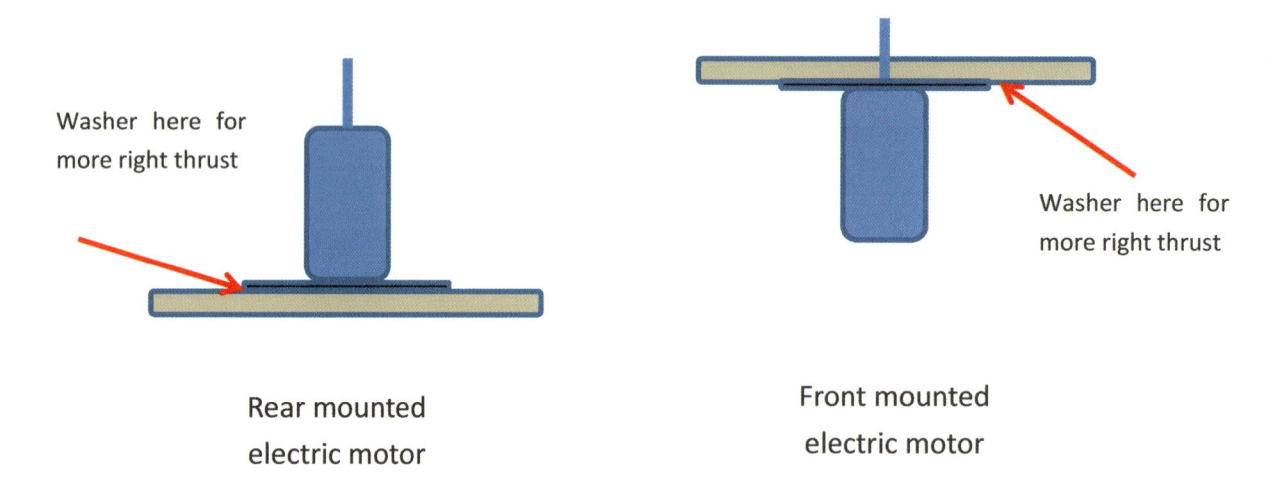

Washer here for more right thrust

Rear mounted electric motor

Front mounted electric motor

33.   The next area to look at is the control throws you have set on your aircraft. If your transmitter (Tx) supports the function of Rates, you will need to make use of them. You need to set up some relatively low movement of your elevator and ailerons for aerobatics – strange as it may seem! Having loads of elevator movement is a hindrance not a help as the aircraft becomes overly sensitive to control inputs. You should aim for a deflection of around 10°-15° for elevator and ailerons and about 25°-30° for the rudder. These may be a lot less than you are used to. You should retain your existing settings on your higher rates. Exponential (EXPO) is another function you will find useful in combination with Rates. EXPO is applied differently between different Tx makes but what we are aiming to achieve is a lower response to stick movement around centre so that small corrections are not seen as a jerky flight path. If your Tx supports it, it is best to have all 3 control rates controlled by one switch. See para 503.

34.   Now, you are ready to fly your first aerobatic manoeuvre.

PITCH, ROLL AND YAW

35. If you are not familiar with these terms, I've described what they mean below.

Pitch is the term used to describe the effect the elevators have on flight. Pulling back the elevator stick causes the aircraft to pitch up and pushing the stick forward causes the nose to pitch down. The same things happens when the aircraft is inverted but to the pilot on the ground it looks like the opposite happens!	Pitch
Roll is the term used to describe the effect of the ailerons in flight. Moving the aileron stick to the right will cause the aircraft to roll to the right and vice versa. This also applies when the aircraft is inverted. However, when the aircraft is flying towards you it appears as if the controls have reversed. They haven't. You will have been taught to adjust for this when you were being taught to fly i.e. saying "prop up the wing" or push the aileron stick towards the lower wing to roll out of a turn.	Roll
Yaw is the term used to describe the effect of the rudder in flight. Push the rudder stick to the left and the nose will yaw to the left and vice versa. When inverted, the rudder acts in exactly the same way but to you it looks like the opposite is happening. There are some techniques for determining which way to push the rudder stick to get the desired reaction from the aircraft.	Yaw

STARTING AEROBATIC MANOEUVRES

36.   All aerobatic manoeuvres consist of loops, rolls and some element of stalled flight. The loops and rolls can be full, half or some other amount. Start by flying what is called "The Line".

The Line

37.   In precision aerobatics, we fly the aircraft along a line that is usually parallel to the runway from which you have just taken off. The distance of the line out from you will depend on the size of aircraft you are flying. A typical 50-70 size model will need to be flown some 70-80 metres (m) out. This is much further out than you will be used to flying. The reason for this is that you will not end up with the aircraft right overhead you if something goes wrong with your direction of flight during a loop say. You also get a better view of the shape of the loop with the aircraft further out.

38.   To find out how far 80 m is, get someone to hold you model in the air so you have a side view of it and walk 80 m away. That's how big your model should appear when at the right distance. It is quite difficult to fly at exactly 80 m out because of the effect of the wind but we'll deal with the wind later on!

Flying a Loop

39.   Let's start with a loop. The size of the loop you can fly will depend on the power to weight ratio your aircraft. Assuming a modest power to weight ratio then you will probably need full power for a loop. For an IC engine, you will also need to apply power a bit before you need it to allow the engine to respond in time while for an electric motor the response will be much faster. See the dotted line in the diagram below on when to apply power.

40.   Pick a point on the horizon, it could be a tree, building or electricity pylon, that you can use as your centre point for the loop. For an IC powered aircraft, as the aircraft comes to this point smoothly apply power and as you reach your aiming point, ease back on the elevator stick taking care to avoid applying any aileron and keep the power coming up to maximum – see the dotted line in the diagram below. For electric powered aircraft, begin applying the power increase as you start to ease back the elevator stick at the entry to the loop.

Reduce power smoothly to idle

Increase power smoothly to "cruise"

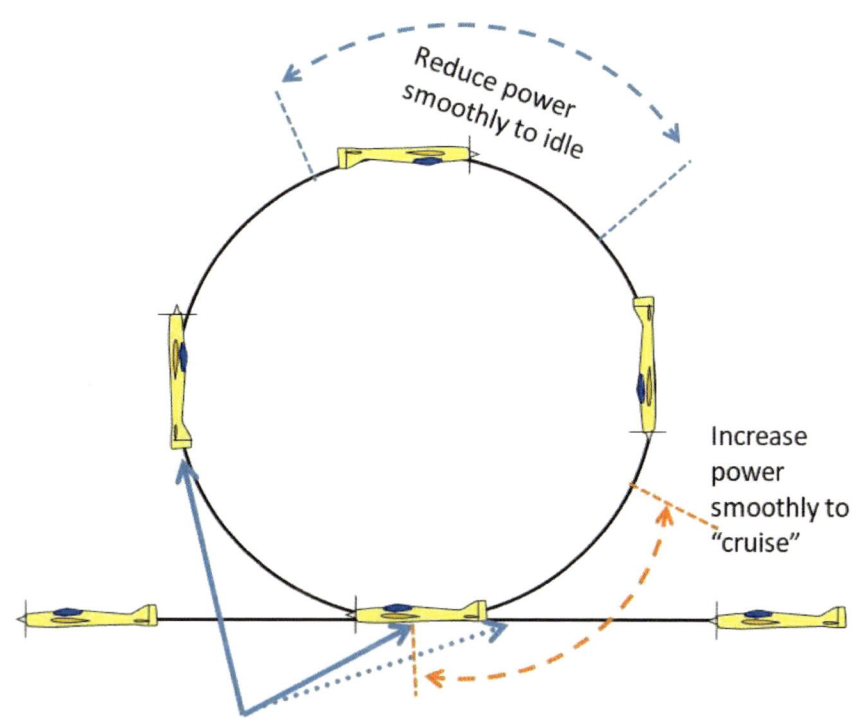

Increase power smoothly to maintain airspeed

41. As the aircraft reaches the top of the loop, smoothly reduce the power but don't snap the throttle shut! You are aiming to have the throttle closed by about the 2 o'clock position if flying from right to left at the beginning of the loop. (If you are flying the other way, the position will be 10 o'clock.) Be prepared to gently ease off the amount of up elevator you applied as you approach the top of the loop for reasons I will explain later. Continuing round the loop, begin to apply power smoothly from the 4 o'clock position aiming to be back to 2/3 power by the time the aircraft comes level and at that point return the elevator stick to neutral and fly away S&L. Do not allow a climb or dive to mark the exit!

Flying a Roll

42. When you first fly a roll, you will notice that the nose drops all the time the aircraft is rolling. In your early stages of aerobatics, instead of rolling from S&L, pull up to a 45° climb and apply full power. Once established in the climb, release the elevator input then quickly apply and release a little up elevator just before you start the roll. You should aim to pitch the nose up around 10°-15°. Return the elevator stick to neutral and apply just aileron to roll the aircraft. This is where low rates are very useful. If you have a low enough rate, you can apply full aileron and the aircraft should roll at around one roll per two secs or so.

43. As the aircraft becomes inverted, just push a bit of down elevator so that it comes in an equal amount either side of the aircraft when inverted. The amount you have to push will vary but try using the same amount you used to pitch the aircraft nose up by 15°. If the elevator is not applied equally either side of inverted, the aircraft direction of flight will alter. You will only get this right by trial and error. Return the elevator stick to neutral. If you find it too difficult to use elevator to begin with then as you have a safety margin with your 45° climb, you can safely ignore the elevator input until you feel ready to do so.

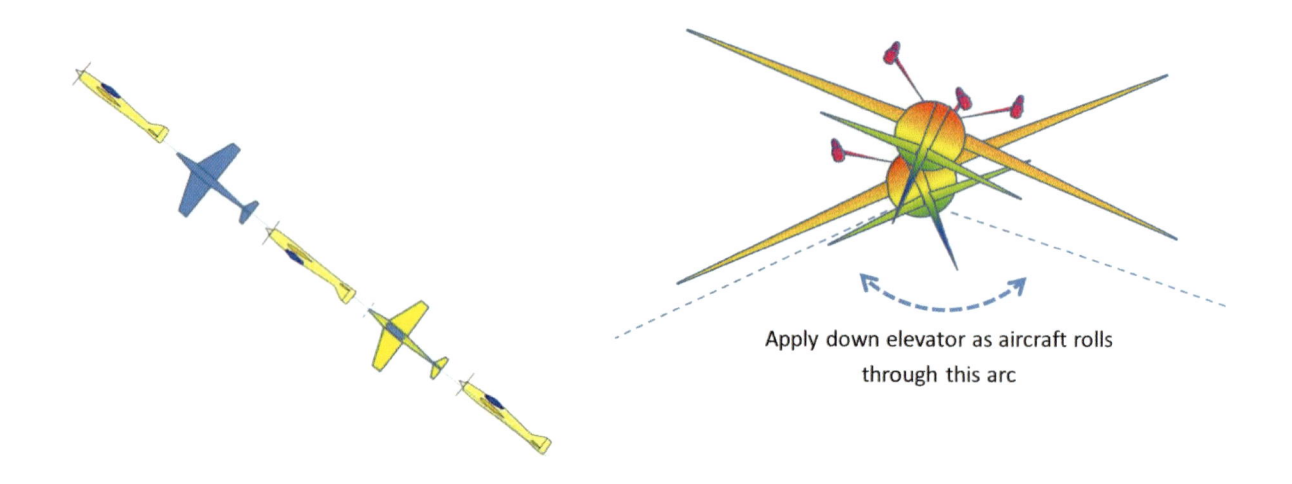

Apply down elevator as aircraft rolls through this arc

44. As the aircraft approaches upright, be ready to return the aileron stick to neutral and pull the elevator stick back to return the nose to the 45° line on which you started. Having a slower roll rate will help you to time the elevator inputs.

45. As you start to get more confident about rolling, you can bring the 45° climb down to 20° and eventually dispense with it so that you are rolling on the horizontal line.

Some Guidance on How to Improve

46. Once you are comfortable rolling and looping, the next thing to try is to fly a combination of roll and loop.

Half Loop Half Roll – The Immelmann Turn

47. Try flying a half loop and then, when you reach the top of the loop, immediately carry out a half roll. Be prepared for the nose to drop while you do this. (For the moment, just apply a quick pulse of down elevator, return to neutral and carry out the half roll to upright.) Later on, you will learn how to use rudder in rolls to prevent the nose dropping. This manoeuvre is called an Immelmann Turn in aerobatics. It is used a lot to turn the aircraft around and fly back the other way.

The Immelman Turn

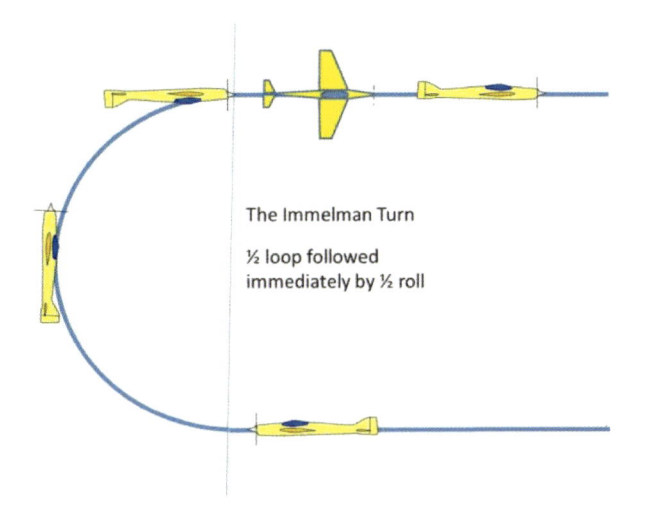

½ loop followed
immediately by ½ roll

Half Roll Half Loop - Split S

48.   Having got your aircraft high up, coming down is achieved by flying a Split S. This is the reverse of the Immelmann Turn

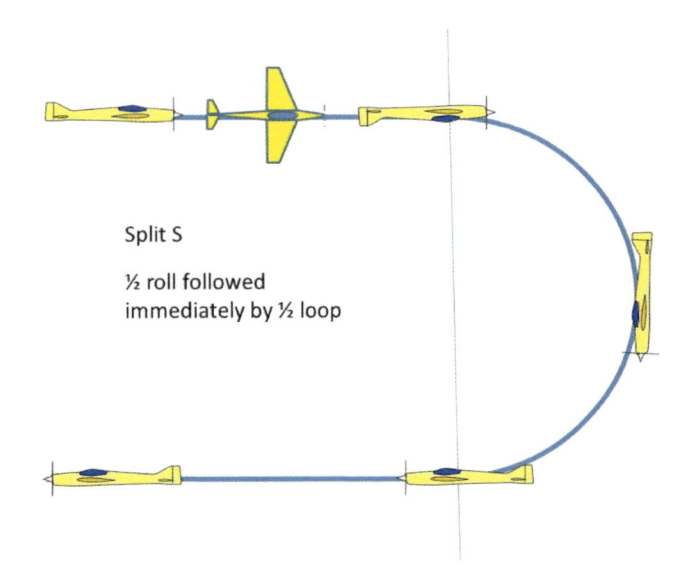

Split S

½ roll followed
immediately by ½ loop

49.   As with the roll, as you start the half roll into the Split S, the aircraft's nose will drop. We'll deal with this later on when you are ready to use rudder during the roll. For the time being, a short application of up elevator just before you roll will help to keep the nose from falling too far. (NB: release the elevator before rolling or the result will be a barrel roll.) The saving grace for this manoeuvre is that as soon as you have completed the half roll you can start your half loop.

WHAT NEXT?

50.   The term precision aerobatics means that you need to work towards the term precision. Your loops should start and end on the centre line marker. You must exit the loop at the same height as the entry height.

51.   Your rolls should start and finish with wings level. Rolling more slowly helps to stop the aircraft more precisely.

52.   If you find that this level of precision is something that really interests you then you are ready to progress from these taster bits to taking the next step. Read on and you will learn that there is a great deal more that you can learn to improve your aerobatic flying. On the other hand, you might be quite happy with what you can now do and want to consolidate before doing anything more complicated.

53.   Either way is fine. The main point is to enjoy your flying.

CHAPTER 3. SOME BASIC CONCEPTS

INTRODUCTION

54. All aerobatic manoeuvres are made up of a roll or loop, a combination of the two and some stalled manoeuvres. For competition, these manoeuvres are all flown within the confines of what is called the Aerobatic Box. All manoeuvres have to remain within this Box, apart from during take-off and landing, in order to score points. The Box includes a line along which the aircraft is supposed to travel between the two ends of the Box and the aircraft should not exceed the height of the Box.

NOTE: Distances on the ground are denominated in metres (m) while height above ground is in feet (ft). To convert from m to yards multiply m by 1.094.

55. So, in this Chapter, I go into more detail on various aspects of aerobatics. I will describe:

- The Aerobatic Box

- Flying the Line

- Flying manoeuvres

- Planning your flight

- Some aerobatic conventions

- The effect of gravity

- The effect of wind (see Chapter 5 for more detailed information on this topic)

- The Canalyser or T Can

THE AEROBATIC BOX

56.   The Aerobatic Box which is a chunk of sky within which you need to fly in order to score maximum points. Here's what the Aerobatic Box looks like.

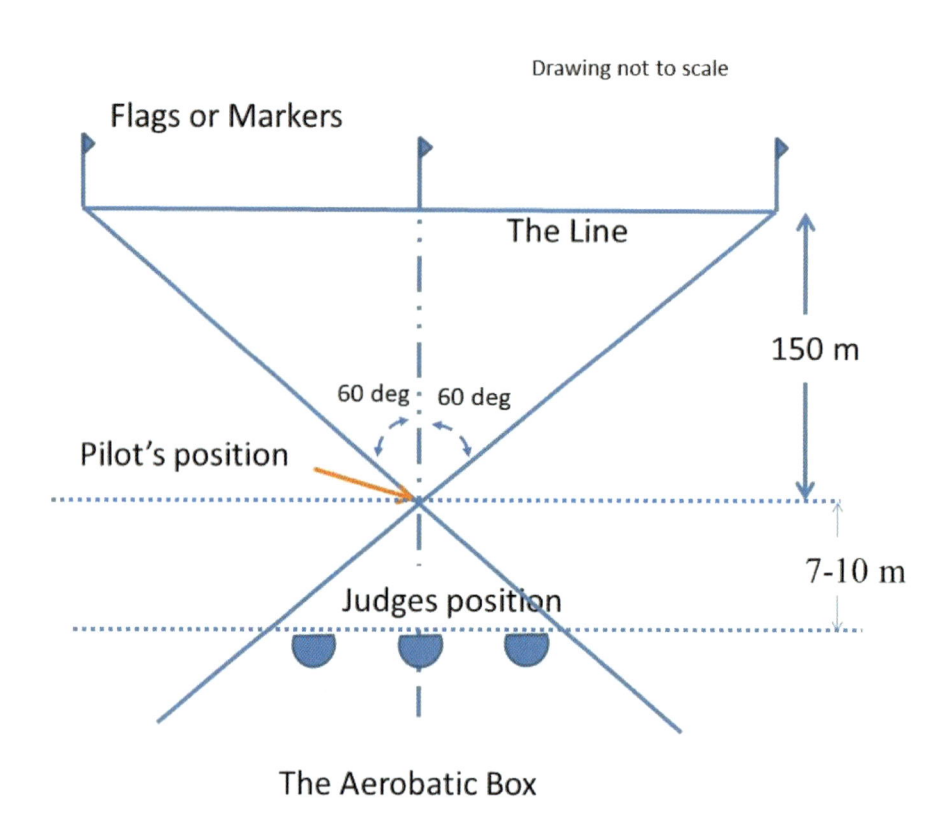

Drawing not to scale

The Aerobatic Box
(Flags or Markers, The Line, 150 m, 60 deg · 60 deg, Pilot's position, Judges position, 7-10 m)

57.   "The Line" is the expected path of the aircraft over the ground as it flies to and fro between the two end flag markers. The centre flag marker is used to judge how well centred your centre manoeuvre really is. At your flying site, make use of anything that helps you to judge the three points. These could be trees, buildings, electricity pylons and so on.

58.   The pilot stands at the apex of the three lines marking the straight ahead and then a line at 60° either side of straight ahead. The take-off and landing area is typically around 10 m out from the pilot.

59.   The maximum height is defined by an angle of 60° to the horizontal from where the pilot stands, so that means at 150 m the maximum height will be 852 ft. Height is always expressed in feet in aviation! It is surprising how steep 60° looks when you are standing on the ground as the pilot!

60.	The judges sit 7-10 m behind the pilot and as close to centre as they can. Judges are spaced 2 m apart. Sitting next to them is an assistant (called a scribe) who records the score for each manoeuvre that is judged. In order to prevent other judges hearing the marks awarded, the judge will whisper the score so the scribe needs to listen hard for the score! The aim is to prevent another judge hearing the score and being influenced by it. Manoeuvres are marked out of 10 with various marks deducted from ½ a point to all the points (zero) depending on the severity of the error. This system allows the judge to focus on the manoeuvre without having to look down and write a score in the score sheet. However, the introduction of automated scoring tools means that many competitions no longer need scribes as the judge can award marks by operating the system to deduct marks as the aircraft flies the manoeuvre so the chance to be a scribe may die out. This is a pity as you can learn a lot about what makes a great manoeuvre compared with a poor manoeuvre. At your first competition, do ask to scribe. Judges don't bite and are only too happy to assist a newcomer. Even if you just go to the competition to watch, have a go at scribing.

61.	When you are first learning a manoeuvre, flying it on its own is probably quite enough complication. As you get more practiced, and more confident, you can plan to fly the end manoeuvre as the turnaround at each end of the field – hence the term turnaround schedule. Remember though, **you** set the pace at which you wish to develop your aerobatics, although it's always helpful if you have either a more experienced mentor at hand or a group of you to help and encourage each other.

FLYING THE LINE

62.	Now before we fly any manoeuvres, practice flying on a line parallel to the runway in use. Try and arrange this so that you have an easily identifiable marker on the horizon right in front of you to use as a centre marker that you can see as you fly across the sky. You also want markers that are easily identified 60° either side of centre so that you can see where the ends of the Box are. If there are no distinguishing features at your flying site see if you can persuade your club to allow you either to paint some lines on the ground or peg out some two-inch-wide tape so you can see the centre and two side lines and can gauge the position of your aircraft.

63.	When you first start you may find it is quite difficult to fly a consistent line but that is the basic starting point for aerobatics. The other fact that will be different is that you need to fly much further out than you are used to. Why? Well, if you look at the Aerobatic Box diagram, the closer in you fly the less distance and height you have in which to carry out your manoeuvres. Remember you need to fly three manoeuvres, one at each end and a centre manoeuvre, and that dictates the distance out you should fly.

64. The size of your aircraft also determines how far out you need to fly. So, depending on the size of your aircraft, the distances to fly are as follows:

- 50/70 size aircraft – 70/80 m
- 110/120 size aircraft – 110/120 m
- 2 m size aircraft – 150/175 m

65. The biggest difference in transitioning from a club pilot to being able to fly an aerobatic schedule is that you will be able to fly on a constant line and link aerobatic manoeuvres together while maintaining that line.

Flying Manoeuvres

66. When flying in competition, the judges start with a score of 10 and apply downgrades for errors or if you infringe the Box boundaries. A manoeuvre is defined by a straight line before the manoeuvre, the manoeuvre and a straight line after the manoeuvre equal in length to the entry line. If the manoeuvre is completely outside the Box, the score awarded is zero. If only 10% of the manoeuvre is outside then you are downgraded 1 point or 10%. If 80% of the manoeuvre is outside the Box the downgrade is 8 points or 80% and so on. In determining how much of the manoeuvre will be marked, the judges include the line before and line after in their assessment. So, the actual spin completely outside the Box might warrant only a 20% - 30% deduction i.e. only 2-3 points. Remember also that the judges are looking at the travel of the CG around the manoeuvre and not the attitude of the aircraft.

67. It is a good idea to spend time flying to and fro at the appropriate distance out for the size of your model to get used to this way of flying. If you train yourself to fly in an Aerobatic Box area from the beginning it will make it easier if you decide to take up competitive flying. Try and pick a tree or other feature on or close to the two edges of your Aerobatic Box.

68. Every aerobatic manoeuvre must have the following features:

- A line before – that is a section of straight flying – it is always level.
- The manoeuvre.
- A line after – that is a section of straight flying equal to the first line so that the manoeuvre is centred – again always level.
- You could ensure that you stick to this by counting e.g for two seconds count "one, two" or "one thousand two thousand" before and after you complete the manoeuvre as shown in the diagram

below. That is provided you had at least two secs of level flight before you entered the manoeuvre! If there are a number of lines, as in say a 4-point roll, count through every one with the same speed. On a climbing manoeuvre, say two half rolls on a 45° climbing line, you must make sure you have added enough power to keep the speed constant so that the lines between the part manoeuvres really are the same length when based on timing. Remember that with a downwind element, the ground speed will be higher than the up-wind element so you should compensate for this in your timing count as it's the distance covered over the ground that matters for geometry purposes.

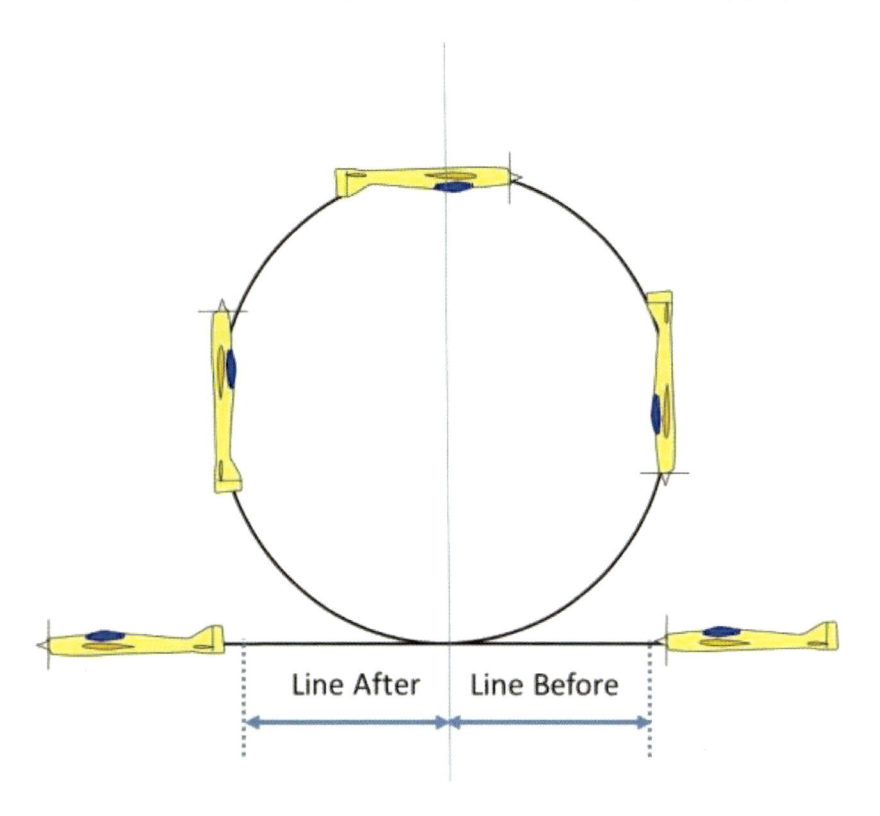

69. Also, **don't fly too low** - stay at around 100 ft or so (equal to three houses high) for a 50/70 size model or 150 ft for a 2 m size. It makes a big difference to your adrenaline flow since, if you make a mistake, you have height in hand. We've all scared ourselves with the wrong input at the wrong time and you also stand a good chance of avoiding the dreaded sudden "one-point landing" if you have that extra insurance of height. Remember that the "top of the Box" is at around 850 ft when you are at 150 m distance out so don't feel that a bottom height of 150 ft will cramp your style! The vertical size of the Box is another reason for a good power to weight ratio for an aerobatic aircraft. Ideally, you want sufficient power so that your aircraft has "unlimited vertical performance" i.e. it keeps going upwards at least as fast as it was flying straight and level at half power. **Not flying low also reduces the effect turbulence will have on your aircraft. On really, turbulent days it pays to fly a little higher.**

70.   If you are relatively experienced in flying aerobatics, your end manoeuvres can be any combination of stall turn, half Cuban Eight, half reverse Cuban Eight (see Chapter 7 for description). A half reverse Cuban Eight has the advantage of increasing the length of line you can fly level before your next manoeuvre or before you hit the centre line, so where you have the option, it is the better one to use. Alternatively, if you are new to aerobatics, then you can use a procedure turn to replace the end manoeuvre and that gives you time to collect your wits before returning in the other direction! A procedure turn, or P Turn, is started by turning 90° away from the flight path then reversing the turn to fly a 270° turn to bring you back onto the same ground track, what we call The Line, as shown in the diagram below. In a crosswind or headwind, you will need to compensate for the wind so that the path flown brings you back to the line.

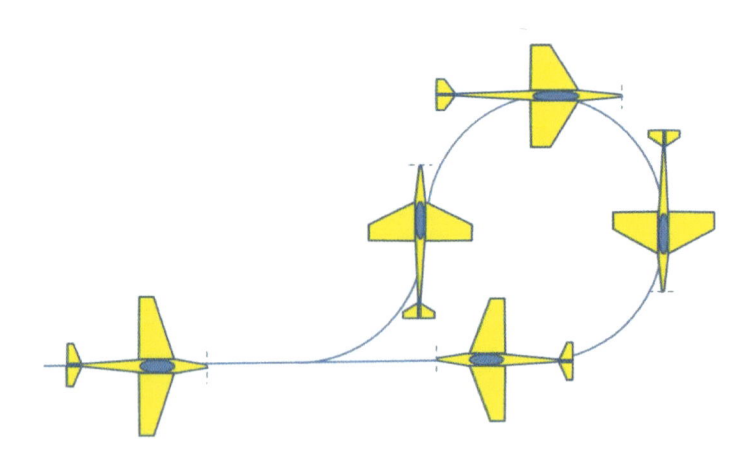

71.   You will quickly find that an error in one manoeuvre places you in a more difficult position to start the next one. However, if you want to fly competition aerobatics then you will eventually need to fly all the manoeuvres in the right order. You can choose to miss out a manoeuvre, and get a zero score for it, if you have got seriously out of position in order to position correctly for the one after rather than continue to make life difficult for yourself!

72.   Whatever you do, avoid flying a race track since you will either be too far out or too close in. You must always aim to be at the optimum selected distance out at all times.

73.   When you can fly that line at a consistent distance out and at the same height in both directions then you're ready to move onto the next bit. Come back to practicing just flying this line from time to time as it will help you to become more accurate in your aerobatic flying. Most aerobatic pilots do this when they've been away from flying for a period of time.

74.   The one thing I would urge you to do is to strive for accuracy. Like all things in life, what you first learn is always difficult to unlearn! It is easy to do sloppy aerobatics but everyone will see that and you won't feel satisfied.

If, when you start your loop, your loop is off centre, readjust it so that the loop is centred. That skill will be essential if you are aiming to achieve either a BMFA B Certificate or fly in a competition – not only does it look better and shows that you have full control over your aircraft you also score higher points. Be critical of your flying, it's the only way to improve!

75.   This is one reason why flying in competition is so helpful in that you can see the mistakes others make and can learn from them as well as getting advice on fixing your mistakes.

PLAN YOUR FLIGHT

76.   How often do you think about what you are going to fly and how you are going to fly it before you get airborne? If you want to fly proper aerobatics, you need to think about what you are going to do before you get airborne. Competition pilots use a small model aeroplane, called a stick model, to "fly" through their schedule before getting airborne so that they can remind themselves what the aircraft will look like as they go through the schedule, what wind corrections they will need and so on. You can either make your own or buy one. See the example below. I got this one when I was flying a biplane but it works fine for monoplanes as well!

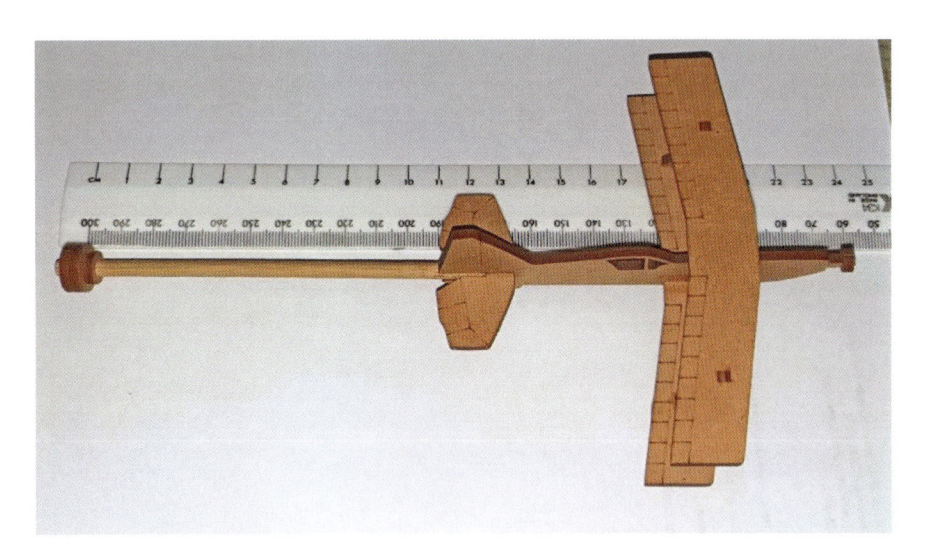

77.   So, as part of your process of flying aerobatics you need to get used to being more deliberate with your pre-flight process. By all means use the stick model to talk your control movements through the manoeuvre. Simple things, like which way am I going to apply rudder to keep tracking into the crosswind, is easier to settle when the aircraft is on the ground than trying to do so when it's airborne.

78.   The other thing to do is to memorise the schedule you are trying to fly. Knowing what your next manoeuvre will be will help you to fly the aircraft out of one manoeuvre into the correct position to start the next manoeuvre. You can use a friend to call the next manoeuvre but it's better to have memorised it as well.

79.   All practicing aerobatic pilots know exactly what they intend to do before they get airborne. That is part of the discipline of flying aerobatics.

SOME CURRENT AEROBATIC CONVENTIONS

80.   It is worth flagging up some conventions early as it helps to have these in mind when reading about how to fly various manoeuvres. If you ever end up flying in a competition, you must follow these if you are not to lose points unnecessarily.

81.   At this stage, the ones you are most likely to come across are:

- **There must be a line before and a line after every manoeuvre**. A line means a period of steady level flight. The length of line before and the line after must be equal. That means they can be long or short but both must be the same for that manoeuvre,

- **Between rolls in opposite directions there must be no line**. For example, two consecutive quarter rolls flown in opposite directions must have: a line; a quarter roll to the left; an immediate quarter roll to the right; and then a line,

- **Between rolls in the same direction, there must be a line.** For example, lines between two consecutive half rolls in the same direction must be short and of equal length so you would have: a line; a half roll; a line; a half roll; a line. All lines must be of the same length.

82.   The full range of judging guidance is contained in the FAI Sporting Code in Annex 5B, the Manoeuvre Execution Guide[12] in the F3 Aerobatics volume.

---

[12] FAI Sporting Code https://www.fai.org/page/ciam-code

The Effect of Gravity

83. You will experience the effect of gravity most noticeably when performing manoeuvres with a significant vertical component such as a loop.

84. You will be familiar with the four forces acting on an aircraft in flight already. Two of these forces are fixed to the aircraft axes but lift and gravity aren't. So consider how the apparent direction in which gravity acts changes in a loop as shown in the diagram below:

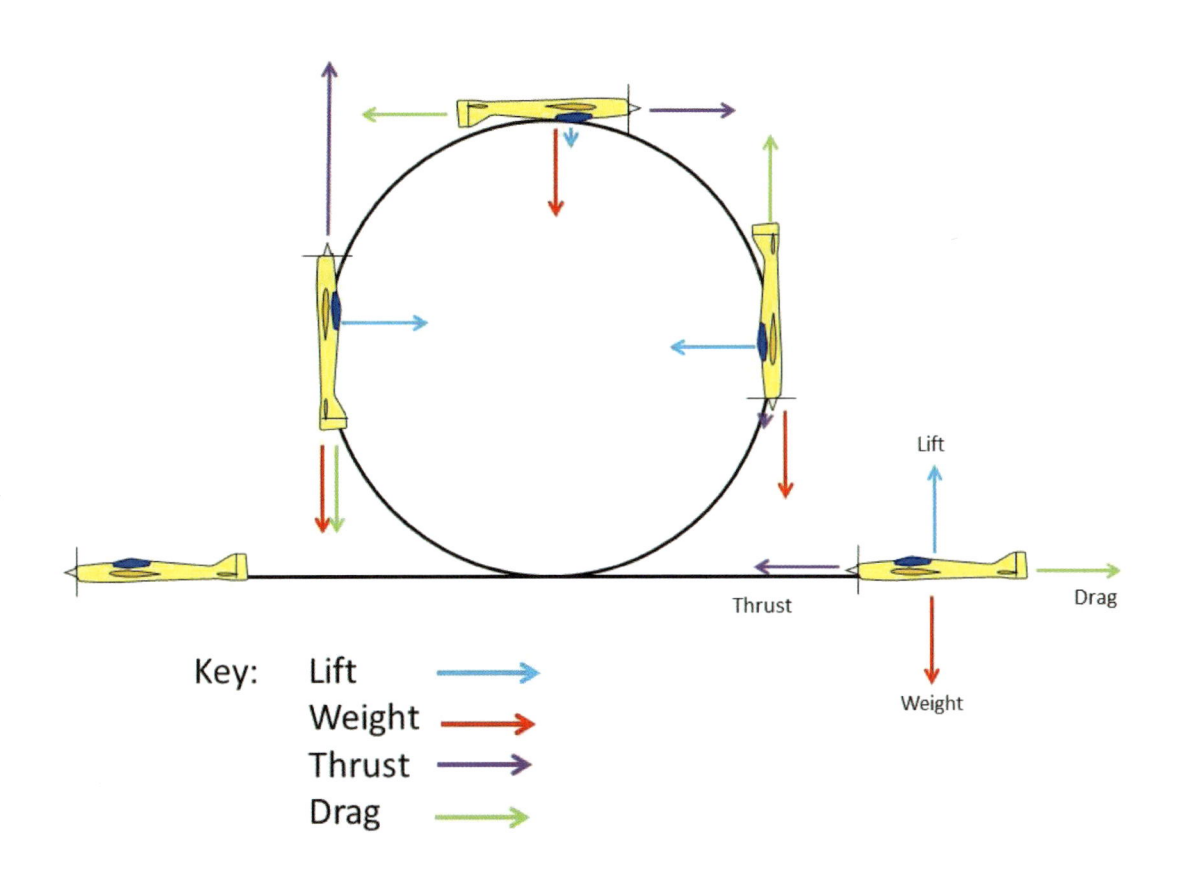

85. As your aircraft travels round the loop, gravity impacts each of the other 3 forces requiring you to make significant changes to the aircraft controls. At the top of a big the loop, we may well have to reverse the direction of lift, push down elevator, to balance gravity. We'll go into that in more detail later on in Chapter 5.

86. The arrows in the diagram above represent both the amount of the force, by their length, and the direction in which that force is acting. **We call this a vector since that combines both force and direction**.

87. When rolling with the aircraft flying straight and level to start with, when viewed from inside the aircraft, gravity appears to rotate! Of course, it's the aircraft that rotates and as the lift vector rotates, we need to be ready to reduce it by pushing forward on the stick as the aircraft rolls inverted and easing back to neutral as the aircraft rolls back past 90°. We also use rudder to generate lift from the fuselage and, by virtue of pointing the nose up, we add an element of thrust to the lift force.

88. This diagram shows that with the aircraft in knife edge, the thrust vector (purple line) can be resolved into a horizontal thrust force (orange line) and a lift force (green line).

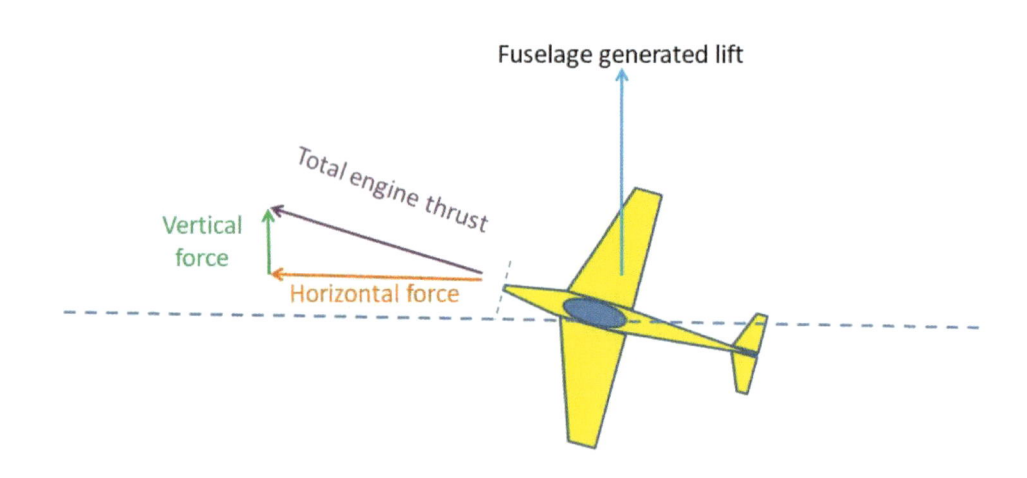

89. This "engine generated lift" is added to the "fuselage generated lift" (blue line) to support the full weight of the aircraft.

90. Once you have understood the forces that impact on the way your aircraft flies, you can then move on to understanding the basic aerobatic manoeuvres before moving on to flying the manoeuvres as a schedule.

AIRSPEED AND GROUNDSPEED

91.   I have met pilots who are confused by these two terms so I thought it best to bring up the issue. Skip this if you already are well versed in the difference between these two terms.

92.   Just consider you have a young friend who is keen to run up the down-going escalators. You are standing beside the escalator watching as he starts running up the escalator. When he matches the speed at which the escalator is coming down, he appears stationary to you but he is running quite fast. **So, in this context his ground speed is zero but his airspeed is his running speed**.

93.   He stops running and comes down, takes the up escalator and then runs down the down escalator at the same speed as he was running up it. **His airspeed is the same but his ground speed is now twice as fast**.

94.   That is relative motion and is what we deal with every time we take off from one environment, the ground, and enter the other environment, the air. Our aircraft's airspeed is determined by whether the aircraft is climbing or diving and how much power we have selected. The air within which the aircraft is flying is travelling over the ground and will generate what we see as a wind speed. If the wind direction happens to be at an angle to our runway, we then have a crosswind. None of this has any effect on the way the aircraft flies, but to us, anchored on the ground, our fixed reference tells us that the aircraft slows down when it flies into wind and speeds up when it flies downwind. The aircraft is oblivious to this as all it can sense is its speed through the air and the fact the air is moving is immaterial to the way it flies.

95.   To us though, wanting to fly aerobatics and to see the sort of shapes that we wish to fly in aerobatics, we have to compensate for the fact that the aircraft is operating in a different environment from the solid land on which we stand. So, we have to change the way the aircraft flies to see the manoeuvre shape we want!

CORRECTING FOR THE WIND

96.   Schedules are flown on a line that is usually, but not always, parallel to the runway being used for take-off and landing. This almost always means there will be a head and crosswind and coping with both is an integral part of flying precision aerobatics. The good news is that learning to cope with unkind winds will open up the number of days you feel confident to go up to your field and fly. When you see an expert aerobatic pilot flying in very windy conditions it looks as if there is no wind! Don't worry. Lesser mortals are affected to a greater or lesser extent. The key point is that you should be aware of the difference between track, the path over the ground of your aircraft, and heading which is the direction in which your aircraft is pointing. The greater the crosswind angle and strength, the greater will be the divergence between the aircraft heading and the track you need to fly over the ground. You should expect to be affected by crosswinds and when an onlooker thinks you are not affected it

means you have definitely got better! The way to get better is to **fly and practice often and in all sorts of wind conditions**.

Effect of Headwind

97.   Let's first consider the effect of just a headwind on the loop. As you fly into the wind to start the loop, this will have the effect of reducing the aircraft's ground speed for a given air speed. Clearly as you get to the top of the loop, the ground speed will increase as well. If you do nothing about this then the loop will finish downwind from where you started it.

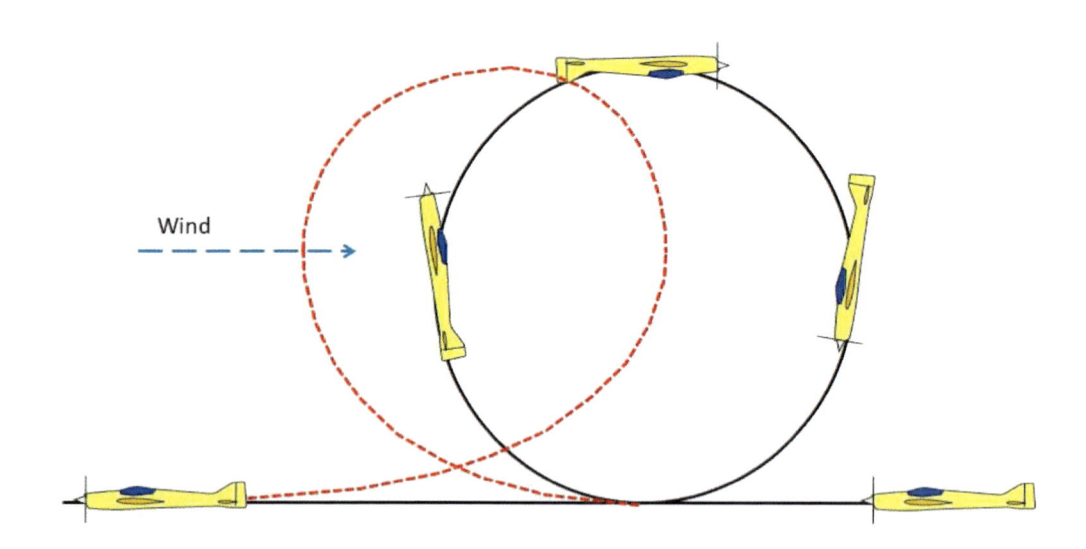

98.   Look at the diagram above. In order for the loop to appear round (black line) you have to fly a distorted shape (dotted red line) so that as the block of wind in which you are flying takes the aircraft downwind the loop appears round as the dotted red line is blown backwards and sits on top of the black line. If you were to fly exactly the same shape but in still air it would look like the red dotted line. Notice that in still air, you would finish the loop well upwind. This oddity is due to the pilot standing on the ground and the relative motion of the wind over the ground.

99.   The other thing to note is that at the 9 o'clock and 3 o'clock positions, the aircraft's nose is tilted into wind – the position you see is slightly exaggerated to make this point clear. Since it is the path of the CG of the aircraft

that is judged you have to have the aircraft inclined into wind at these two points to maintain the shape of the loop.

Effect of a Crosswind

100.   As you have set up the aircraft track to be parallel to the runway in use, as soon as you start the pull up for your loop if you do nothing about the heading of the aircraft you will end up with a loop that will be flown at an angle to the ground track. In other words, as you loop, your aircraft will come in to you and then go out from you depending on whether the wind is blowing into your face or your back. What is needed is a loop that is aligned with the ground track.

101.   Let's say you are flying right to left with the crosswind blowing in your face and we are looking down on the aircraft. You will have set the aircraft to fly nose in to the wind at an angle that allows the aircraft's ground track (dotted blue line) to parallel the display axis to set the flight path by using the rudder to yaw the aircraft's nose into wind. Once you have the desired heading, release the rudder. Consequently, the aircraft tracks correctly but with the nose pointing to the right of track but importantly is in balanced flight. Once you release the rudder there will be no yaw and will fly this heading without any further input from you.

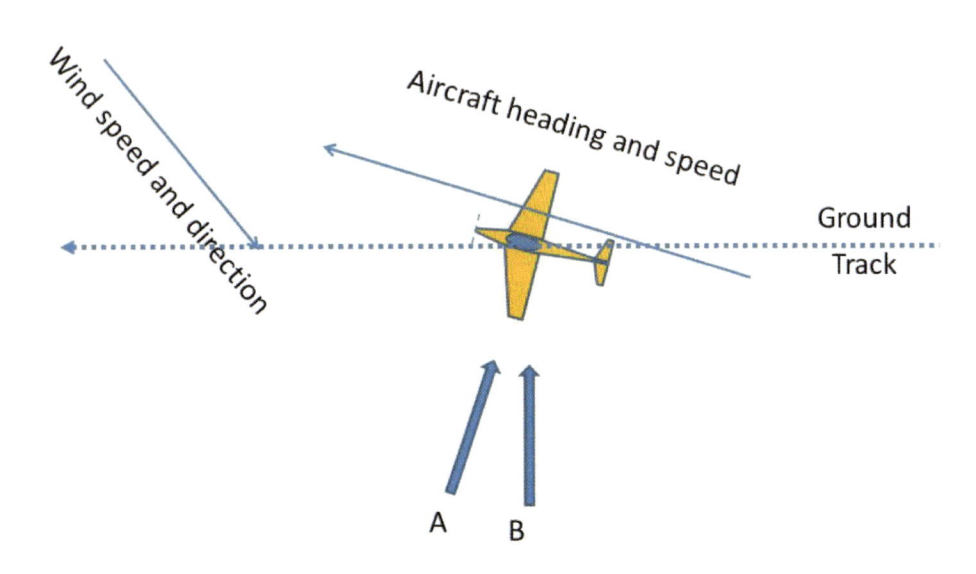

102.   It is important to realise that the aircraft is not flying in a yaw. The fact that it has to head to windward of the track line is of concern to you and not the aircraft. Note that, once you have established the required heading,

by use of the rudder, you can centralise all three flying surface controls and the aircraft will fly that heading, and hence the track, without any further control input other than to correct for any turbulence the aircraft might experience.

103.   This is relative motion and it is caused by the aircraft flying in one environment, the air, relative to the pilot and judges sitting on the ground in a fixed position while the wind blows over them. This creates a crosswind if the desired ground track you want the aircraft to follow is at an angle to the wind direction. It is worth getting your mind around this concept. You need to feel comfortable with why we sometimes have to fly the aircraft in the way we do in order to make the shape correspond to the one we wish to see.

104.   If you just loop from this position, the aircraft will perform a loop in the plane at the same angle as the aircraft's heading and not the track. So, the aircraft will end up flying a distorted loop when viewed by the pilot i.e. think of looking at a circle that is turned at 30° to you. The viewer at A will see a perfectly circular loop whereas the viewer at B will see more of an oval loop.

105.   I cover how to correct for this in the Chapter 5.

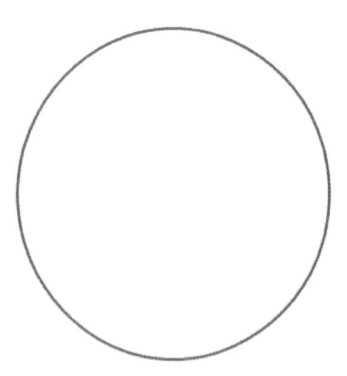

The view from Position A   The view from Position B

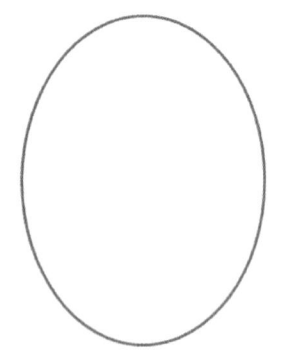

The Effect of the Wind Gradient

106. The diagram below shows how wind speed changes from ground level to around 400 ft. Note that at true ground level i.e. **ground level here is the ground at the level immediately under the aircraft wheels and not your height when you are standing**, there is zero wind speed. Think of this as the **ground's** boundary layer. If you find that hard to understand, think of the rain drops that remain on your windscreen as you drive along at 70 mph and need your wipers to clear them. This is because the rain drops are inside the lowest level of the windscreen's boundary layer

107. A second factor to consider is that the wind direction changes with height. This is more marked on strong wind days. You may have seen that the clouds move in a different direction, up to 30° or so sometimes, from the wind direction at ground level. So, it is important to remember that as you climb for any vertical manoeuvre, not only will the wind speed increase but the wind direction may also change. This change can be as much as 20-30 degrees from the wind direction at ground level. So, if you find that you are having difficulty in performing a nice round loop on a strong wind day, those are some of the reasons.

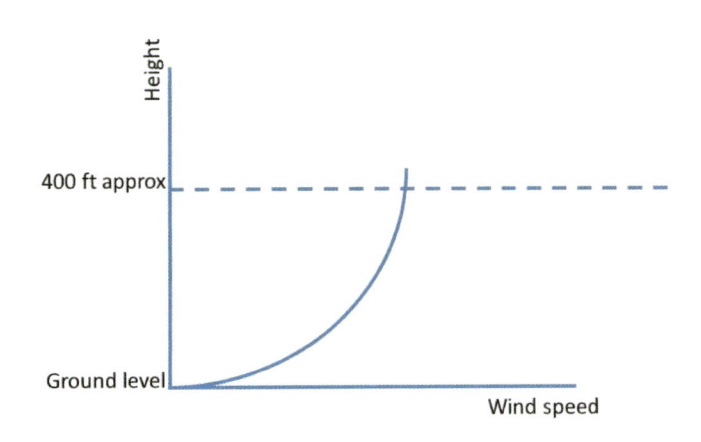

108. There is another effect to consider when landing in a strong wind. As the aircraft descends to the final part of the landing, the flare can be defeated by the dropping wind speed as the aircraft gets close to the ground. Since the aircraft has mass, and because it's moving it has momentum, it cannot change speed instantaneously – unless it's a very light foamy! The effect of a sudden drop in wind speed will, therefore, be felt as a sudden drop in airspeed by the aircraft as it takes time for the mass of the aircraft to respond.

109. If the effect is to drop the aircraft's airspeed below its stalling speed it will stall and "arrive" or you will suffer a heavy landing. The way to defeat this is either to approach at a higher airspeed (your ground speed will

be low in a high wind) or steepen the approach path from about 50 ft above the ground. The aircraft picks up airspeed as the wind gradient is robbing the aircraft of it resulting in a roughly similar airspeed as you approach the ground for the landing flare.

THE CANALYSER

110. The canalyser, also called a T Can, is a small wing that is fitted close to or on a monoplane's canopy area and around the main wing's and the fuselage's thickest point. They first appeared a bit before 2010 and initially were quite small. They have grown somewhat since. The ultimate canalyser is the top wing of a biplane!

111. Fitting a canalyser has the effect of greatly increasing the rudder's authority. Indeed, by combining a canalyser with the deep fuselages that are in vogue today you can carry out a knife edge loop with a relatively small rudder deflection.

112. This photo shows the typical location of a canalyser.

113. Why does this happen? The answer is a little technical but is all to do with the vortices that are generated at the canalyser tips.

114. The canalyser behaves like a small wing and influences the flow over the rear of the fuselage and horizontal and vertical tail surfaces. It does this because of the pair of trailing wing tip vortices that it generates and their interaction with the surfaces behind the canalyser. This has the effect of increasing rudder authority

115. Hence, the huge improvement in rudder power, allied to the tall fuselage, makes knife edge flight for these airframes very easy. Note that the tail plane and elevator also become more effective. In the next photo, compare with the biplane behind it showing the different relationship between the biplane wings.

CHAPTER 4. SETUP AND TRIMMING

INTRODUCTION

116. In this chapter, I've set out the sorts of things that you need to work through as part of the setup and trimming process. This chapter tells you what to do and the Annex A (Set up and Trimming) contains the same information but in much more detail to explain why and how to make the adjustments.

117. There is an excellent guide to trimming on the GBRCAA website[13]. In fact, you get the Association's own guide, as well as 3 others: Mike Chipchase; Pete Goldsmith and Bryan Hebert. At this stage, the GBRCAA Trimming Guide is probably the least complicated, so I would recommend that you use that guide but the others are there for you to explore as you get more experienced.

118. Bryan Hebert's Triangulation Trimming Guide is a particularly rigorous guide but you need to go to his website for the full information[14] but you need an airframe with adjustable wing, and tail, incidence. In Bryan's guide, he places much emphasis on a more forward CG than most pilots use allied to a slightly higher main wing incidence. However, following the crawl, walk, run philosophy, I would only try to use Bryan's techniques when you have some experience of flying precision aerobatics and you have an airframe with adjustable incidences for both the main wing and the tail plane although the latter is of lesser importance.

119. Zero gravity trimming is worth a passing mention. What this term means is that you adjust the elevator trim so that the aircraft trimmed to fly a vertical downline hands-off. What that means is that you need to maintain a pull force on the elevator when flying S&L and a push force of the same magnitude when flying inverted. I do not recommend using this type of trimming when you are first learning how to fly aerobatics as it will complicate matters for you.

120. Everyone is capable of flying precision aerobatics even if you just have something like a Wot 4 but it does need you to set up your model in a very methodical way. At the end of the day, the pilot's skill, and the amount of practice they do, will be the dominant factor in achieving the desired result but the right aeroplane, correctly set up, is a huge help! What follows refers to setting up precision, or traditional, aerobatic aircraft but not 3D aircraft.

121. For many pilots, trimming is limited to checking the CG is within the range shown on the plan/ARTF[15] instructions, followed by a test flight using the Transmitter trims to get the aircraft to fly straight and level. If that

---

[13] Trimming Guides http://www.gbrcaa.org/?page_id=1072
[14] Bryan Hebert Triangulation Trimming - https://www.ckaero.net/pages/triangulation-trimming
[15] Almost ready to fly. Also, aircraft are offered for sale in an unpainted state called Almost Ready to Cover (ARTC).

is all you do, then you are in for a surprise as there is a whole range of things that you can change or adjust that will make your aeroplane fly better. The difference between flying an aircraft that has been set up as the instructions and one that has been trimmed to optimise its performance can be quite stark. This requires working through a process so that at the end you will end up with an aircraft that feels completely different and much nicer to fly at no cost.

SERVO SETUP

122. The best way to ensure that you are making full use of the power and resolution of your servos is to spend a little time on setting them up correctly. Some makes of servo are better than others as regards their resolution and the slop or backlash in their gear trains. Check for smooth movement over the entire range and do not use servos that are jerky or slower one way than the other. Seek advice on the GBRCAA Forum on good servos to use in your model.

123. Start by looking at what you want to produce in the way of movement on your control surface. If you are intending to fly traditional, or precision, aerobatics then you do not need vast amounts of throw. Most beginners to aerobatics are always surprised at how little control surface movement is required – more is not better with control throws!

124. **Neutral Position**. You should aim for the control horn to be at 90° to the pushrod connecting the servo to the control surface by repositioning the servo arm on the splined output shaft until it's either there or very close and only then using the sub trim for final adjustment. The pushrod and control surface horn should also be at 90° to each other.

125. **Torque and Resolution**. To maximise the servo's torque, or turning power, and resolution (accuracy and repeatability of servo commanded position) make sure that you have 100% (some go to 120% or more) servo movement for the maximum control surface movement that you need. What you must avoid is reducing servo arm movement using the Tx to achieve the required **maximum** control surface movement. It's fine to use Rates to control the control surface movement provided that maximum rates give the maximum servo arm and the maximum control surface movement needed e.g, sufficient elevator for spinning.

> NB. For a rudder pull-pull cable arrangement to work properly, it is essential to get the geometry correct. That is, the distance between the rudder control horn holes must be exactly the same as the distance between the servo arm holes.

126. **Pushrod Connectors**. The pushrod ends should not exhibit any slop when connected to the servo arm or control horn. See Annex A for more information on this topic.

127.　**Twin Elevator Servos**. Some F3A aircraft have dual mini servos mounted in each tail plane half to drive their elevators. Even good quality servos will not always keep the movement of the two elevators together all the time. Annex A para 490 contains more detail on setting up twin servos.

Servo Centring

128.　The ability of a servo to centre accurately is essential if you are to be able to trim the aircraft accurately. As an example, early in my aerobatic life I used servos that did not centre accurately and the result was I could not rely on the aircraft flying level after pushing or pulling to fly level! **Money spent on good quality servos will make the biggest difference to your flying ability.**

Control Throws

129.　For almost all precision aerobatic manoeuvres, you'll find that approximately 10° each way for ailerons and elevators is all you'll need. The rudder will need around 25°. That's not much movement but it's enough when you have the CG in the right place. You will need more elevator movement for stalling, usually around 20°-25°, with around 35°-40° for the rudder for spinning. So, the rule is to mount your pushrod so that you can achieve the maximum control surface movement with maximum servo arm movement. You can then use RATES to access smaller control movements. See Annex A on how to convert degrees into mm or inches.

Hinges

130.　OK, we've got our servos sorted out and the pushrods connected up and the next area to examine is the hinging. The key issue with hinging control surfaces is that it is accurately done. The main faults are:

- hinge slots not in the middle of the wing/tail plane/fin and the aileron/elevator/rudder control surfaces.

- too big a gap between the wing or fuselage and the control surface. The gap should be as small as possible consistent with the control surface movement not being inhibited.

- the pushrod holes in the control horn must line up with the middle of the hinge line when the surface is at neutral – see diagram below. Otherwise, you will get some non-linear movement introduced – i.e. more up than down or vice versa – and that will make accurate flying more difficult.

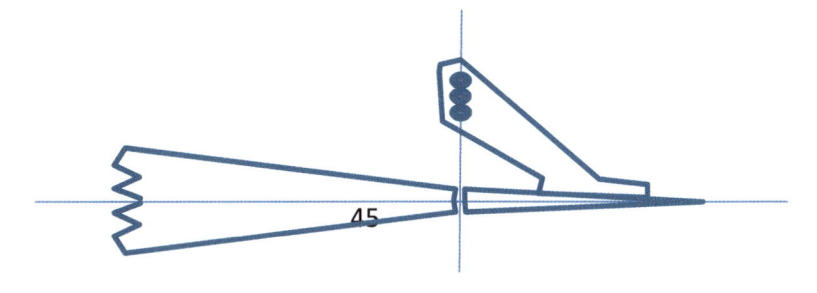

INITIAL SETTING OF CENTRE OF GRAVITY (CG).

131.   Many club pilots set the CG for their first flight and never think about it again if the flight was a "success". Fine tuning the CG position can transform a difficult to fly aircraft into one that is solidly stable but a pleasure to fly.

132.   I used to do that as well until I was discussing the fact that I was running out of elevator movement for the final flare for landing. My mentor suggested moving the CG back a bit a little at a time to see what difference that would make. So, as I couldn't move the Rx battery in this setup, I armed myself with some sticky weights (pop down to your local tyre fitters and see if you can beg some 5g and 10g sticky lead off them – but be prepared to pay a nominal sum) and stuck on 5 gm weights as far aft as I could on my Wot 4. I will now describe how you check for the optimum CG position. You will be amazed at the difference in the model's behaviour when you find the optimum position for the CG.

133.   Remember, the CG position is the single most powerful trimming tool you have!

134.   So, where should you set the CG? You will usually get a range for CG position. I usually opt for the middle position, and if the information is accurate and your maiden flight ended with a normal landing, you have at least established one safe position. You can now move the CG to help with some problems with the aircraft's handling but more of that later. Provided you move the CG small amounts you are not going to run into any instability problems.

ONE CHANGE AT A TIME

135.   When you make any changes to your model setup, make sure you make only one change at a time. This will avoid the problem of wondering which change has resulted in either an improvement or a problem.

TRIMMING FOR STRAIGHT AND LEVEL FLIGHT AND FINE TRIMMING THE CG

136.   OK, the CG is in the mid position, the control throws are set and we have some lower rates set as well. Typically, CG can be anywhere between 27% and 35% of Mean Aerodynamic Chord (MAC). If you have an un-tapered wing then the MAC is the same as the chord of the wing. Multiplying the chord length by 0.3 (30% of MAC) will give you the position of the CG as X inches/cm back from the leading edge as a starting point. However, if you have a tapered wing then finding the MAC is a little bit more difficult. Use the diagram below as a template to draw out your tapered wing on a piece of paper either full size or scaled. A line drawn at right angles to the

MAC line and projected to the root rib will give the CG position at the root. It's worth mentioning that Bryan Hebert specifies a CG of between 25%-28% of MAC allied to greater wing incidence.

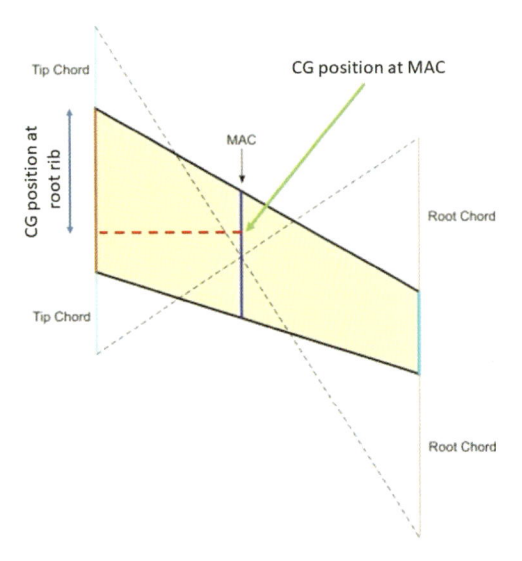

137. The first thing you'll do when you get your newly set up aircraft airborne is to trim for straight and level (S&L) flight. For a typical sports aerobatic model, you'll want around 60%-70% power. If you are flying a pattern type aircraft with a lot better than 1:1 power to weight ratio (i.e. if you release it at full power pointing vertically upwards it will accelerate away) you'll only want 50% power.

138. If you can adjust the trim steps on your Transmitter set them to 3 or 4 steps per click for the first flight allowing you to trim quickly. Reset them to 1 step per click for the second flight to fine tune your setup. If you are flying a specialist aerobatic design then you can start with 1 step per click from the beginning.

139. For aerobatic aircraft, you do not want high levels of stability in pitch but equally you don't want an unstable aircraft. Some pilots like a neutral stability aircraft but I prefer a slightly positively stable aircraft.

- A positively stable aircraft will tend to return to the position from which it has been disturbed e.g. if from straight and level (S&L) flight you pull the nose up and then release the elevator input the nose will pitch down and try and regain the last trimmed position.

- One with neutral stability will tend to stay in the same position in which you have put it.

- One with negative stability will tend to diverge in the direction in which you started it moving. So if flying S&L and you pull up the nose and release the elevator, the aircraft will continue to pitch nose up so you will need to use down elevator to achieve the required flight path. In fact, the aircraft will always want to diverge from whatever position you command and it can become "twitchy".

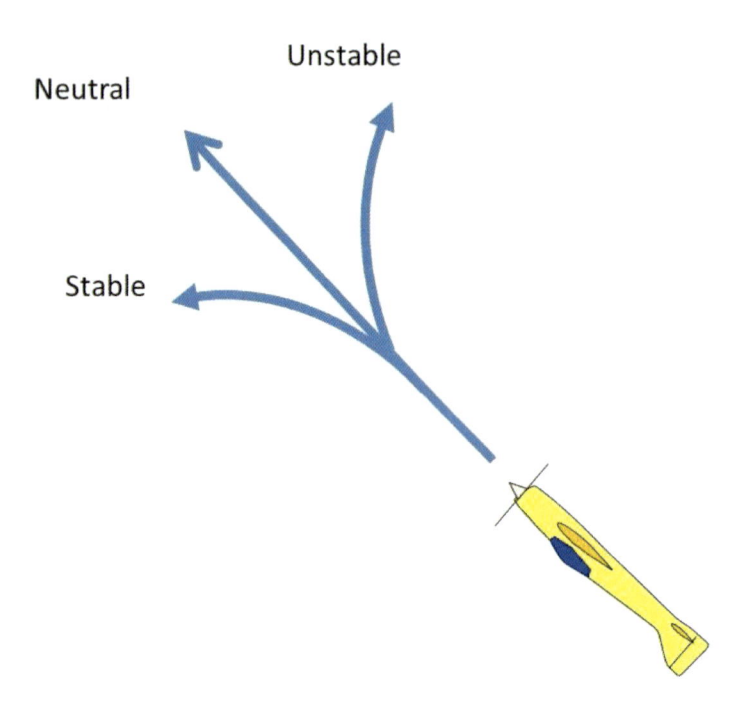

140. Think of stability as a set of solid cones, resting on a flat table represented by the red line, with the following properties:

- Stable – if you push the top of the cone by a small amount and then release it, the cone will return to sitting flat on the table,

- Neutral – if you push the cone by a small amount, (arrow pointing into the page) it will continue to roll on the table but won't return to its original position.

- Unstable – if you can manage to balance the cone on its point, good luck by the way, then the slightest nudge will cause it to topple over.[16]

---

[16] An unstable model is unlikely to survive its maiden flight unless you are very lucky! The only unstable aircraft in the real world are the 5th Generation fighters that use computers to fly them according to the pilots' control inputs e.g. the Eurofighter Typhoon.

Stable   Neutral   Unstable

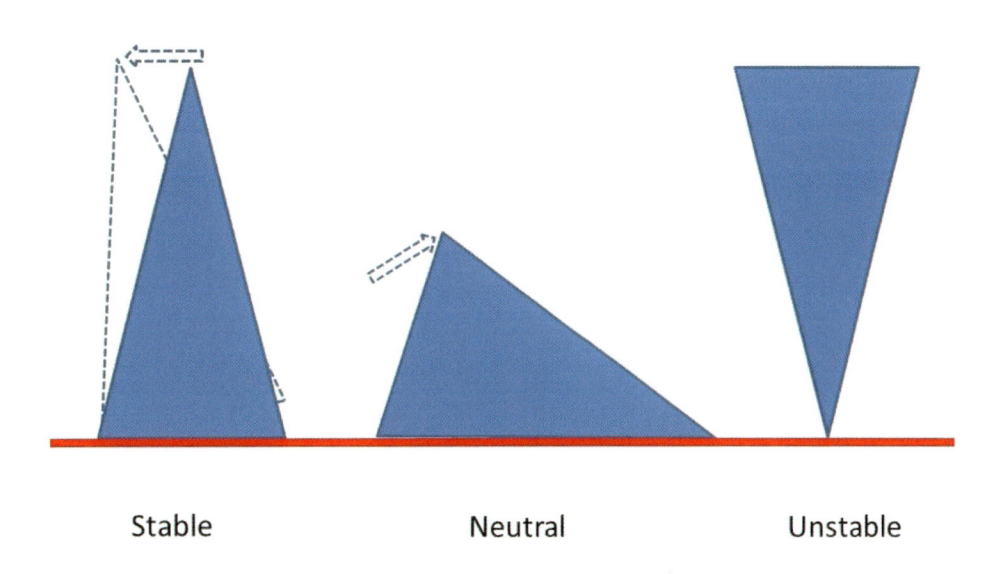

141.   Re-read the notes at para 21 where I discuss how to establish an optimum CG for your aircraft.

142.   A point that is sometimes overlooked in electrically powered aircraft is the variation in weight of the flight pack. For 10S flight packs there can be considerable difference in weight between packs from different manufacturers. Even packs from the same manufacturer will vary in weight a certain amount. Weighing your available packs and marking them as Low/Medium/High weight will allow you to position them to give the same CG position. Mark the High and Low weight pack positions and then, when you secure the pack in place, you can be sure the CG will be where you want it. Alternatively, add weight to all the lower packs to give the same pack weight for all packs you use.

143.   IC engine powered aircraft usually have their tanks in front of the CG and the CG is set with an empty tank. So, you will end up with the CG forward of the desired point with a full tank with the CG gradually moving back to the set position as the fuel is exhausted. This can have an effect on the aircraft's handling. Many specialist aerobatic aircraft have the tank mounted on the CG thus avoiding this problem. However, you must then have a pump to provide the engine with a steady flow of fuel particularly when the aircraft is pointing vertically upwards. You can buy aftermarket fuel pumps for two and four stroke engines. These can be worked either from crankcase pressure pulses or else, particularly for four strokes, by engine vibration.

ENGINE/MOTOR THRUST LINE

144.   Our next task having settled on our CG is to sort out the engine/motor thrust line.

145.   Review the text I wrote at para 31 as regards correcting for thrust line alignment.

146.   A refinement for more specialist aerobatic aircraft is to carry out a check of the aircraft's attitude when no power is applied. You do this by **carrying out a power off vertical dive to check the aircraft is tracking straight in the yaw sense.** Use the rudder trim to ensure that the aircraft tracks straight down without deviating to the left or right of vertical. This ensures that any yaw introduced by adding power is not due to an airframe issue. Now you can check if engine side thrust is correct by pulling to the vertical while applying full power and see if the aircraft goes straight up or veers to the right or to the left. (It is unlikely that at this stage you will be using a contra rotating propeller set-up but, if you are lucky enough to have such an aircraft, the motor should be set with zero side thrust and, usually, 1° down thrust.)

147.   Once you have reached the point where your aircraft's flight path is not **immediately** affected by the application or reduction in power than you have the optimum solution!

LATERAL BALANCE

148.   Lateral balance is another bit of trimming that is often only done in the static situation, i.e. when not flying. The static balance measurement may not be completely accurate but may look OK. However, in flight, any slight difference in weight between the left and right side of the whole aircraft will become apparent by the heavier side causing the wing on that side to drop when subjected to a high "g" force and what will mean the heavier wing will drop when significant g is applied. So, as you pull up for a loop, the heavier wing will drop and the aircraft will appear to screw out of the loop towards the heavier wing. You will see the same thing in an outside loop.

149.   In order to test for this condition in flight, the best way to do so is to fly a vertical downline with the throttle closed and pull back sharply on the elevator stick. It is important to ensure that you don't inadvertently apply aileron (Mode 2) or rudder (Mode 1) when doing this test. Either note which wing drops yourself or get a friend to check for you. Repeat the test between 5-10 times to be sure that it is always the same wing that drops. Now you know which wing is heavier, you can add small weights to the lighter wingtip and repeat the test until you are satisfied that the lateral balance is correct.

150.   You can now proceed to fly pitching manoeuvres safe in the knowledge that any deviation from wings level is not due to lateral imbalance but to your control inputs!

VERTICAL DOWNLINE

151. There are a number of manoeuvres in aerobatics where you want the aircraft to descend on a vertical downline, without pilot input, with the throttle closed – Square Loop, Spin and Stall turn to name but three. Most aircraft will not do this if you have set them up to be stable as they will tend to pitch to the canopy. (This is where Zero Gravity Trimming (see below) comes into its own as you trim the aircraft to fly vertically downwards hands off.)

152. These days, aerobatic aircraft are normally set up with the tailplane at 0° with the wing at 0.8° approximately. (This is sometimes referred to as decalage.) The reason the aircraft almost always pitches to the canopy on a vertical downline is that in level flight the relationship between the aircraft's weight, acting through the CG, and wing lift, acting through the Centre of Pressure causes a nose down pitch and so the tail plane/elevator provides the balancing down force at the tail to maintain the aircraft's equilibrium. This is the trimmed state of the aircraft for straight and level flight hands off where gravity acts at virtually 90° to the aircraft's longitudinal axis. Now, when you push the aircraft into a vertical descent and allow the elevator stick to return to the centre, with gravity acting along the longitudinal axis the aircraft's natural stability will try and return the relationship between the wing and the tail but there is no gravity to achieve a balance. So, given that the tail is trimmed to provide a down force, the lack of weight to balance lift results in the nose pitching up in the direction of the canopy.

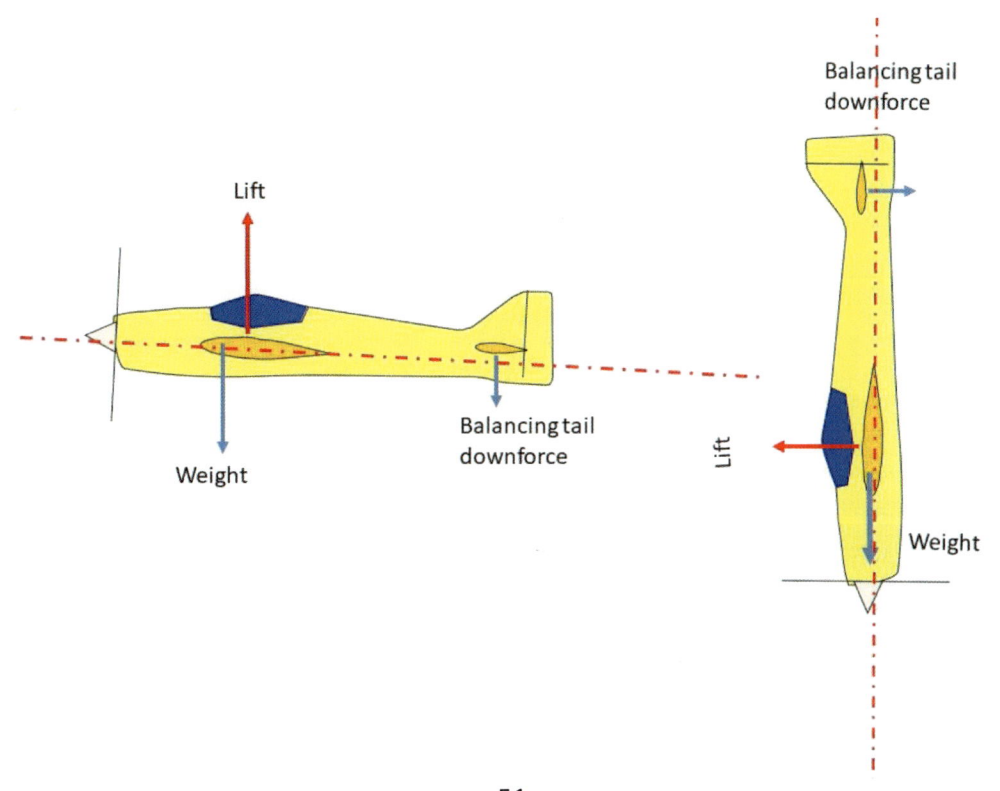

153. The most common way to achieve a vertical downline is to use your Tx to mix a small amount of down elevator to the fully closed throttle. The aim is to eliminate the down force generated by the tail plane/elevator so there is no pitch up force. Start with a small amount of elevator mixed to closed throttle and fly it to check functioning before making further changes. Do this in calm weather.

154. Remember, this is merely a starting point as you will have to make changes to the downline on windy days by using your elevator stick. Also, make sure this mix is on a switch so that it is not active when you want to flare for landing at which point a sudden nose down pitch with a closed throttle is not what you want!

VERTICAL UPLINE

155. Where there is a vertical downline there must also be a vertical upline! What we are trying to achieve with this setup is to get the aircraft to track vertically upwards by itself – well almost! We saw above that we were trying to eliminate the yawing effect of adding power and we do this by climbing the aircraft vertically, looking at it in plan form, and checking that, once set to the vertical with the rudder, no further rudder input is needed.

156. For the aircraft to be trimmed to fly S&L the wing incidence has to be positive to generate lift. In a vertical upline, this will pitch the aircraft towards the canopy. One way of resolving this is to increase the down thrust of the motor/engine so that when full power (or a lot of power) is added, the down thrust will maintain a true vertical. As for the vertical down line, since we will almost always have a wind blowing, we will need to adjust the aircraft's attitude "on the day" to compensate. So, either an over or under rotation to the vertical will be necessary.

WING INCIDENCE

157. Most sport aerobatic aircraft do not have any provision for fine tuning either the wing or tail plane incidence. As I mentioned earlier, we normally set up our aerobatic aircraft with the Tail plane at 0° and the main wing at +0.8°. To do this, you will need an incidence meter. Just enter "wing incidence meter" into a search engine and you will find a number of examples. You can choose either an analogue or digital read out. Most sport aerobatic aircraft will need to have either the trailing or leading edges packed up with balsa if you want to change their basic wing incidence setting. Provided you have an incidence meter, it is not difficult to do.

158. If you find that the "sit" of the model in the air is not to your liking, you can use wing incidence to resolve that e.g. if your aircraft sits with its tail lower than you'd like, increasing wing incidence will have the effect of raising the tail and vice versa. You will, of course, need to re-trim the aircraft to fly straight and level after changing the wing incidence.

159. You do not need to worry too much about wing incidence at this early stage. Indeed, you may not even notice the finer points of changes in wing incidence. However, as you progress, and perhaps purchase a model

with such adjustability then you can turn to a number of the trimming schemes, particularly that of Bryan Hebert, that I have pointed to earlier. They will give more details on how wing incidence combined with moving the CG can be used to cure a number of faults in the way your aircraft handles.

GEOMETRIC ACCURACY

160.   The instructions for your model may well have indicated how you should maintain geometric accuracy for your model as you assemble or build it. I cannot stress this enough. If you build in a geometric inaccuracy, e.g. the fin is not at right angles to the tailplane or the tailplane is misaligned with the wing, then expect the aircraft to display some poor characteristics when you try and fly precision aerobatics. It really is worth its weight in gold to get the geometry as accurate as you can manage. Note that not all ARTF models can be relied on being accurately made. A little bit of "adjusting" may well be needed but time spent doing this will be well rewarded.

KNIFE EDGE TRIMMING

161.   Most sport aerobatic aircraft which do not have deep fuselages (in the vertical sense) can be made to fly in knife edge (that is with the wings vertical and relying on the fuselage and engine power to keep the aircraft flying at constant height) but are not particularly suited to knife edge (or KE) manoeuvres. There are a few aircraft designs that can be trimmed to fly without interaction between the rudder and the aircraft's flight path with the CG in a particular position. The rest need some amount of mixing to achieve a low work load for the pilot. The mixing in this case has Rudder as Master and either or both of Aileron/Elevator as Slave.

162.   Aileron can be mixed to rudder to reduce any tendency to unroll or over roll while Elevator can be mixed in to prevent pitch in the direction of the canopy or towards the undercarriage which if not corrected in the mix will drag the aircraft off its desired heading. You need to do these tweaks using small amounts of mixing initially and with a switch to switch the mix in or out. It is quite often the case that the mixes for left and right rudder Knife Edge will be different both for amount and direction.

AILERON DIFFERENTIAL

163.   You may have come across this with some of your models. When right aileron is applied, as the aircraft rolls to the right it may yaw to the left slightly. This looks like its tail has dropped. This is caused by there being more lift and hence drag on the wing with the down-going aileron lifting the wing than the up-going aileron reducing lift on the other wing helping to lower it. The problem can be solved by using the aileron differential function in your Tx. **Specialist aerobatic aircraft rarely display this trait**. When inverted, differential works against what you are trying to achieve and since you spend half your time inverted in aerobatics it's usually not recommended.

164. The usual way of checking for the need for aileron differential is to fly the aircraft directly towards yourself aligned with the wind direction. Then pull to the vertical while applying appropriate power, pause to establish truly vertical flight and then half roll quickly using only the ailerons. Do this several times and rolling in both directions. Note in which direction the aircraft yaws.

165. If after a half roll to the right, the aircraft yaws to the right, then the right wing has more drag than the left wing and we would want to reduce the aileron throw on the wing and vice versa. It will take some time to sort this out as there may well be other problems in the structure of the aircraft also contributing to this effect e.g. a slightly twisted fuselage.

166. The adverse yaw is caused by more induced drag on the wing with the greater lift and not the aileron drag. When using differential aileron to cure adverse yaw you reduce the deflection of the surface on the wing with the higher lift. This reduces both drag due to lift and profile drag, i.e. reinforcing the drag reduction. Conversely, increasing the (upward) deflection on the other wing increases the profile drag, but decrease the lift and, hence, the lift induced drag, i.e. introducing opposing effects that would tend to cancel out.

GOOD TO GO?

167. When you can let your aircraft fly from one end of the line to the other with your hands off the sticks and it will climb and descend vertically in straight lines, you are now ready to start flying aerobatics with a properly trimmed aircraft. From now on, all the problems are down to you and not the way the aeroplane flies!

168. Having reduced your workload by having a properly trimmed aircraft, you now will be looking to fly more accurately and to fly existing or new manoeuvres to a much higher standard. Initially, you will find that as you try to fly in this new way, you will feel a higher workload. The more you fly, the more your workload will reduce as you begin to do more things subconsciously and you will be able to start thinking ahead of the aircraft. That will probably cause you to think that the trim is not quite right after all so come back to the trimming section until you get it right. It is probably best to keep your flight to no more than ten minutes and then to spend at least that long, if not longer, reviewing how you got on, what you did right, what you did wrong and what you need to do in your next flight. It can help to keep a note book to jot down these thoughts and plans. This will help you to make progress in a more methodical way which, in the long run, will help you to progress at a faster rate.

169. Remember, changes in temperature and humidity will twist a wooden structure and your careful trimming will be defeated. So, trimming is a regular task to make sure the aircraft helps and does not fight you.

CHAPTER 5. THE BASICS OF AEROBATIC MANOEUVRES

INTRODUCTION

170. This chapter is for those who are trying to understand what is required to fly large smooth aerobatic manoeuvres. Not many clubs will have practising competition aerobatic pilots. If you are lucky enough to have one at your club, and they are willing to help you, then do use them.

171. For those who don't have a resident guru, in this chapter I'm trying to help you to understand what goes on in a range of aerobatic manoeuvres. I include some advice on the Tx functions that can help you with these manoeuvres:

- Top, middle and bottom lines

- Loops

- Use of the Throttle

- Use of Rudder

- Rolls

- Stall Turn (aka the Hammerhead)

- Stalling

- Spinning

- The issue of Weathercocking

- Inverted Flying

- Hand Held or Tray Mounted Transmitter

- Transmitter Functions

TOP, BOTTOM AND MIDDLE LINES

172.   Precision aerobatics are conducted on three horizontal lines both for reference and for use. In Chapter 3, para 56, I introduced the Aerobatic Box. Within that Box, we talk about the top line, meaning the one that is at 60° above the horizontal, and a bottom line. The bottom line is usually flown between 100-150 ft or around 3 houses high. It follows that there is also a middle line in between these two. For example, if you were going to fly a Vertical Figure of Eight you might enter in the middle, fly a loop and then fly an outside loop. The middle line would then be the height you entered the Figure of Eight i.e. halfway between the two circles that make up the Eight.

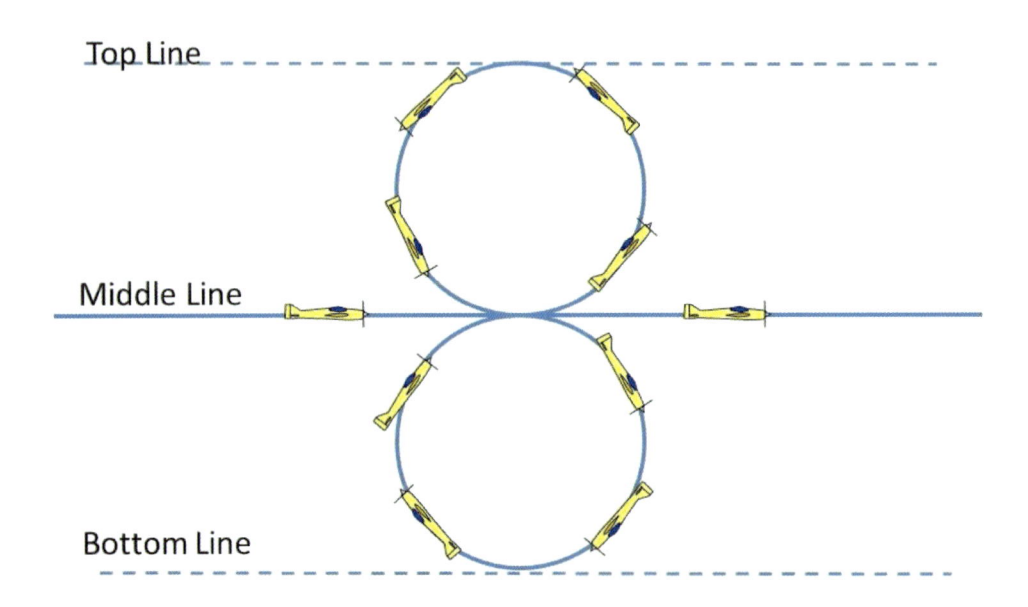

173.   Why are these lines important? Well, one of the skills in precision aerobatics is to fly a long level leg. By level I mean no climbing or diving or losing direction while the line is being flown. It is very important that you get into the habit of flying like this. Say you have to fly a half loop manoeuvre at one end of the Box and need to fly to the other end to fly another half loop, you must maintain height and direction to enable the second half loop to have the same diameter and for the exit point to be at the same height as the entry to the first half loop and be on the same Line.

174.   It is also not just height keeping we need but also the ability to fly along the track on the ground that could be 70 m, 110 m or 150 m away from where you are standing. That requires correction for any crosswind that is blowing by flying the aircraft so its nose is pointing to the windward side of the required track line. I have covered this in more detail in Chapter 3 para 100.

175.   I cannot stress enough the importance of accuracy in flying in order to achieve precision aerobatics. While it may seem boring to practice flying along a line at top, middle and bottom levels, it is a skill that can only be learned by constant repetition. Even top pilots usually have an exercise routine that they fly regularly to make sure that this vital skill is maintained. Without this skill, flying precision aerobatics becomes extremely difficult and, more to the point, you will not score as highly in competition as you might think you ought.

176.   One of the skills that is invaluable to develop is a level of self-criticism applied to the accuracy of your flying. Asking a friend to give you this view isn't always too helpful unless they also know for what they are looking. The average club pilot is unable to provide useful input to an aspiring precision aerobatic pilot simply because the level of accuracy we require is not something that they recognise. This isn't meant to denigrate them just a statement of fact. I would say that most club pilots could raise their flying standard if they were so inclined and given a little help.

LOOPS

177.   In Chapter 3, I described the forces acting on an aircraft in the loop as an example of how gravity affects the other forces acting on the aircraft. I also described the effect of wind on manoeuvres. So, this is how to overcome these issues.

178.   Flying a loop is much more than applying full power and hauling back on the stick! One of the reasons that aerobatic models are fairly lightly built and have powerful engines/motors is so that you can fly large manoeuvres, accurately, at a constant speed. That means the control response is the same all the way round the manoeuvre from the pilot's viewpoint and, for the spectator, the manoeuvre looks really nice. This means you have to use the throttle throughout the manoeuvre to adjust for the changing effects of gravity and wind. The other point about manoeuvres is to think about their size. The size of a manoeuvre is scored by its matching size relative to the size of manoeuvring zone and the relative size of the other manoeuvres performed throughout the schedule.

179.   While a 2 m standard aircraft will be powerful enough to enable you to fill the Aerobatic Box you may need to choose a manoeuvre size that suits the power of your aircraft. So, a bigger manoeuvre envelope will get a better score than a small manoeuvre envelope – remember that size is a judging criterion. The downside is that you need to fly the aircraft all the way round as well as be ready to correct for the any changes in wind speed and direction as the aircraft climbs and descends. I hope you can now appreciate the reason for trimming to avoid any pitch or

yaw changes as power is changed. There is quite enough going on without having to deal with those issues at the same time!

180. Let's assume that your aircraft is flying from right to left as you come in to perform a loop.

181. **To deal with the effects of gravity**, these are the issues you need to address:

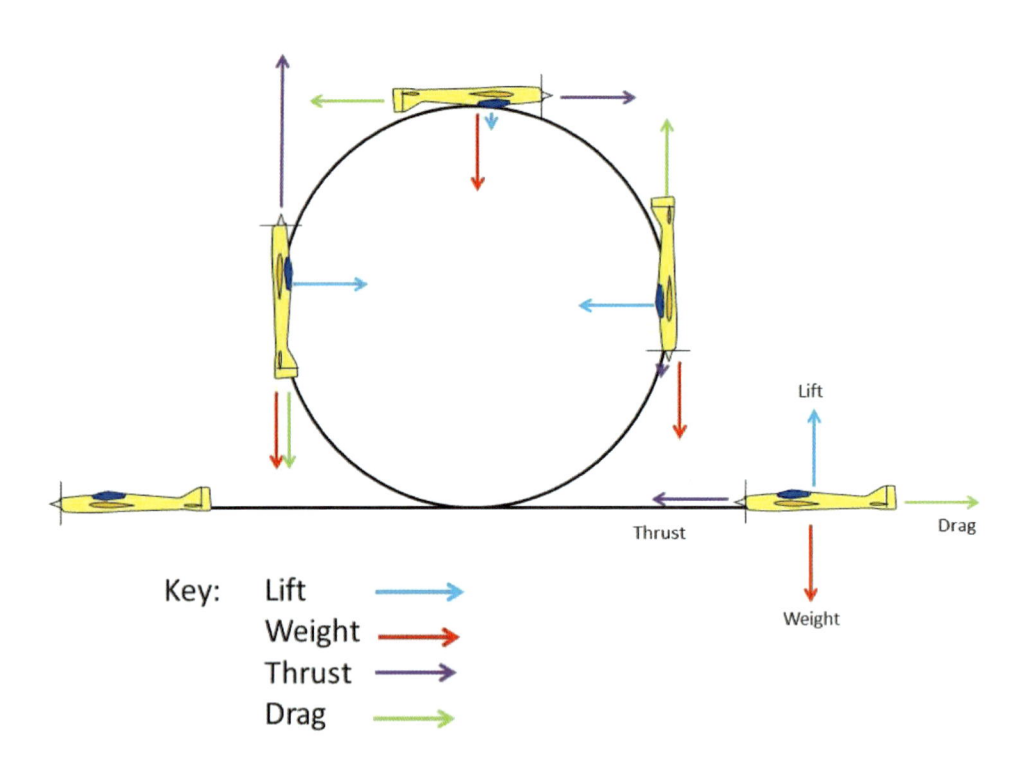

Key: Lift →
      Weight →
      Thrust →
      Drag →

- 1st Quarter – As you start the loop in the first quarter:

    o you have to increase lift to overcome gravity in order to climb (ease stick back)

    o more lift creates more drag (more power needed)

    o as the aircraft rotates to go up less lift supports the weight (more power needed)

    o at the end of the 1st quarter, engine power is the only force opposing gravity and drag so the maximum amount of power is needed here

    o the lift force is what makes the aircraft follow the path of the loop

- 2nd Quarter – As you start the second quarter of the loop:
  - Gravity is now assisting the roundness of the loop so ease off on the amount of lift needed from the wing to fly a round loop i.e. you must ease off the pull on the elevator stick.
  - Less lift reduces drag.
  - As you get round the second quarter, the effect of gravity acting as "drag" also reduces so start reducing throttle to prevent the aircraft accelerating.
  - Be ready to reduce lift further to maintain the loop's geometry (may even have to add a touch of down elevator to maintain the loop's shape).

- 3rd Quarter. – Now:
  - Gravity continues to act with lift and maintain the shape of the loop but it is increasingly adding to engine thrust. So, smoothly close the throttle until it is fully closed by the time your reach 2 o'clock (or 10 o'clock if you are looping the other way).
  - Continue not to pull too hard on the elevator as well because Gravity is still your friend.

- 4th Quarter. – Like the fickle friend it is:
  - Gravity now starts to work against lift and the roundness of the loop so increase the pull on the stick to maintain the loop geometry.
  - Gravity reduces its help to the engine thrust so, by the time you reach 4 o'clock, (or 8 o'clock if looping the other way) start advancing the throttle so that you are back to cruise setting just before you are level and exiting the loop.

Reduce power smoothly to idle

Increase power smoothly to "cruise"

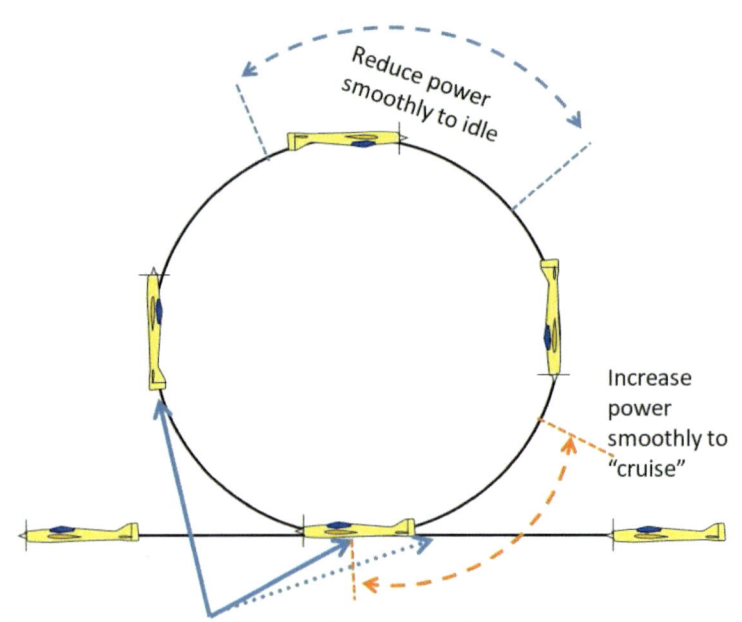

Increase power smoothly to maintain airspeed

182. **To deal with the effect of a headwind**, let's assume that you are flying with a wind that is blowing at 30° across your desired line. This is what you will need to do address the headwind component:

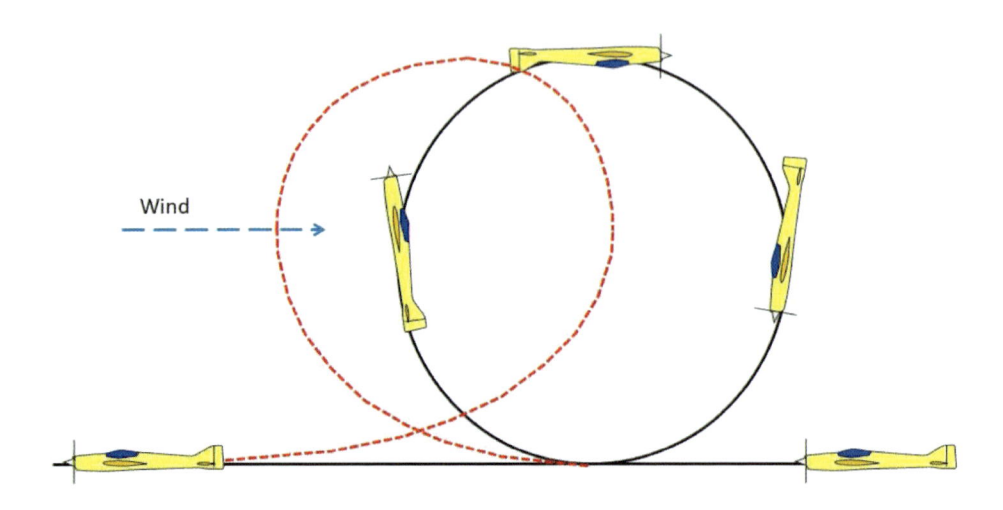

Wind

- 1st Quarter
    - A gentler pull up into the loop than in still air, as the headwind will blow your aircraft back onto the proper looping track, and make sure the aircraft is inclined into wind as it reaches the end of the first Quarter so it is not blown backwards at that point

- 2nd Quarter
    - Continue with slightly less up elevator as in the still wind condition until you reach the end of the second Quarter

- 3rd Quarter
    - Now you need to apply more up elevator to get the aircraft to follow the correct path.
    - The power should have been smoothly closed to either idle of a touch above by no later than the 2 o'clock position (or 10 o'clock if looping the other way)

- 4th Quarter
    - Continue with the extra elevator pull but adjust it so that your aircraft meets the proper bottom position for the loop.
    - From about 4 o'clock onwards, increase the power, possibly adding more than necessary if there is a strong wind to drive the aircraft forward sufficiently to end the loop at the centre point and at the same height as your entry height.

183. **To deal with the effect of the crosswind**, consider the situation I described in Chapter 3. The diagram below is another way of looking at the problem you are trying to overcome. Let us assume that you are going to fly around a cylinder. Use a large cardboard tube to represent your cylinder. If you have a stick model use that to "fly" around the cylinder firstly, coming in at right angles to the major axis of the cylinder. That would represent the case of looping without a crosswind. Now yaw your stick model so that it is coming in at an angle to the cylinder and then "fly" around it. See how the aircraft has to be rolled slightly all the way round to maintain the correct relationship between the wing and the surface of the cylinder.

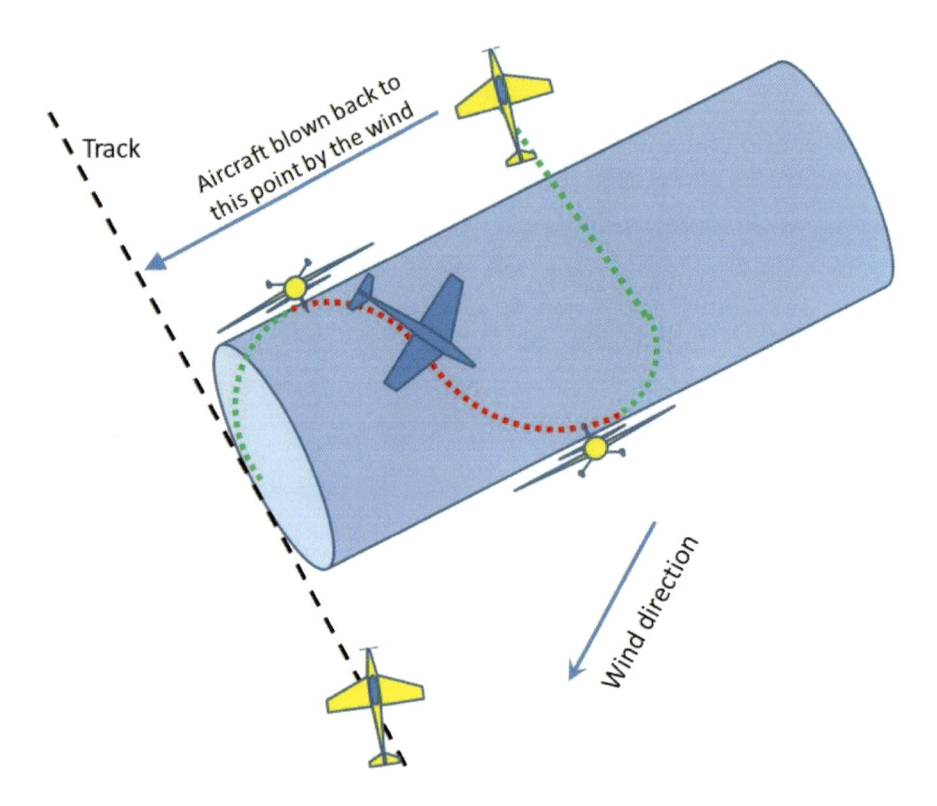

184. In the diagram above, I have shown this case. The aircraft's path in still air is shown by the dotted line. The green dotted line is the path under the cylinder while the red dotted line is the path above it. When there is a crosswind, the aircraft will be blown back along the cylinder the whole time so that at the end of the loop the aircraft position is as shown by the blue arrow.

185. There are two options on how to counter it:

- In the **first way**, where heading is not too far off the desired track, as you start your pull up, you need to do two things. Gently squeeze in some right rudder to keep the aircraft tracking correctly in the vertical plane. What you are trying to do is to fly a slightly barrel loop to prevent the wind blowing the aircraft towards you as your ground speed reduces as you pull up. The effect of the wind will be such that the loop will not appear to be a barrel loop. Note also that wind speed will probably be higher and the direction alter slightly as you travel upwards through the loop and you will face a decrease in wind speed and change in wind direction on the way down.

- In the **second way**, where there is a significant crosswind, the great advantage is that you maintain the wing in the plane of the loop as it would be in still air and is what the judges are seeking. **What you are trying to achieve is to fly around a cylinder that is at right angles to The Line.** That means that as the aircraft pitches up it must also roll so that the wings always remain parallel to the surface of the cylinder. To achieve this, you need a very small application of aileron as you fly the loop. This would result in a barrel roll in still air as your wings would cause the aircraft to move in the direction of the roll, but here, this is exactly what we want to achieve! As you start the pull up apply a small amount of roll in the direction from which the wind is blowing in order to keep the wings in the correct plane of manoeuvre, in this case it would be a slight roll to the right (see diagram below) so that the wing looks as if it is "level" or in the same plane, all the way round. After the first ¼ loop, the wings should be parallel to the Box edge line. You don't need much and do it smoothly so it appears in the correct plane. Once you've established the bank keep your eye on the flight path and either take some bank off or add a touch more to keep the loop in the right place. Develop the habit of making sure the wings are level as you go through the top of the loop. Bear in mind that as the aircraft climbs the wind speed and direction may vary so you should be prepared to counter the effect this will have on the flight path so you may need to vary the amount of bank you are using. Do make sure your wings appear level at the beginning, the top and bottom of the loop so to the judges it doesn't look as if your wings are banked!

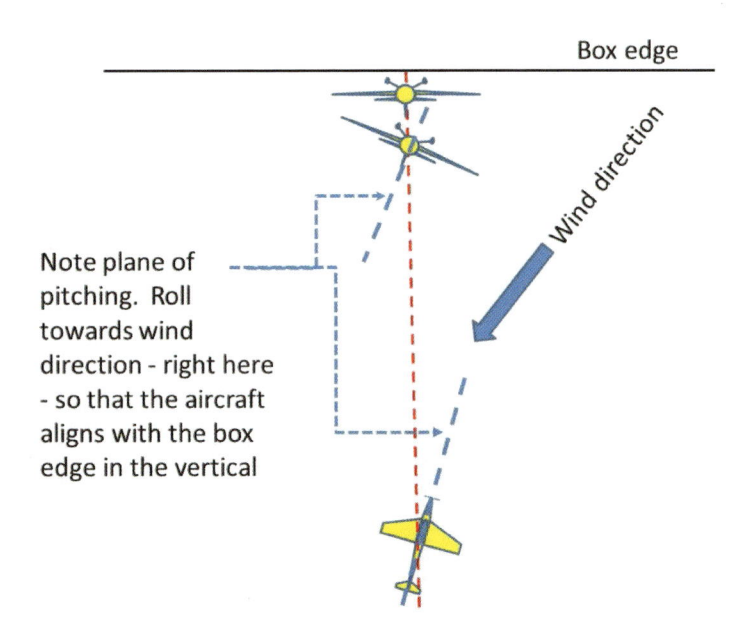

Note plane of pitching. Roll towards wind direction - right here - so that the aircraft aligns with the box edge in the vertical

Box edge

Wind direction

186. Choose which ever technique suits you – both work but the second technique will score you higher points. You may choose a combination of the two as well.

187. Remember, you **roll towards the direction from which the wind is blowing** to correct this issue provided you are looping. It is the opposite if you are flying an outside loop.

63

188. So, there is a lot going on in a simple manoeuvre such as a loop. Break it down into smaller digestible chunks to begin with. Deal with each issue in turn beginning with gravity before you go for the full process I've described above.

189. These techniques will give you a start point for flying your loop but since each aircraft type will have different drag characteristics, and an IC engine will need to throttle up earlier than an electric motor, you will need to adjust your throttle and elevator controls to achieve a nice round loop that looks like it is being flown at the same speed all the way round. You'll know when you've got there because it will look effortless to a spectator, and in due course, it may even feel perfectly normal to you!

USE OF THE THROTTLE

190. As you will have gathered by now, the throttle is not an on-off switch. Throttle management is a key component of precision aerobatics and it can take quite a long time to get proficient at throttle use. To help us, we use the Throttle Curve function. If you have never used this, please read up about it in your Tx manual or else ask someone who knows how to set up throttle curves.

191. For the avoidance of doubt, when I talk about power, what I mean is the physical force, or thrust, generated by the motor/engine. Motor/engine rpm is not always easy to correlate with the linearity of thrust, hence, the need to use the Throttle Curve function. Using this function, we can get our throttle stick to provide the required linearity in response that we are seeking from use of the throttle stick. So, regardless of where the throttle stick is at any one time, moving it a little only provides a little more, or less, thrust and not a sudden surge of power. A linear response to throttle stick position is what makes throttle control during aerobatics much easier to achieve.

192. As I mentioned earlier, most specialist aerobatic aircraft have engines/motors specified that provide over a 1:1 power to weight ratio. The objective is to allow the pilot to maintain a constant speed while flying manoeuvres in the vertical. This requires the relationship with throttle stick position and actual engine/motor power to allow the pilot to feel almost a linear relationship between throttle stick position and required power. For such models, we usually set half power or half throttle stick, as the datum power for S&L flying. Most club aerobatic aircraft do not have this abundance of power so tend to need about two thirds power to give us the required S&L speed. This then means that there is insufficient excess power for the pilot to be able to fly vertical manoeuvres at constant speed but for starting off in precision aerobatics this is an acceptable trade-off as it doesn't cost you any more than you have spent on your current aircraft.

193. For an electric motor, you can use your wattmeter to find what the various levels of power being produced by the motor for throttle stick position. In this case, we are not measuring rpm but the actual power being consumed. You could also rig up a balance to read the amount of thrust being produced but for our purposes what

the wattmeter says is probably good enough. So, if you wanted half power at half throttle, it is relatively easy to set.

194. For an IC engine, this is not so simple since rpm isn't a good measure of power on its own. For a start, the most sensitive part of the throttle tends to be at the low end while from three quarters open to full power rarely produces as much of a power increase. If you have a spring balance, then using that in the model restraint line will give you a reading on what maximum thrust is and then you can adjust the mid-point accordingly. I have flown models where the power is all down at the bottom end and others where it's all at the top end. For our purposes, we need much more adjustable power.

195. Throttle management for an electric model is even more difficult than for an IC model as you don't have the engine noise to let you know how much power you have selected. Therefore, it is easy to overuse power when you first start flying precision aerobatics with electric motors and burn up your flight pack.

196. The lack of engine noise in an electric model also makes selecting your "cruise" power accurately more difficult. Until I got a Tx that provided a beep function for throttle stick position, I was either setting too high or too low a power setting. With the beep set to sound at "cruise" power, I could be sure I had the same power set either when reducing power from maximum or increasing power from idle.

197. The usual curve for electric motors looks something like this in the THROTTLE CURVE Screen:

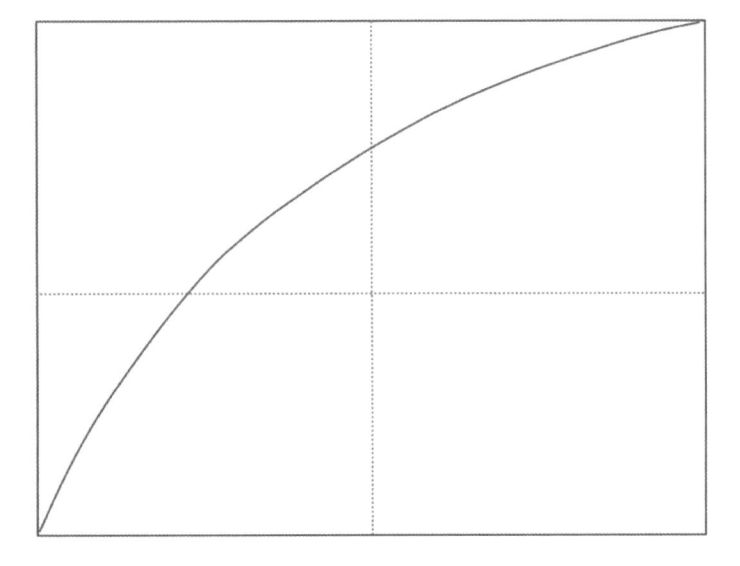

198. Or like this, where a plateau in the curve is positioned at your desired cruise power setting.

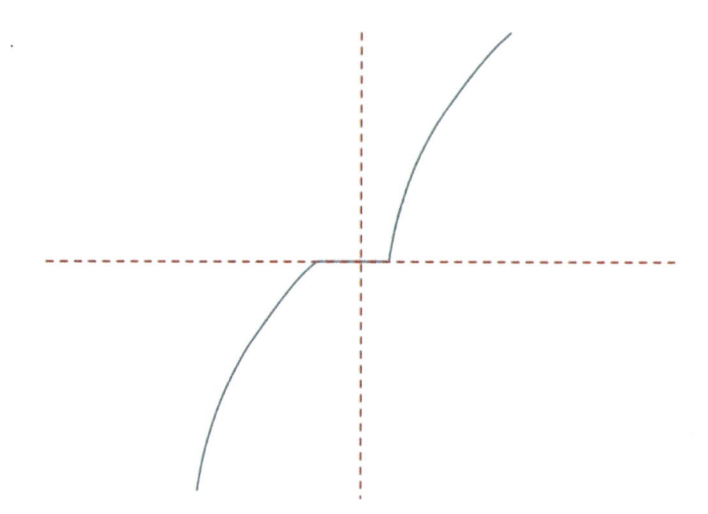

199. It is also useful to set an idle for an electric motor so that the propeller is just turning i.e. the lowest sustainable speed that you can set. This will help you during landing by providing an instant response, just like an IC engine, to the throttle rather than the more usual situation of moving the throttle several clicks before getting the ESC to provide power. Depending on your ESC, this can give a burst of power just when you don't want it! For example, when your aircraft is on approach with the throttle closed and you want a touch more power to overcome an under-shoot situation. A sudden burst of power at that point makes your landing look very untidy! Idle can be selected by using the second Throttle Curve capability in your Tx and raising the bottom curve point until you reach the lowest sustainable rpm for the motor.

USE OF RUDDER

200. If you haven't noticed this already, the rudder will keep getting mentioned almost all the time! So, if you are used to letting your rudder and throttle alone for most of the time you are flying, this is going to have to change! The rudder is used almost all the time to cater for amongst other things:

- Staying on your desired ground track – once you have settled on S&L for your manoeuvre, you use rudder to keep the aircraft pointing in the right direction and not aileron. That's because you attract penalties each time your bank is altered in a manoeuvre, apart from rolling ones.

- Carrying out wind correction on the way up and down vertical or 45° lines.

- Knife edge manoeuvres.

201. Now, while all this is going on, you need to keep the wings level.

You Need to Use All the Controls – (almost all the time)

202.   Now, if you are not used to using rudder and throttle almost continuously when you fly, you will be surprised by just how important proper control of these functions are in aerobatics. It is essential that you become used to using all four primary controls together pretty much all of the time if you are to achieve the sort of control that will allow you to fly your aerobatic patterns regardless of wind direction and strength.

The good thing is that learning to fly precision aerobatics will help you with flying all your other aircraft!

Rolls

203.   There are essentially five types of roll:

- Normal speed roll

- Slow roll

- Point rolls

- Rolls in opposite directions either point or full rolls

- Snap or flick rolls.

Normal Roll

204.   The key point to remember with rolling is that you will need eventually to coordinate aileron, elevator and rudder inputs. Initially, if you are performing normal rolls, you can get away with just using aileron and elevator. I would say that a normal roll in aerobatics will be one that takes around 2 seconds to perform with a slow roll roughly double that. Normally, you set slightly higher power than required for S&L flying before you start the roll. It is easier to perform slow and point rolls if you raise power from your cruise mode as the increased airspeed gives your flight controls more power which is what you need.

Elevator Only Rolling

205.   Just before you apply aileron to start the roll, apply a quick dab of up elevator to pitch the aircraft about 10° nose up. Make sure you release the elevator before you start the roll. It is worth using a rate that gives the desired roll rate with full stick applied as you do not need to worry about maintaining a constant roll rate then! As the aircraft rolls, the nose will drop and you need to apply sufficient down elevator for an equal amount of time either side of the inverted position as shown in the diagram below. How much elevator? Sufficient to bring the

nose up to 10° nose up. The aircraft nose will then again start to fall and you then need to apply sufficient up elevator as you complete the roll to bring the nose level.

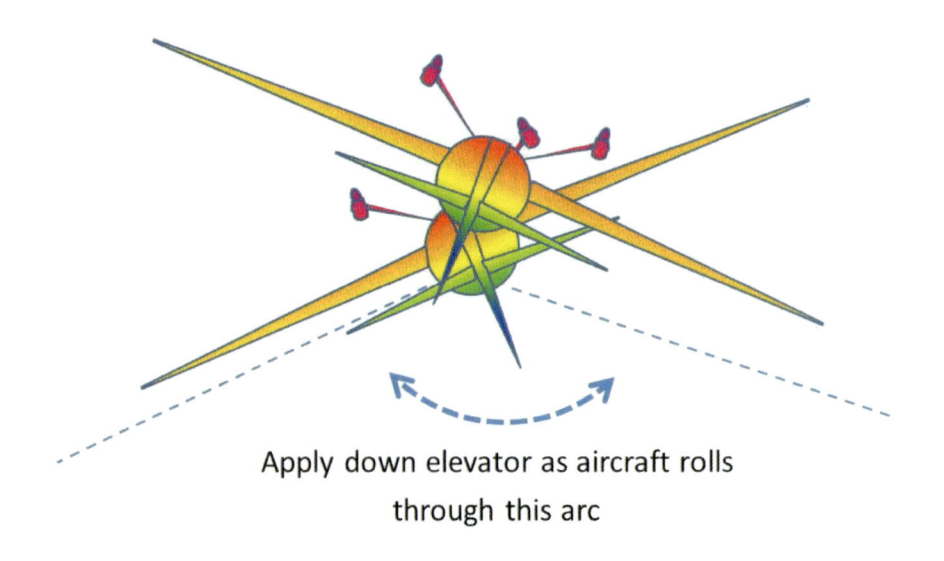

Apply down elevator as aircraft rolls through this arc

Elevator and Rudder Rolls

206. The type of aircraft you fly will determine how much you need to use the rudder when the aircraft starts to lose its wing generated lift and has to rely instead on lift being generated by the fuselage and engine. Also, with the wings vertical, different airframes will exhibit either a pull to the canopy, a pull to the undercarriage or be neutral. This can be countered either by mixing elevator to rudder movement or manually using the elevator.

207. These days in precision aerobatics, most standard rolls in competition tend to be of the slow variety. This is for two reasons. First, it gives the pilot more chance of stopping the roll accurately for either full or part rolls. Second, it helps to use a rate that gives a low rate of roll with full aileron and thus helps with the need for a constant roll rate.

208. When you first start practicing rolling, a nice safe way to do this manoeuvre is to pull up to a 45° climb adding appropriate power and then carry out the roll. As you get more confident, reduce the 45° climb progressively until you feel comfortable rolling on the horizontal.

209. The table below shows the aircraft attitude with the required control inputs:

Start from straight and level flight with the wings level. Decide which way to roll and remember that rudder goes in the opposite direction to aileron when rolling from upright. Open up a bit more power.	
In this case, we're rolling **right** so we need **left** rudder coming in as the roll starts and a touch of **up** elevator. The role of the elevator is both to keep the nose up and to prevent the rudder from yawing the aircraft off heading. So, keeping the nose at the correct level is a function of both rudder and elevator at this bank angle.	
As the aircraft continues to roll to 90°, progressively **reduce** the elevator to zero and the rudder to that **required** to maintain level flight. This is sometimes referred to as "Top Rudder" which is a term from full size aviation where the pilot will be lying on his side and top is obvious!	
Once passed 90°, you must start to **introduce down** elevator progressively **reducing** the amount of **left** rudder	
As the aircraft reaches the inverted position, you should have progressively **reduced rudder to zero** and **pushed elevator** to the amount needed to maintain level inverted flight.	

The roll has now passed inverted so when rolling from inverted rudder goes in the same direction as aileron. So begin applying right rudder while reducing the amount of down elevator. This again is to balance the effect of both rudder and elevator both to maintain height and heading.	
As the aircraft reaches the 90° bank position again, you should have **released all the down elevator** and have the **right rudder** to sufficient needed to maintain height. This again could be referred to as "Top Rudder".	
As the aircraft continues around the roll and reaches the 45° bank position, you should have started to pull in some up elevator and reduce the amount of right rudder so that again the elevator and rudder maintain the correct nose position while also maintaining heading.	
As the aircraft reaches wings level all the rudder and elevator input is bled off so that the aircraft returns to straight and level flight and remember to centralise the ailerons! Rolling fast requires faster changes in rudder and elevator throughout the manoeuvre. Rolling slower, both looks nicer and gives you more time to feed in and out rudder and elevator inputs.	

210.   It is worth thinking about breaking the whole sequence down into four quarter rolls and hold left rudder knife edge, inverted and right rudder knife edge to help to get through the whole manoeuvre in bite sized chunks. You will need to centralise the ailerons at each of the four points of course!

Useful tips.

211.   **When rolling from upright to inverted**, the rudder stick goes in the opposite direction from aileron stick for the first half of the roll.

212. **When rolling from inverted to upright,** the rudder stick goes in the same direction as aileron stick for the first half of the roll.

Slow Roll

213. For a true slow roll follow the procedure in the table above but remember you will need an even slower rate of roll. This can again be put on a rate so full aileron gives a constant slow roll at the desired roll rate. Always increase power before you start a slow roll. **It's the roll that's slow not the aircraft!** A higher airspeed gives you better control over the manoeuvre.

Point Roll

214. Point rolls demand rudder and elevator. The 4-point roll (4 x 90° roll segments) is easier to perform as you every time you stop you only need either rudder or elevator. The 8-point roll (8 x 45° roll segments) requires both on four occasions and since you have to hold the point position for a short time, accuracy is the name of the game otherwise the manoeuvre looks horrid! The table above shows how you can perform these rolls. Just remember to centre the ailerons to mark each point! The roll rate needs to be constant and the pause at each point has to be of the same duration.

Rolls in Opposite Directions

215. One of the requirements in the FAI rules for rolls in opposite directions is that there should be no gap between them. So, the roll must be reversed immediately i.e. there must be no line between opposite rolls. This applies whether the manoeuvre comprises full rolls, part rolls or a combination of the two.

216. However, if you are required to fly a combination of rolls with some in the same and others in the opposite direction, then there must be a line between all rolls or part rolls in the same direction and no line when the rolls change direction. Whilst these intricacies may not trouble you at the moment, it is as well to be aware of this peculiarity in the FAI aerobatic rules.

Flick or Snap Roll

217. The flick roll or snap is a violent roll with the wing stalled – **a horizontal spin if you like**. The manoeuvre is carried out well above the normal stalling speed and uses the elevator to raise the wing's angle of attack to its stalling or critical angle. The elevator needs to be moved as fast as possible so that the aircraft does not have time to do more than show a pitch up.

218. In precision aerobatics, however, the judging criterion is that the aircraft must be seen to break its line of flight and then autorotate. You may or may not need to have more elevator movement than I described for normal aerobatic flying to ensure the elevator power is there to get the wing to the critical angle – it's a case of suck it and

see! You will also need to apply rudder and aileron to achieve the desired rotation and speed of rotation. You can have positive snaps, up elevator, or negative snaps, down elevator. Remember that for a negative snap, the rudder will go in the opposite direction to aileron!

219. Unless specified, you can snap to the left or right. The same holds true for positive or negative snaps.

Effect of Crosswind on a Roll

220. The good news on a horizontal roll is that provided you have set the aircraft's heading to provide a ground track on top of the line, you need take no further action regarding the impact of a crosswind on a roll.

221. However, if the roll is on a vertical or 45° line, then the crosswind strength and direction may change as you climb or descend. If there is only a minor change in wind speed and direction, you may get away without any correction. Otherwise, you will either have to increase or decrease the aircraft's heading with respect to the changes in wind speed and direction to maintain the desired track.

222. To increase the track angle if rolling in the direction of the crosswind, apply a little up elevator at the 3 o'clock and down elevator at the 9 o'clock points and a little left rudder at the 6 o'clock and a little right rudder at the 12 o'clock points. To decrease track angle, the opposite applies.

STALL TURN (AKA HAMMERHEAD)

223. The stall turn is a bit of a misnomer since the aircraft wing does not stall! However, the aircraft must come to a complete halt in this manoeuvre. This is a matter of timing and use of power. Turn too early and the aircraft will skid round the turn and perform more of a wingover. Turn too late and it will either perform a tail slide or, more likely flop either forwards or backwards.

224. The use of power during the manoeuvre is key to success. Never perform a stall turn with the throttle closed as you are guaranteed to get a flop either forward or backward. The reason is that with sufficient power on, both the elevator and rudder will have authority from the propeller slipstream when the aircraft comes to a stop. The elevator maintains the aircraft's attitude in pitch, while the rudder maintains attitude in yaw and initiates the stall turn proper.

225. As in any aerobatic manoeuvre, the wind plays its part to complicate matters. For a pure headwind, the aircraft if pulled to a true vertical will get blown back by the wind. So, you need to lean the aircraft into wind by using a bit of down elevator sufficiently to allow the CG to track vertically upwards as in the diagram below.

226. Equally, once turned around and facing the ground, the nose of the aircraft must also be positioned to point into wind i.e., you need to push some down elevator to achieve this. Again, adjust the amount of elevator to give as true a vertical down line for the CG as you can manage.

227. So, if done properly at the end of the Box, **the aircraft will maintain its position relative to the ground** during the up and down line but it is accepted that during stalled flight you have no control over the aircraft and it will be blown down and crosswind. However, with correct positioning you should not be blown out of the Box.

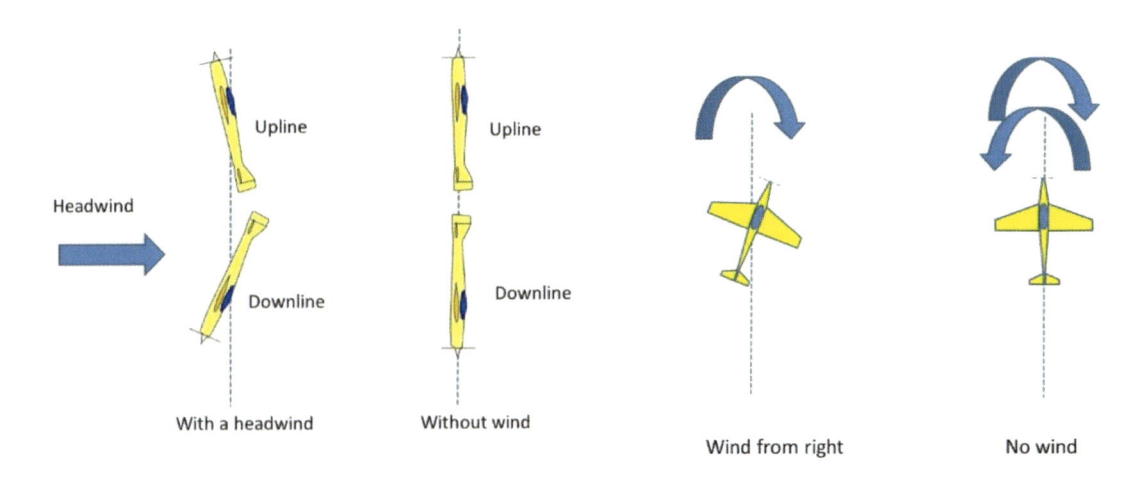

With a headwind   *Without wind*   *Wind from right*   *No wind*

228. If you have to correct for a side wind as well, which is usually the case, then you will have already adjusted the aircraft's track so it is pointing into the side wind to hold its position along the ground track. As you pull up to the vertical (or headwind adjusted vertical), in addition to increasing power to give you the same speed upwards as horizontally, you will need to do two things:

- Check whether you have enough yaw on into the side wind to stop the aircraft being blown off the desired track line. You use rudder to yaw the aircraft as shown in the diagram above. Once at the correct angle, you can centralise the rudder but be ready to correct the aircraft's attitude if required. As wind increases with height you might need more rudder input to maintain a true vertical.

- Gently roll the wings in the direction of the side wind as you pull to the vertical so that they are in the vertical plane as in the diagram below which shows the view looking down on the line from above. This is the same as when you loop in a crosswind as you are flying a quarter loop entry.

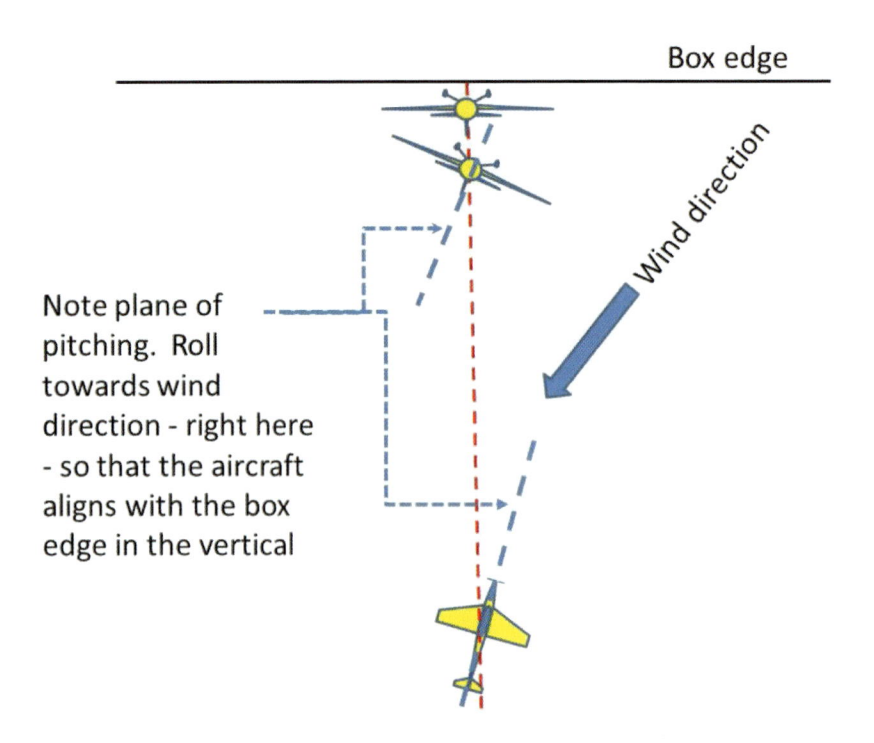

Note plane of pitching. Roll towards wind direction - right here - so that the aircraft aligns with the box edge in the vertical

229. So, we have the aircraft tracking vertically upwards having compensated for both the head and side wind components. The next activity occurs when you have judged that the vertical line you have flown is sufficient. What is sufficient? Well, that's where viewing some YouTube videos of aircraft flying stall turns in F3A schedules will help you to decide. Suffice to say, that you probably will not go high enough to begin with. So, as you reach the height from which you want to slow the aircraft:

- Reduce the throttle to around ¼ power and wait for the aircraft to slow down. The exact amount of power needed will vary from model to model so just try different power settings around ¼ throttle.

- As the aircraft comes to a stop, apply rudder in the direction of the side wind and as the nose drops through 90°, close the throttle completely and push sufficient down elevator to position the nose of the aircraft pointing into the headwind component (see earlier diagram).

- Just before the aircraft reaches the required yaw angle into wind move the rudder stick to just past centre (again exactly how much requires practice on your aircraft), so that the aircraft stops rotating without swinging around the CG, and then apply rudder the other way to maintain the required yaw angle to stabilise the descent attitude.

230. Earlier on I mentioned the need on most aircraft setups to arrange a bit of down elevator with the throttle fully closed. This is so that in still wind conditions, the aircraft will travel vertically downwards. If there is a headwind, then you will need to compensate with more down elevator than you have already mixed in to the fully closed throttle.

231. The earlier diagram illustrating the side wind situation shows the stall turn towards the side wind direction. If you turn away from the wind, the aircraft has to turn a lot more than the 180° to arrive at the wind-corrected attitude and the stall turn will not look as if it has pivoted around the CG. What the judges are looking for in a stall turn, as the aircraft comes to rest, is a pivot around the CG before heading downwards. The rules state that "*Drift caused by wind as the model slows and stops prior to, during and after the pivot must not be downgraded*". The pivot does not have to be 180° since it is the path of the CG in the vertical that is being judged. In still wind, when a 180° pivot would be expected, you can choose which way to turn. So, **in a crosswind always perform the stall turn towards the wind direction**. This reduces the chance that as the aircraft drifts with the wind, the perception is that the flight path is not a pivot around the CG but more of a wing over. Whilst the rules state that you will not be penalised for wind drift when the aircraft is stalled, it makes it easier for you and the for the judges to see that you have pivoted around the CG.

(NB. If you are flying the BMFA B Test schedule, all stall turns need to be made away from any crowd line irrespective of the crosswind direction.)

232. The recovery to level flight needs to have the same radius ¼ loop as the entry ¼ loop. However, if the stall turn is flown as an end manoeuvre, the pull-out height need not be the same as the entry height as a turnaround manoeuvre can also be used to adjust height into the next centre manoeuvre.

233. A key part of the pull out is to ensure that the aircraft's wings are in the right position. If you are seeing them almost in plan form then as you pull out the aircraft will come in straight for you! If you see them turned the other way too much then on pull out the aircraft will fly away from you. With the wings in the correct position, as you pull out the aircraft will track along The Line. Remember that in a crosswind with the aircraft descending and the nose yawed into wind, as you pull out you will need to roll the wings level by slightly rolling towards the side wind direction as described previously.

STALLING

234. Remember that the wing stalls when it reaches the critical angle of attack – that is the angle between the wing and the direction of the airflow well ahead of the wing. You can reach this critical angle either by slowing down the aircraft gradually or by approaching it very rapidly and at a very high speed. The latter is called an accelerated stall or a high-speed stall. It can happen when a pilot tries to pull out too close to the ground and applies full up elevator, stalls the wing and, usually, spins into the ground. Any wing stalls regardless of the speed

at which the aircraft is travelling once you exceed its maximum angle of attack. Recovery from the high-speed stall is immediate on releasing the elevator back pressure fractionally to get below the critical angle of attack. If you are in normal speed stall, then you need to take more deliberate action. Returning the elevator to neutral is usually sufficient for aerobatic model aircraft.

235. If you find that your aircraft will not stall, here are some courses of action:

- Increase the amount of up elevator you can get. Normally around 30°-35° should be sufficient to stall the aircraft. If that doesn't work go to the next point.

- If you have left your CG set a long way forward, try moving it back a little at a time until you get the aircraft to stall.

236. If you were sitting in a full-size aerobatic aircraft, you would feel some juddering as the high-speed stall is approached. This is a requirement for safety since this gives the pilot warning that he is approaching the critical angle of attack. We model pilots don't get this warning!

SPINNING

237. Well, the stall is the precursor to the spin. **If the aircraft does not first stall, it will not spin!** So, you must stall the aircraft in order for it to spin. In aerobatics, spin entry is watched very carefully to see if the pilot lets the aircraft fall into the spin naturally or forces it into the spin. **In the latter case, he scores zero**.

238. So, to enter a spin, we first of all need to pick the spot at which we are going to spin the aircraft. This could be either right in front of you and on the centreline or at either Box end. Once the aircraft is spinning, you have no control over it and it will drift downwind until you initiate recovery.

239. Key points on spinning are:

- You must maintain a straight line following a horizontal flight path i.e. allowing the aircraft to visibly climb to slow down loses you points. So the aim is to approach the spinning point slowing down and creep up to the point at which you wish to initiate the spin, closing the throttle completely shortly before you begin the final smooth backward movement of the elevator stick making sure the aircraft flight path remains horizontal at all times although the aircraft nose will be pitching higher and higher.

- The stall is denoted by the nose dropping and as soon as the nose drops watch carefully to see in which direction the aircraft wants to spin. Apply full rudder to spin in that direction. Going against this initial spin will cost you around 5 points!

- Applying rudder once both wings have stalled has the effect of unstalling the outside wing (right wing if using left rudder) while keeping the other wing stalled. So, the combination of elevator, rudder and unstalled outside wing, which is providing a lift force, cause the aircraft to spin. The inside wing provides no lift as it is stalled.

- You are allowed to use aileron to help the spin but only once the aircraft has started to turn into the spin. Too much aileron will speed up the spin rate making it more difficult to recover on the correct heading. (A way to achieve a repeatable amount of aileron is to mix aileron with rudder and either use a switch to enable this as part of your spin condition, or use stick position switches to look for full up elevator and full rudder before applying the selected amount of aileron. The amount of aileron to be mixed to rudder is very small, typically less than 5%. If you wait for the nose to drop to signify the stall and then apply rudder with its tiny amount of aileron, there will be no reaction in roll as the wing is still stalled but as soon as the outside wing becomes unstalled the small aileron deflection will start working.)

- Spin recovery must be on the desired track. The penalty is 1 point per 15° off the required heading. So, you must decide at what point to neutralise the controls and/or apply opposite rudder to stop the spin. Practice this so that you can stop your spin exactly on the desired track every time! (NB. Spin initiation is on aircraft heading and not track although they will be the same when there is no crosswind. So, if you perform a three-turn spin **to the right** while your heading is left of track, you will need to complete **just over three turns** to exit on track. If you perform a three-turn spin **to the left** instead you would need to complete **less than three turns** to exit on track.)

- Once the spin has stopped, you are looking for a good vertical down line for around 2 secs before starting a smooth ¼ loop pull out to horizontal that you should maintain for 2 secs. My earlier comment about mixing a bit of down elevator with fully closed throttle to give a still air vertical down line only works in still air! Be prepared to adjust the vertical down line by pitching the nose in the direction of the wind to give a true vertical descent of the CG – that's what the judges are looking for.

240. If you cannot get the aircraft to stall, it will never spin and using full aft stick, rudder and aileron will result in a flick entry to the spin. For aerobatics, this is scored as zero. You may need to increase elevator travel to get sufficient elevator power to get the wing to stall. You may want to use the dual rates to give you this additional elevator throw. If you have trimmed your CG as I described earlier, that pretty much guarantees that the aircraft will stall and, hence, spin once you have carried out the above actions. If the aircraft keeps coming out of the spin into a spiral dive, consider using aileron to help. With some aircraft in-spin aileron is needed (in the same direction as the spin) but sometimes out-spin aileron may be needed.

241. In aerobatics, they never specify which direction, i.e. left or right, you must spin, just whether the spin is upright or inverted. However, they might specify that you have to change direction of the spin. I don't propose that you should go this far at this stage! For the time being just focus on the upright spin with recovery to upright flight.

242. When it's done right, a spin is a beautiful manoeuvre to watch.

The Issue of Weathercocking

243. The definition of the **noun** weathercock is: a weathervane in the form of a cockerel fitted to the top of a building. The definition of the **verb** weathercock is: tend to turn to head into the wind (referring to a boat or aircraft).

244. However, once an aircraft is no longer connected to the ground, something a boat cannot achieve(!), it generates its own wind by virtue of its airspeed. The aircraft is unaware of the speed and direction of the movement of the air mass in which it is flying except when it is climbing or descending through an air mass that is changing speed and direction, e.g., usually when taking off and landing.

245. You may be told that when you slow the aircraft up to stall or spin it, that it will weathercock into wind. This will only be true if the path of the aircraft moves from one mass of air flowing in one direction into another moving in a different direction – a very unlikely situation in the short distance it takes for the aircraft to slow down at the height you will be flying it to stall it.

246. What is happening is that you have not got the wings absolutely level. This is hardly surprising since the aircraft is at 800 ft and at least 150 m away from you and we may only have 5° of bank on! At the normal speed of the aircraft the curved flight causes by the small bank angle is not noticeable to the pilot. If you had a ground observer standing on the line looking at the aircraft flying towards them, they would see a slight "banana" shape to your flight path. As soon as you reduce the aircraft speed to stall it, the radius of turn reduces dramatically (radius of turn is dependent on velocity squared) and you see the aircraft turn into wind. The diagram below shows the lift force exerts a turning force when the wings are banked. The total lift force (blue arrow) can be resolved into a vertical lift force (green arrow) and a turning force (red arrow.)

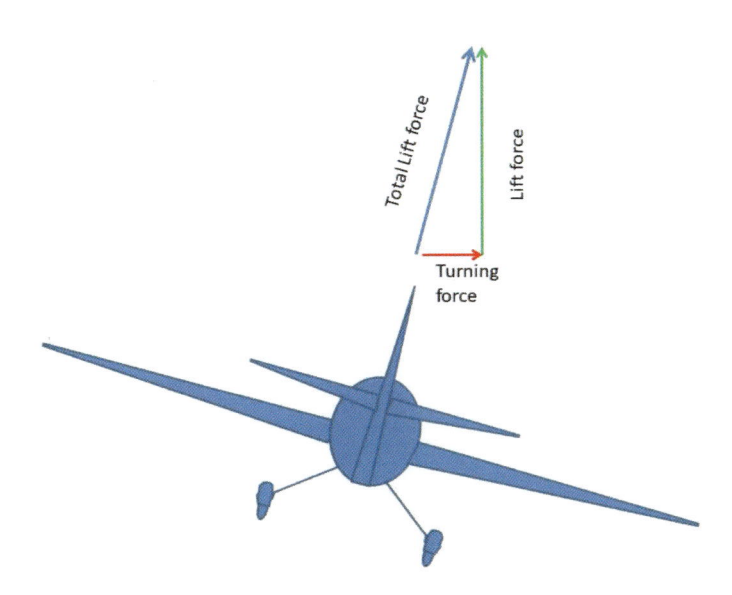

247. Hence, the view that the crosswind has blown the aircraft so that it weathercocks into wind. It is true that the aircraft has turned into wind **but the cause is the bank and not weathercocking**!

248. What the judges are looking for is the aircraft **heading** to remain unchanged as the aircraft is slowed down to the stall and enters the spin. The number of spin turns is counted relative to your entry heading.

249. You are not downgraded for having the aircraft track off the display line as the aircraft slows down, unless you end up outside the limits of the Aerobatic Box. Remember that if the wind speed is greater than the aircraft's stalling speed, the aircraft will be seen to travel backwards before stalling. This does not mean the aircraft is flying backwards just that's how it looks to you, anchored to the ground, with the aircraft going backwards relative to you. The aircraft is still flying forwards at just above stalling speed. The moment the aircraft stalls and enters the spin, the aircraft will drift directly downwind at the prevailing wind speed. You are not penalised for this while the aircraft is in the spin as the judges are told explicitly not to mark anyone down for one of the laws of Physics!

250. A more rigorous explanation is contained in Annex B.

INVERTED FLYING

251. Although not strictly an aerobatic manoeuvre, you are going to be flying inverted when doing aerobatics for around half the time. So, it's worth practising it until you get used to it. Some pilots have a real fear of flying inverted and either avoid it or keep it to a minimum.

252. The easiest entry into inverted is to fly a half loop at one end of your Aerobatic Box. This automatically gives you extra height to allow you to experiment with flying a long straight track to the other end of the Box and then fly another half loop to return to upright flight. If you found it easy to fly a straight, level track all the time you were inverted then you are ready to move onto the next stage.

253. If you need a lot of down elevator to maintain inverted flight then the CG is probably too far forward so try moving it rearwards a little at a time. You can also reduce the Tx's Exponential on down elevator and thus get more down than up at the same stick displacement (See para 261, Transmitter Function below).

254. If you didn't find inverted flying easy, then read on. Well, why are you having difficulty? Firstly, you will have the elevator effect reversed and the only way that you can get used to this is to keep practicing flying inverted. Secondly, if you haven't already noticed, the ailerons work in the same way as when you are the right way up. Thirdly, the rudder effect, like the elevator, is reversed. Well, what's the problem there you ask? Remember that we are using rudder to hold our track over the ground to cope with crosswinds. So the question is, which way do you move the rudder. Easy when you are on the ground to say "well, it's the other way of course" but when you are flying it seems to get a bit more difficult.

255. I heard this tip from a friend. Imagine you are viewing your model from behind and you want the tail to move to the left – just apply left rudder and vice versa. It was so simple but removed so much confusion from my mind. Try it and see how you get on. This technique is particularly useful when you are flying the aircraft vertically upwards and looking at its underside.

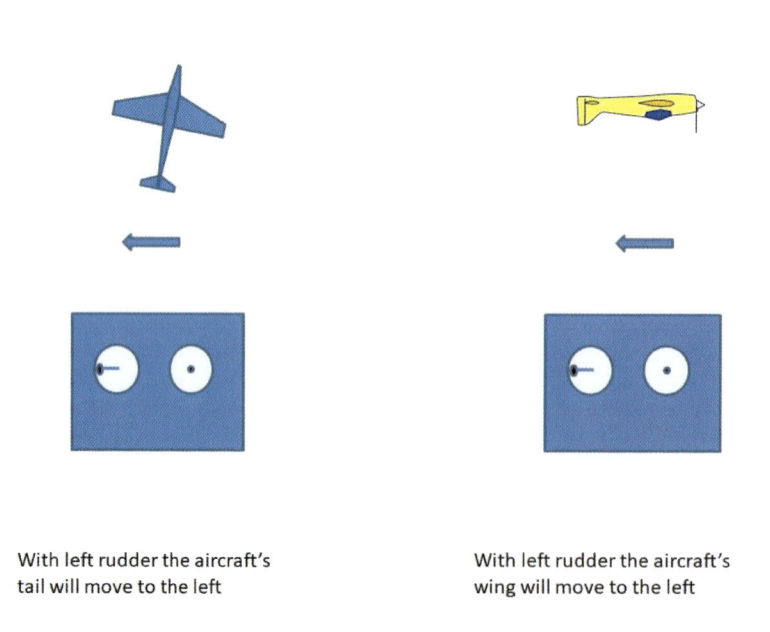

With left rudder the aircraft's tail will move to the left

With left rudder the aircraft's wing will move to the left

256. If you can't get on with that tip, here's another. Look at the wingtip nearest you and decide whether it needs to move forward or back to yaw the aircraft onto the correct heading. Just move the rudder stick in the same direction as you want the wingtip to move. This works whether you are flying left to right or vice versa and you don't even need to think about moving it left or right! This technique is particularly useful when you are flying along the line inverted level, or in a 45° climb or descent.

257. When you feel comfortable flying a long, straight, inverted flight path, you should try flying inverted "Figures of 8". That's a good way of building up your inverted flight experience and confidence. You should also train yourself to roll upright if things start to go wrong when you are inverted. Pulling up elevator is a panic reaction and rarely ends well!

HAND HELD OR TRAY MOUNTED TRANSMITTER

258. One thing I have found that helped me in flying aerobatics, and inverted flying in particular, is using a Tx tray. Now, there will be lots of people who have grown up flying with thumbs only or thumb and forefinger but holding the Tx. If you trained to fly using a tray then you can ignore this bit. I used to fly with a neck strap and using thumbs only when I started competition aerobatics. Then I noticed that as I got tense, I twisted the Tx towards my body and found that the movement of my thumbs became restricted. Try it and see!

259. I also struggled to fly inverted without porpoising up and down. I was encouraged to try a tray and initially it all felt very strange. I persisted and it took me roughly three months to re-train myself to fly with the tray. Needless to say, during that time my aerobatics suffered – even more than they did when I flew them with scrunched up thumbs! However, what I found as soon as I started flying with a tray was that I could use the stable base of the Tx on its tray as a way of bracing my fingers in order to fly very smooth and accurate inverted flight. That's what convinced me to persevere with the tray as everything else felt a bit odd. So, my recommendation is to try flying with a tray but give it several weeks before you decide whether to continue with the tray or to go back to holding the Tx.

260. In my case, it took me three months to get my flying back to the standard it had been when flying thumbs only. **The gains since then have been enormous**. The only time I fly thumbs now is if a tray isn't available.

Transmitter Functions

261.   If you have never used the Rates or Exponential or Mixing functions on your transmitter, now is the time to do so! You are unlikely to achieve the precision of control required for precision aerobatics if you do not make use of these functions. The aim of using these functions is as follows:

- **Rates** allow you to set the small control movements that you will need for smooth aerobatics but also allow you to stall and spin the aircraft using larger control movements. If you have a 3-way Rate switch it can be used to set Spin, Land and Aerobatic flight modes

- **Exponential**, or Expo, is designed to alter the response of the control around the neutral point. For our purposes, we want control surface movement around neutral to be lower so check your Tx manual to find out if you need negative or positive Expo (e.g. Futaba uses negative and JR/Spektrum use positive). Set Expo to between 15% and 36%.

- **Spring tension**. Most transmitters allow the user to alter the spring tension for the sticks. One of the recommendations I followed was setting spring tension as high as possible to improve the feel of the stick. When you are tense, a weak spring is difficult to feel so you cannot easily "feel" how much control movement your fingers have demanded.

- **Mixing**. We use mixing to help control some aspects of the model's behaviour when mechanical fixes have not worked. As an example of mixing, on some of your aircraft you may have used a mix of rudder to aileron to overcome control coupling in Knife Edge flight.

262.   Other functions that you will find are indispensable when you move up to fly more complicated schedules are available on high-end Txs. These Txs are more expensive than standard 6 Channel Txs but when you need these functions there is no alternative. If you are prepared to do a lot of programming of the transmitter yourself, you could look at one of the Open Transmitter code products on the market. These are considerably cheaper than the normal branded transmitters but are more complex to set up. It's best to join a user group where you can get help on how to programme these transmitters.

263.   The functions to which I refer are:

- **Stick alert** – can be used to sound a beep when the throttle is at your desired cruise speed setting.

- **Stick position switches** – allows you to control a function by triggering it by moving a stick in a particular direction distance e.g. you can have small rudder movement until you apply full rudder for a stall turn say and then you get extra rudder.

- **6 or more Mixes** – for example setting up a mix with throttle to elevator to help produce a vertical down line.

- **Throttle Curves** – most transmitters have one but you may want at least two and possibly more to cover landing (with idle setting) and flying in high winds where you want more power. High-end Txs also give greater control of the throttle curve shape

- **Servo Matching** – a very useful function when aligning twin elevator servos to make sure they are absolutely in synchronisation when they operate over their whole range.

- **Voice Alarms** – useful when you want multiple alarms for low Rx pack voltage, low flight pack voltage, height. Some transmitters also support voice messages that can be triggered by operating a sprung loaded switch – useful for having the next manoeuvre name called out by operating the switch.

- **Pre-set Mixes** – the most useful is rudder to aileron/elevator which covers knife edge trimming.

- **4 Aileron Setup** – makes setting up a biplane with four aileron servos an absolute doddle!

- **Minimum of 8 channels** – setting up a biplane with twin elevator servos, 4 aileron servos, rudder and motor would be compromised otherwise since you need to be able to adjust individually every servo you use.

CHAPTER 6.   SOME PRACTICE ROUTINES

INTRODUCTION

264.   Now that you have trimmed your aircraft and have had the chance to study some if not all the manoeuvres described, it's time to put some of this information to work for you. I've suggested some basic training routines below that will help you to develop your flying skills so that, when you are ready to start flying some aerobatic schedules, you will at least not have to worry about the basics. The practice routines in this Edition are different from Edition 1 to reflect the changes in the Clubman Schedule.

265.   The priorities I would recommend you adopt when flying these exercises are as follows:

- First, become familiar with the manoeuvres in each routine and observe where you are having difficulties.

- Second, analyse those difficulties and check the relevant sections of this book to try and work out what you need to do to rectify them. A club mate who is willing to work with you to observe what is happening and tell you what happened is very useful.

- Third, try and make corrections for the wind so that your manoeuvres are carried out parallel to your line and on The Line. This is where you get used to not banking the aircraft but using rudder to correct the heading.

- Fourth, work on the entry and exit attitudes and position of the aircraft so that as you exit one manoeuvre you are properly set up for the next and do not need to apply late and large corrections.

- Finally, are you really flying straight and level when you have to?

266.   The whole aim of these mini-schedules is to get you used to flying a schedule accurately even with only a few manoeuvres to fly. Go on to the next mini-schedule once you are happy you can fly the current one to a good standard. See Annex D for calling cards for these Mini Schedules.

FLYING A RECTANGULAR CIRCUIT

267.   Before you say "I can do that already", are you able to fly straight and level exactly parallel to the take-off direction going upwind and downwind, fly 90° turns, or rather wind corrected turns, that allow the aircraft to track at 90° to the upwind and downwind legs while maintaining a constant height?

268. You may find that the aircraft height varies constantly while the direction of flight is less than that desired. It is vitally important to get these basics right before moving on to the next exercise as otherwise you will be spending all your time flying the aeroplane as opposed to flying the manoeuvre with the aeroplane. There is a big difference!

FLYING THE LINE

269. This will be the first time you are going to come into conflict with your club mates who will be busy flying rectangular patterns since what you want to do is fly up and down on the same line with a reversal at each end. So, best to do this either when there is a gap in flying or ask them to give you a 10 min slot when you can fly on your own. 10 mins is quite long enough as you will be concentrating hard and that is tiring. As a point to note, you get 8 minutes to fly the FAI Schedules – this includes taking off and flying 17 manoeuvres. In point of fact, timing starts as soon as the helper puts the aircraft wheels on the ground for take-off! In International Competitions, only manoeuvres are judged so provided the last manoeuvre was inside the 8 mins limit the pilot is OK since landing can be outside the 8 mins as both landing and take-off are not judged.

270. Check what distance out you need to fly. Then get one of your club mates to hold your aircraft up while you pace out the distance you will need to fly at and take a good look at how big your model looks to you. That is what you need to keep in your mind's eye when you are flying it.

271. If you can persuade one of your buddies to pace out the distance to the line and then stand there and watch carefully as you fly to and fro and arrange some sort of signalling procedure to tell you that you are either too far out or too close in until you can get the model on, or at least close to, the line almost all the time.

272. You can choose whatever turn round you wish to perform e.g. stall turn, half reverse Cuban Eight (see Chapter 7) or procedure turn.

INVERTED FLYING

273. If you are comfortable with inverted flying then move onto the next exercise.

274. If inverted flying is still challenging you, re-read the guidance in para 251 above and keep practicing till flying inverted feels "normal".

275. Remember the two tips I mentioned in Chapter 5 (paras 255 and 256) that help you to keep the aircraft flying in the correct direction using the rudder. It is difficult to break the habit of rolling the aircraft to change its heading but you must get used to using rudder and keeping the wings level at all times. If you don't get use to this early on, if you go on to fly in competition you will lose a lot of points unnecessarily.

276. Repeat this for your 10 min slot and keep repeating it till you feel comfortable flying the length of the line inverted and on the required heading. You may find that it's not quite as easy as it seems especially when it comes to maintaining direction and keeping wings level!

277. Try flying inverted rectangular circuits to the same standard as your upright ones and then try inverted Figures of 8 with the cross over right in front of you.

278. By the way, if you are really concentrating then 10 mins is the maximum you want to fly otherwise your flying will deteriorate. Better to land and think about what went well and what didn't. Sometimes jotting down your thoughts is a useful way of checking on your progress and reminding you what you need to work on next time. Just flying around aimlessly is not really making best use of your time

1st Mini Schedule

279. You have been patiently building up your skills so the next exercise is to put together a mini schedule and fly that for a bit. Try this schedule first. It is focused on looping and inverted flight. You should aim to go to the edge of the Box but, at the same time, remain within it:

- **Take off** and do a 180° turn onto your line, and then fly a procedure turn, or Half Reverse Cuban Eight (See Chapter 7 para 311 for how to fly a Half Reverse Cuban Eight) to return to centre. Once you complete your turnaround, your flight path should be level and on the correct heading without needing too much correction with rudder to hold The Line.

- **Loop on centre** – by that I mean bang on centre and not a bit before or a bit after. This is where someone to count down to centre is a boon. It can be quite difficult to force yourself to commit at a specific point but best to get into the habit early! Your loop needs to be as large as you feel comfortable flying in the conditions. Revise the section on looping in Chapter 5 starting at para 177.

- **Half loop**. On completion of the loop, fly out level and on the right heading and perform a half loop as close to the edge of the Box as you can manage.

- **Inverted flight**. Fly inverted level until you reach the centre.

- **Loop on centre**. Perform another loop, this time you will fly downwards. Again, wind correction would be good to build in. After the loop, that should end at the entry height, continue inverted flight towards the Box end.

- **Half Loop**. Fly a half loop to bring you to the same height at which you started the mini schedule.

- **Loop on centre** and **r**epeat the mini-schedule.

280.   What you are aiming for in this exercise is to get your loop geometry right, make an attempt to correct for any head and crosswind component, practice your inverted flight all while keeping on the line.

2ND MINI SCHEDULE

281.   The second mini schedule I suggest brings looping and rolling together:

- **Take off** and do a 180° turn onto your line, and then fly a procedure turn, or Half Reverse Cuban Eight (See Chapter 7 para 311 for how to fly a Half Reverse Cuban Eight) to return to centre. Once you complete your turnaround, your flight path should be level and on the correct heading.

- **Loop** on centre. – aim to start the loop bang on centre and not a bit before or a bit after. This is where someone to count down to centre is a boon. It can be quite difficult to force yourself to commit at a specific point but best to get into the habit early! Your loop needs to be as large as you feel comfortable flying in the conditions. Revise the section on looping in Chapter 5 starting at para 177.

- **Half Reverse Cuban Eight** at Box end (See Chapter 7 para 311 for a description of how to fly this manoeuvre). This manoeuvre is used to turn the aircraft round and this is also referred to as an end manoeuvre. You can enter and exit an end manoeuvre at different heights without being penalised. So, whilst it is nice to get the entry and exit at the same height for the Half Reverse Cuban Eight, it is not essential to do so. The main points on this exercise are to: keep the wings level before and after the half roll, make sure you leave a line after the half roll and maintain the 45° climb angle, and get the wing orientation correct as you complete the half loop in order to bring the aircraft back along the desired track.

- **Four Point Roll.** Think of this as a stepping stone to a slow roll (see Chapter 5 para 214). The Half Reverse Cuban Eight gives you the maximum room for flying this manoeuvre. However, don't wait too long before you start the roll as otherwise it is all too easy to end up at centre and just about to start the first quarter roll! Refresh your mind on which way to move the rudder as you roll to avoid moving it in the wrong direction. If you are still having difficulty with this, go back to practising the roll on a 45° upline.

- **Half Cuban Eight.** This manoeuvre is described in Chapter 7 para 329. This manoeuvre gives you the maximum length in which to perform the preceding Four Point Roll. Remember my comments on wings being level and lines before and after the half roll.

- **Repeat** starting with the Loop. Land after no more than ten minutes flying time to review how you got on.

282.   What you are aiming for here is to get used to more complex manoeuvres involving looping and rolling.

3ʳᴰ Mini Schedule

283. This mini schedule introduces the Immelmann, slow roll and Split S and outside loop from the bottom up

- **Take off** and do a 180° turn onto your line, and then fly a procedure turn, or Half Reverse Cuban Eight (See Chapter 7 para 311 for how to fly a Half Reverse Cuban Eight) to return to centre. Once you complete your turnaround, your flight path should be level and on the correct heading without needing too much correction with rudder to hold The Line.

- **Immelmann** – see Chapter 2 para 47 and Chapter 7 para 335. In this mini schedule, since we are flying the Immelmann as an end manoeuvre, do go as far to the edge of the Box leaving just enough space for the half loop to remain in the Box. If the aircraft appears to move to the left or right of the desired track in the half loop, you didn't have the wings level before you started! Remember that there is no line between the end of the half loop and the start of the half roll. Remember that you must use rudder for this half roll and that, as you are rolling from inverted, the rudder stick goes in the same direction as the aileron stick.

- **Slow Roll.** This manoeuvre is not normally flown at height but, in the mini schedule, you can use height as your safety blanket in case things go wrong with your Slow Roll! See Chapter 5 para 213 for a description of how to carry out the Slow Roll. Initially, aim for about a two second roll but gradually build this up to between three and five (really slow!) seconds.

- **Split S.** Refer to Chapter 2 para 48 and Chapter 7 para 345 and carry out this manoeuvre as close to the Box edge as you can without going outside the Box.

- **½ roll to inverted, outside loop from the bottom, ½ roll to upright.** After the ½ roll leave a short pause (say "pause") before pushing down elevator on centre to perform an outside loop from the bottom. Remember that as you come down on the 2ⁿᵈ half of the outside loop, resist the temptation to pull up elevator! Just keep saying "down elevator" from time to time. You should pause (say "pause" again) and ½ roll to upright once you have finished the outside loop and collected your senses!

- **Repeat** starting with the Loop and then land after no more than ten minutes flying time to review how you got on

284. You are aiming to achieve accuracy in climbing and descending manoeuvres, practicing corrective actions for head and crosswinds. You also have the opportunity to practice the slow roll at a height that will give you the confidence to make an error but still recover in good time.

4ᵗʰ Mini Schedule

285.   This mini-schedule introduces 2 manoeuvres that you may not have flown before and introduces your first full roll in an aerobatic schedule:

- **Take off** and do a 180° turn onto your line, and then fly a procedure turn, or Half Reverse Cuban Eight (See Chapter 7 para 311 for how to fly a Half Reverse Cuban Eight) to return to centre. Once you complete your turnaround, your flight path should be level and on the correct heading without needing too much correction with rudder to hold The Line.

- **Loop on centre** – aim to start the loop bang on centre and not a bit before or a bit after. This is where someone to count down to centre is a boon. It can be quite difficult to force yourself to commit at a specific point but best to get into the habit early! Your loop needs to be as large as you feel comfortable flying in the conditions. Revise the section on looping in Chapter 5 starting at para 177.

- **Humpty Bump (1/2 roll up)**. See Chapter 7 para 347 for a description on how to fly this manoeuvre. Being an end manoeuvre, you do not need entry and exit heights to be the same. With this Humpty Bump, aim to start your first ¼ loop leaving enough space for the ½ loop at the top to remain within the Box. This Humpty Bump is referred to as "Pull, ½ roll, Pull, Pull" which describes where the ½ roll should be. You will need to ensure wings level before and during the looping elements but if you have a head and crosswind then refer to para 177 and onwards for how to correct for this.

- **Cuban Eight** (See Chapter 7 para 380) but here we'll be using half rolls in the centre, centred on the 45° down lines. That means you must fly past centre and try and imagine you are looking at a Cuban Eight in the sky before you begin the first 5/8 loop. Remember to fly a short straight 45° downline for the cross over before preforming a ½ roll centred on the cross over and then another short line before you fly a ¾ loop into wind this time. Recap the cross over from above and then pull out to level flight. Fly as big a manoeuvre as you can to giver room to fly the line before and line after the ½ roll.

- **Humpty Bump (1/2 roll down)**. See Chapter 7 para 375 for a description on how to fly this manoeuvre. Again, being an end manoeuvre, you do not need entry and exit heights to be the same. With this Humpty Bump, you should aim to start your first ¼ loop so that the aircraft just remains within the Box. This Humpty Bump is referred to as "Pull, Pull, ½ roll, Pull" which means that the ½ roll will be on the downline. You need to ensure wings level before and during the looping elements. If you have a head and crosswind refer to para 177 and onwards on what you should be doing to correct for this.

- **Repeat** starting with the Loop and then land after no more than ten minutes flying time to review how you got on.

5ᵀᴴ Mini-Schedule

286.   This mini-schedule introduces the 45° upline and provides you with more rolling practice building on the last exercise:

- **Take off** and do a 180° turn onto your line, and then fly a procedure turn, or Half Reverse Cuban Eight (See Chapter 7 para 311 for how to fly a Half Reverse Cuban Eight) to return to centre. Once you complete your turnaround, your flight path should be level and on the correct heading without needing too much correction with rudder to hold The Line.

- **Inverted Flight.** Carry out a ½ roll and fly inverted for at least five seconds then fly another ½ roll to end upright. Make sure that your inverted flight is centred. (see Chapter 7 para 357)

- **Humpty Bump (1/2 roll down)**. See Chapter 7 para 375 for a description on how to fly this manoeuvre. Again, being an end manoeuvre, you do not need entry and exit heights to be the same. With this Humpty Bump, you should aim to start your first ¼ loop so that the aircraft just remains within the Box. This Humpty Bump is referred to as "Pull, Pull, ½ roll, Pull" which means that the ½ roll will be on the downline. You will need to ensure wings level before and during the looping elements but if you have a head and crosswind then refer to para 177 and onwards on what you should be doing to correct for this.

- **Cuban Eight** (See Chapter 7 para 380) but here we'll be using half rolls in the centre, centred on the 45° down lines. That means you must fly past centre and try and imagine you are looking at a Cuban Eight in the sky before you begin the first 5/8 loop. Remember to fly a short straight 45° downline for the cross over before preforming a ½ roll centred on the cross over and then another short line before you fly a ¾ loop into wind this time. Recap the cross over from above and then pull out to level flight. Fly as big a manoeuvre as you can as this gives you the time to fly the ½ roll on the cross over with a space before and after it.

- **Stall turn** – refer to Chapter 5 para 223.

- **Repeat** starting with the Outside Loop and then land after no more than ten minutes flying time to review how you got on.

6ᵀᴴ Mini Schedule

- **Take off** and do a 180° turn onto your line, and then fly a procedure turn, or Half Reverse Cuban Eight (See Chapter 7 para 311 for how to fly a Half Reverse Cuban Eight) to return to centre. Once you complete your turnaround, your flight path should be level and on the correct heading without needing too much correction with rudder to hold The Line.

- **Outside loop.** See Chapter 7 para 367. There must be a pause between the ½ roll to inverted and the start of the outside loop and again after the end of the outside loop and the ½ roll to upright.

- **Humpty Bump (1/2 roll up)**. See Chapter 7 para 347 for a description on how to fly this manoeuvre. Again, being an end manoeuvre, you do not need entry and exit heights to be the same. With this Humpty Bump, you should aim to start your first ¼ loop leaving enough space for the ½ loop at the top to remain within the Box. This Humpty Bump is referred to as "Pull, ½ roll, Pull, Pull" which describes where the ½ roll should be. You will need to ensure wings level before and during the looping elements but if you have a head and crosswind then refer to para 177 and onwards on what you should be doing to correct for this.

- **Slow Roll** centred i.e. the aircraft must be inverted on centre. It is important to make sure that you spend as much time rolling to the left as to the right. It's not a good idea to allow yourself to become handed! See Chapter 7 para 319. Aim for two to three seconds for the roll.

- **Half Square Loop Half Roll Up.** You can start this manoeuvre with just enough space for a ¼ loop to the vertical and still remain in the Box. You need to deal with all the usual wind issues as well as timing when to carry out the ½ roll, which needs to be centred on the up line. Then, carry out a ¼ loop to horizontal. This being a Half Square Loop, you need to fly horizontally half the length of the upline to complete the manoeuvre plus fly the line at the end of the manoeuvre. (See Chapter 7 para 387)

- **Three Turn Spin.** The Spin should be carried out on Centre – see Chapter 7 para 394. Your heading should be correct to maintain the required track. As soon as you have completed the preceding manoeuvre, close or reduce the throttle to slow the aircraft down. We are aiming to stall the aircraft on Centre and then initiate the spin. **Recovery is to be on the required track** i.e. you do not necessarily need to do exactly three turns. For example, if you have the aircraft nose to the right of track and spin left, you will need to spin slightly more than three turns to recover on track. On the other hand, if you spin to the right then you will do slightly less than three turns to recover on track. Remember to fly a down line of around two seconds before executing a smooth ¼ loop.

- **Half Reverse Cuban Eight** at Box end (See Chapter 7 para 311 for a description of how to fly this manoeuvre). This manoeuvre is used to turn the aircraft round and this is also referred to as an end manoeuvre. You can enter and exit an end manoeuvre at different heights without being penalised. So, whilst it is nice to get the entry and exit at the same height for the Half Reverse Cuban Eight, it is not essential to do so. The main points on this exercise are to: keep the wings level before and after the half roll, make sure you leave a line after the half roll and maintain the 45° climb angle, and get the wing orientation correct as you complete the half loop in order to bring the aircraft back along the desired track.

- **Fly 45° upline ½ roll** centred. Choose a point well before centre to pull up to a 45° climb adding power as you do so. A helper counting down to centre (e.g. 3, 2, 1, centre) will help you to centre the ½ roll so that the aircraft will have its wings vertical as it passes Centre. Continue inverted for the same length of time that you flew the line and at the same angle and heading as before the ½ roll. Once inverted, you will need to apply some down elevator to maintain the 45° angle. Then, pull to horizontal inverted ready for the next manoeuvre.

- **Half Loop.** Fly this manoeuvre to just inside the edge of the Box.

- **Repeat** starting with the Outside Loop but only if it has less more than six minutes to fly the routine. Better to land after no more than ten minutes flying time to review how you got on.

287.   This is quite a long mini-schedule but it will help you to get used to full 15 manoeuvre Clubman Schedule.

BUILDING UP TO YOUR FIRST FULL SCHEDULE

288.   If you have worked through all these six mini-schedules and feel confident when flying them, you are now ready to take the next step to fly a full schedule which will be the GBRCAA Clubman Schedule which is the entry schedule to aerobatic competition. Excluding landing and take-off, there are 13 manoeuvres in the Clubman Schedule. Ideally, you should try and memorise them.

289.   You can split up the manoeuvres as mini schedules or else practice flying the whole schedule. Even if you have memorised the schedule, it is a good idea to get a club mate to call centre and the next manoeuvre as you are finishing the preceding one.

CHAPTER 7. FLYING THE CLUBMAN SCHEDULE

290. I will now describe how to fly the GBRCAA Clubman Schedule that is effective from January 2022 onwards. This is intended to help those who are just contemplating starting out in aerobatics but may also be of use to some of you who are already flying this schedule. You can download the Clubman Calling card, the Aresti[17] diagram showing the schedule, the take-off and landing criteria and a video of the schedule from the GBRCAA site[18]. The diagrams are below:

No	GBRCAA Clubman Schedule	K
1	Take-off Sequence	1
2	Inside Loop	2
3	1/2 Reverse Cuban 8	2
4	Slow Roll	3
5	1/2 Cuban 8	2
6	Immelmann, Split S Combo	3
7	Humpty-Bump, Pull, 1/2 Roll, Pull, Pull	2
8	1/2 Roll, Inverted flight, 1/2 Roll	2
9	Stall turn	3
10	1/2 Roll, Outside Loop, 1/2 Roll	3
11	Humpty-Bump, Pull, Pull, 1/2 Roll, Pull	2
12	Cuban 8 with 1/2 Roll, 1/2 Roll	2
13	1/2 Square Loop, 1/2 Roll on Upline	2
14	3 Turn Spin	3
15	Landing Swquence	1

Max Score = 330   Advisory Promotion = 190 (60%)

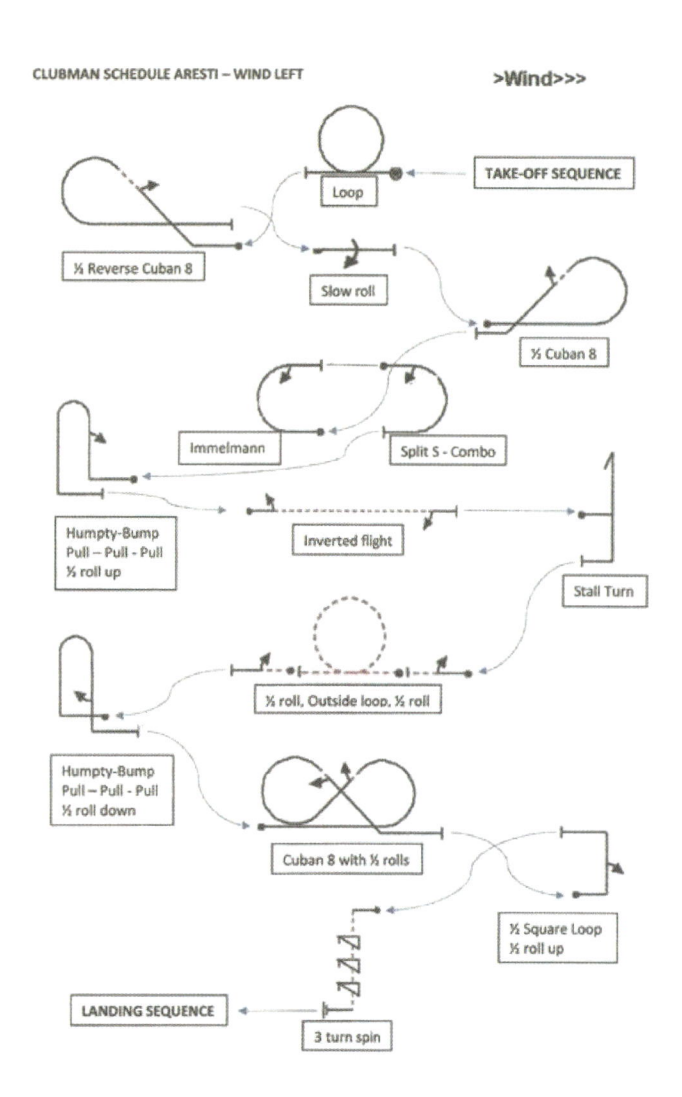

---

[17] Aresti symbols are used for both full size and model aerobatics – See Annex C
[18] Clubman Schedule: http://www.gbrcaa.org/?page_id=84

291. The differences between the old Clubman and the 2022 Clubman Schedule are that there are four more manoeuvres making the total 15 manoeuvres. As before, this includes take-off and landing.

292. As its name implies, the Calling Card is used to call the next manoeuvre to be flown by the pilot. It is all too easy to forget which manoeuvre is to be flown next so, generally, pilots use a Caller standing behind them to call the next manoeuvre. Some modern Txs can help as they can be programmed to use the speech function to call the next manoeuvre by operating a switch. However, they cannot provide information on when you are reaching centre or if you are getting close to the Box edge! I will cover more on the role of the Caller at the end of this Chapter.

293. The right-hand column is headed "K". K is the difficulty factor for that manoeuvre. When flying in competition, judges award a mark between 0 and 10 for each manoeuvre flown and this is multiplied by the K factor to arrive at a score. The judge starts with 10 points and deducts half a point, a point, or a number of points, against four criteria that have been revised in the latest FAI Sporting Code for 2022, namely: geometrical accuracy; constant flying speed; correct positioning within the manoeuvre zone; size matching to the size of the manoeuvring zone. The individual scores when totalled are the overall score for that flight. Points are deducted for each error made e.g. entry without wings level, geometry not right (loop not round), roll rate not constant and so on. The bigger the error the greater the number of points deducted e.g. spin stops less than 15° off heading deduct 1 point for more than 15° deduct 2 points and so on for every 15°. Where a wrong manoeuvre is flown no points are awarded.

294. For each of the Clubman manoeuvres, I've set out the GBRCAA's manoeuvre descriptions and judging criteria, in italics, before describing how you go about flying the manoeuvre. If you have jumped straight to this Chapter and feel you need more help with the manoeuvre, please read the relevant section in Chapter 5. To help you, these are cross referenced in this text.

295. The first point to make is that your straight and level flight needs to be just that. Wandering around the sky in the general direction in which you wish to proceed does not qualify as straight and level flight in the aerobatic context. You also need to work on smooth entry and exit to all turns and manoeuvres. 80° banked turns make it hard to maintain a constant altitude and to come out on the correct heading. 45° banked turns with a smooth roll in and smooth roll out onto the desired heading is where we want to be. This can best be achieved by setting up progressively lower rates and flying the aircraft to see the difference it makes to the stability of the flight path.

296. For example, I have a Wot 4 set up with its lowest rates (I do have a three-position rate switch) to allow full aileron stick deflection to give me a roll of the required rate (around 2-2.5 secs per roll) for the BMFA B Certificate. I have flown the entire B schedule on those very low rates and it does work out OK – you just have to remember to use full stick movement to roll in and roll out of a bank! When I've given others a chance to fly my Wot 4 on these low rates, they look impressively smooth where before they were jerky and looked rushed in the

way they flew. Do experiment to see how the smoothness of your flying can be enhanced by reducing your lowest rates and adjusting the Expo. The key point I make is always to experiment to find out what works best for you. By all means take advice, but if it doesn't feel right for you, find what is and stick to it. Just remember the four judging criteria and find a way to meet them!

297.	The distance out from where you are standing will vary with the size of your aircraft. For a 50/70 size aircraft, you should be aiming to be around 70 to 80 meters out – this may be a good deal further out than you normally fly. Pace out 70 meters and try and get someone to hold your aircraft up in the Pilots' Box while you look back at it. The reason for flying at this range is to give you the room in the Aerobatic Box to fly the 3 manoeuvres (end, centre and other end) required in the schedule without running out of room and having to rush things. A 2 m aircraft will need to be flown at the 150 m line with a 110 size at around 110-120 m.

C-01 Racetrack Take Off Sequence (K=1)

298.	You do not taxi aircraft out to take off (or in for landing) in aerobatic competitions so, even if you don't use a Caller, have a helper to take your aircraft out to the take-off point and recover it after landing. You should brief them to hold the aircraft off the ground till you have signalled you are ready to take-off and only then to place the aircraft on the ground. If you are using an IC engine, it is a good idea to brief you helper that you will run the engine up to max power before he places the model on the ground for take-off.

299.	The take-off is possibly the most important manoeuvre of all, as it is the first manoeuvre you fly in front of the judges, so it is up to you to show us how good you are.

300.	*The model is placed on the take-off area, parallel to the flight line and released. The model rolls along the take-off area until flying speed is achieved, then establishes straight climbing flight parallel to the flight line. The model then turns through 180° in a continuous turn and flies back over the manoeuvring area centre line.* **Take-off judging is completed once the centre line has been crossed** *and the model then performs a 180° turnaround of the pilot's choice, which is not scored.*

301.	*Notes: Box limitations do not apply to this manoeuvre. On rough surfaces or when there is a crosswind, it is acceptable for a helper to restrain the model on the ground until take-off power is applied.*

302.	Judging notes:

- *Model does not track straight on take-off: 1-2 points. (Disregard the effect of the take-off surface e.g. ruts and pot holes on grass sites)*

- *Wings not level after take-off: 1 point per 15 degrees*

- *Rate of climb too steep: 1-2 points above 30 degrees*

- *Model goes behind judge's line after take-off: zero points*

- *Model retouches runway after lift-off: 1 point*

- *Any part of the aircraft structure becomes detached on take-off: zero points for the whole flight*

303.   Your downwind flight path would have been flown at a steady height – no obvious climbing or diving – and using the rudder to achieve the required ground track while keeping your wings level. I found that one of the most difficult things to master as my initial reaction to being off course was to bank and fly to the correct course. In competition aerobatics, you keep your wings level and use the rudder to slide the aircraft into the right position when you are supposed to be flying S&L!

304.   You can choose whatever manoeuvre you would like at the end of your downwind leg to reverse direction. Most pilots use the Half Reverse Cuban Eight since this helps to maintain your flight path direction at the end of the manoeuvre. It also allows you to practice a manoeuvre that will be judged later in the schedule, so, it is well worth flying that as your turnround manoeuvre! See the description on how to fly this manoeuvre at manoeuvre C-03 below.

305.   Like trying to fly a perfect circuit, this first manoeuvre is not as simple as it sounds! However, there are up to 10 marks with a K factor of 1 which means you could earn a score of 10 with a perfect take off manoeuvre. **Note, take-off and landing are not expected to remain within the Box boundaries.**

C-02 INSIDE LOOP (K = 2)

306.   *From upright on the baseline at the centre line, pull through one inside loop to exit upright at baseline height.*

307.   *Judging notes:*

- *Loop should be of constant radius*

- *Entry and exit should be same height and start / finish on centre line.*

- *Loop should be centred on the centre line*

308.   In Chapter 5 para 177, I've described flying the loop. To avoid repetition, it is not included here. Get a friend to watch your manoeuvre and tell you which bits you are getting wrong.

309. The first true aerobatic manoeuvre in Clubman is the loop. For maximum marks, this needs to be round and must start and finish on the centre line at the same height and heading. Remember that you are also being judged for constant speed but in Clubman you are given some leeway on this as not every aircraft will have the required power to weight ratio to enable constant speed to be maintained during the whole loop. This opening manoeuvre looks deceptively simple but throw in a strong headwind or a crosswind and you need to have thought through what the wind is going to do to your flight path so that you can make the necessary corrections to achieve the required geometry in the right place.

310. When your aircraft is in the 4th quarter of the 1st loop, you should be aiming to adjust the flight path so that the aircraft arrives at the centre line at the bottom of the loop flying level and at the same height as entry. You can make use of throttle to help you to make up a bit of ground if it looks like you will be short of centre but do this as early as possible to make it as unobtrusive as possible.

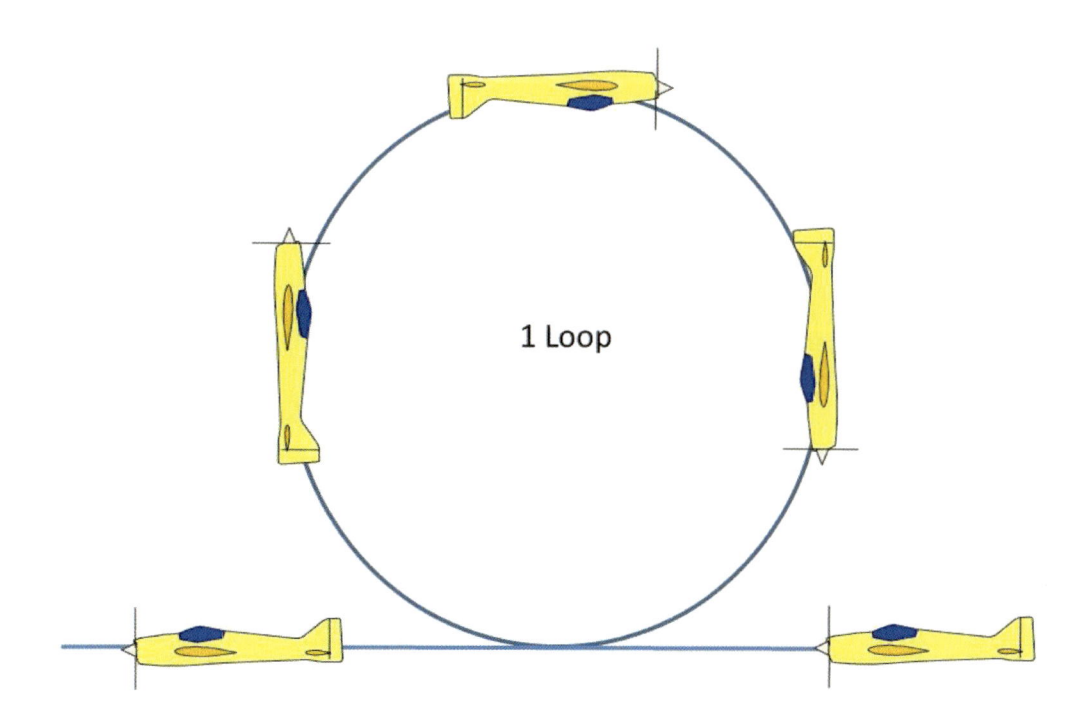

C-03 HALF REVERSE CUBAN EIGHT (K=2)

311.   From upright on the baseline fly a horizontal line then pull through 1/8 of an inside loop into a 45° up line, half roll in the centre of this line. Pull through a 5/8 loop to exit upright on the baseline.

312.   Judging notes:

- *All radii equal*

- *Entry and exit need not be the same height*

- *Half roll should be centred on the 45° up line*

- *Must remain in the Box to avoid deductions*

313.   The manoeuvre, as its name implies, is based on a Reverse Cuban Eight where you pull up to 45°, **pause**, perform a ½ roll, **pause** and then carry out a 5/8 loop to bring you back at the right height and on the correct line for your first manoeuvre. The half roll needs to be centred on the straight line between the two looping segments. The total length of the 45° line must be sufficient to enable you to fly a decent size 5/8 loop. Many pilots have a tendency to start the loop as soon as they have completed the half roll and that reduces the height available for the looping section as well as losing you marks for the half roll not being centred.

Half Reverse Cuban Eight

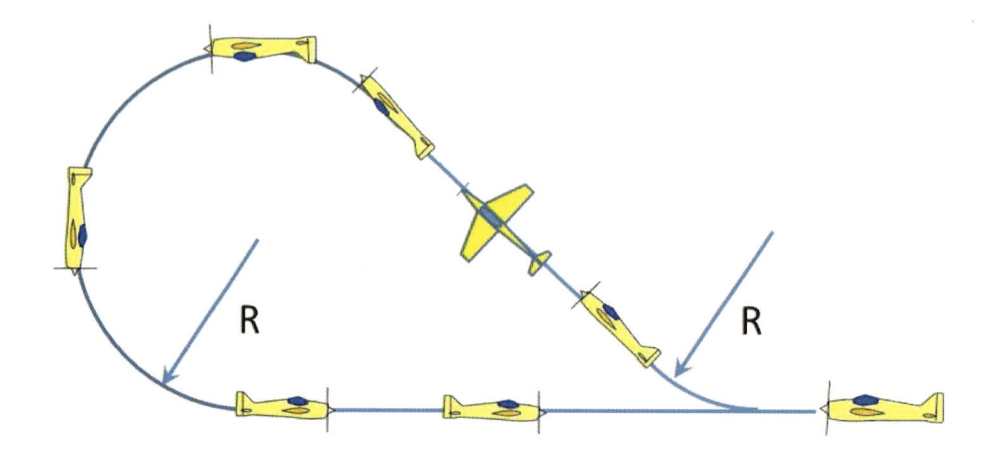

314.   As you leave the loop, you should be assessing whether your ground track is still correct. If your aircraft is being blown in by the wind or you have allowed the heading to drift off during the loop, now is the time to rectify matters. **You need to train yourself to use your rudder to yaw the aircraft onto the correct line while keeping the wings level.**

315. Judging when to start the pull up is key to getting the space right for the next manoeuvre. You will need to practice this until you can be confident that your 5/8 loop will fall just inside the edge of the Box. This will give you the maximum amount of time before you have to start your next manoeuvre and you can also re-check that your heading is correct and if it isn't, use the rudder to correct it.

316. Note that the entry radius R of the 1/8 loop must be the same as the following 5/8 loop. Judging a 45° line is difficult but if you get a friend to hold a 45° set square so that its bottom is level with the horizon (always assuming the horizon is level!) they can then let you know if your climbing angle is correct or whether you are too steep or too shallow. Once you have the 45° flight path set in your mind it helps enormously to get your geometry correct. Remember though, you are looking for the path of the aircraft's CG and not the attitude of the aircraft to be on the 45° line and you should make that clear to your helper.

317. You must also make corrections for both any head- or crosswind components so that your aircraft remains on the correct ground track, the looping sections look round and you remain within the confines of the Aerobatic Box. However, do not take that as the reason not to go to the edge of the Box. Remember, you will be marked on how well you use the available manoeuvring space. As in the case of the loop, you should have thought ahead to how to correct your half loop for head and crosswinds and applied the corrections.

318. You also want to give yourself as much room as possible for your next manoeuvre, the Slow Roll. The big advantage of the Half **Reverse** Cuban Eight, compared with the Half Cuban Eight, is that the aircraft is level earlier and so gives more time for the next manoeuvre.

C-04 SLOW ROLL (K=3)

319. *From upright on the baseline perform a slow roll to exit upright on the baseline.*

320. *Judging notes:*

- *Constant roll rate*

- *Roll should take two to three seconds as a guide*

- *Model should be inverted on centre line*

321. The slow roll is probably the most difficult manoeuvre in this schedule to get right. Review the write-up on how to fly a slow roll in Chapter 5 para 186. Firstly, as I mentioned in the previous section, you need to have left yourself the space to have a line of straight and level flight before beginning the slow roll. Remember also that the aircraft is flying downwind so your ground speed will be higher and you will run out of the Box faster! Once you have come level from the half reverse Cuban Eight, get on with the roll otherwise you stand the chance of

missing centre. For maximum points, the roll must be half way completed with the aircraft inverted and wings level when you cross centre and the roll rate must be constant as must height and heading.

322. The direction of roll is up to you but avoid getting handed by always rolling in the same direction! This manoeuvre requires the use of both elevator and rudder in order to keep the aircraft path level. The aircraft attitude will change as the roll progresses but it's the path of the CG that's being judged. **You might consider setting a rate that gives you a roll rate of one every three seconds with full aileron stick applied.**

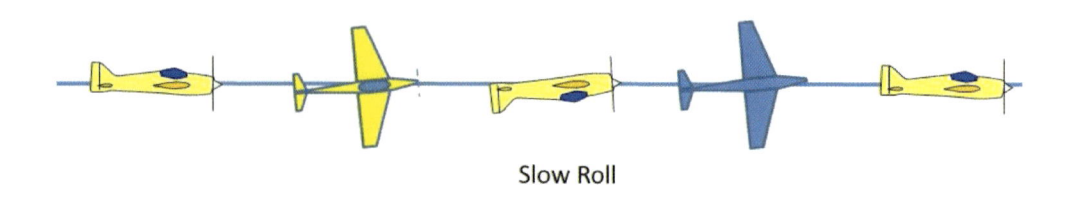

Slow Roll

Notice the aircraft's attitude when flying in knife edge and inverted. You must use the rudder and elevator to counter the loss of height when the aircraft is in those positions.

323. Go back to Chapter 5 para 213 to read the description on rolling. Also, remember to apply a higher throttle setting than you use for normal S&L flight. A slow roll is easier to fly if the aircraft is flying faster as that gives you better control. **It is the roll that is slow not the aircraft's flying speed!**

324. You should be aiming for a roll that takes between two to three seconds. Paradoxically, the slower you roll the more time you have to think and put in the correct control movements – mind you, there's also more time to get confused!

325. Remember that when rolling from upright, rudder stick goes in the opposite direction from the aileron stick. Then once you past inverted, the rudder stick goes in the same direction as the aileron stick.

326. The final part sounds dead easy – stop exactly 360° after you started! However, it took me a fair bit of practice to achieve. Once you stop the roll, remember not to make any adjustments as any move when you are supposed to be flying the "short line afterwards" will immediately lose you a point.

327. As you can see, there's a lot to think about in a slow roll as well if you are to maintain heading, height, constant roll rate and perform exactly a 360° roll. Practice, as ever, makes perfect!

328. The one thing you don't have to correct for during the roll, provided your entry heading was correct, is a crosswind since in a slow roll your heading should remain constant.

C-0-5 Half Cuban Eight (K=2)

329. *From upright on the baseline fly a horizontal line then pull through 5/8 of an inside loop into a 45° down line, half roll in the centre of this line. Pull through a 1/8 loop to exit upright on the baseline.*

330. *Judging notes:*

- *All radii equal*

- *Entry and exit need not be the same height*

- *Half Roll should be centred on the 45° down line*

- *Must remain in the Box to avoid deductions*

331. As you exit the Slow Roll, you should be checking that your aircraft's heading is correct, that you are not being blown in or out by the wind and that your wings are level. Remember to use the rudder to get the aircraft onto the correct track while keeping the wings level with the ailerons.

332. The Half Cuban Eight is flown the opposite way to the Half Reverse Cuban Eight. So, the 5/8 looping element is flown first and then the Half Roll on the 45° down line before pulling level.

Half Cuban Eight

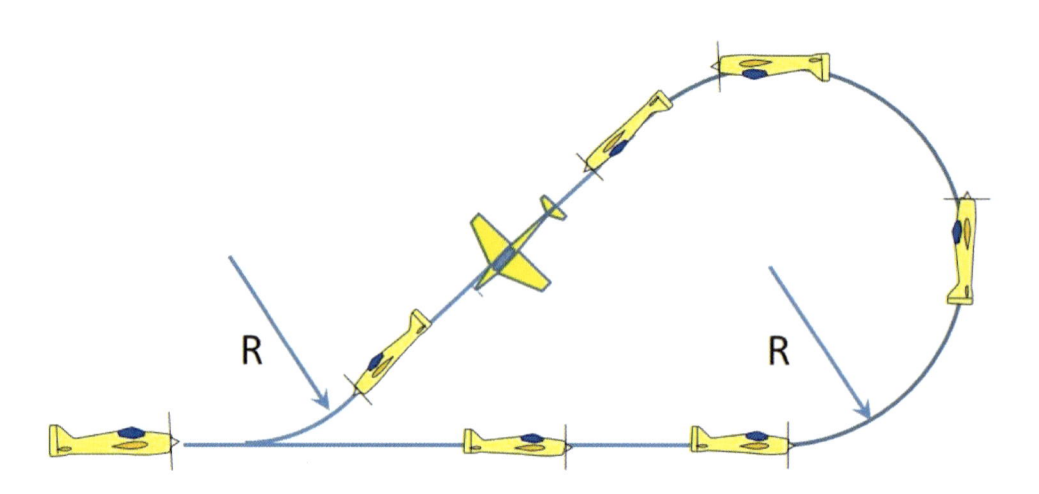

333.   For the Half Cuban Eight, you need to judge where to start the 5/8 loop so that the aircraft just remains within the Box boundary. Like the Half Reverse Cuban Eight, you need to keep the radius of the 5/8 loop the same as the radius of the 1/8 loop that gets you back to straight and level flight. Again, as for the loop, you should have thought through what corrections you need to make to counter the head and crosswinds that will affect the shape of this manoeuvre.

334.   By comparing the two geometries you will see how much earlier you get the aircraft turned around and flying level with the half reverse form of this manoeuvre. The reason for using this combination of turn round manoeuvres is to maximise the length of flight path for the Slow Roll. Since the next manoeuvre does not start until you are well past centre the point at which your aircraft regains level flight is less critical. Nevertheless, you still have the time to assess your aircraft's track over the ground and to use the rudder to make adjustments to get you back on track.

C-06 Immelmann Turn, Split S Combination (K = 3)

335.   *From upright on the baseline pull up into a half inside loop immediately roll to upright, fly past centre on the top line then perform a half roll immediately followed by half an inside loop to exit upright on the baseline.*

336. *Judging notes:*

- *Half roll immediately follows the half loop*
- *Half loop immediately follows half roll*
- *Constant radius through half loops*
- *Roll rates constant*
- *Lines straight, level and wind corrected*

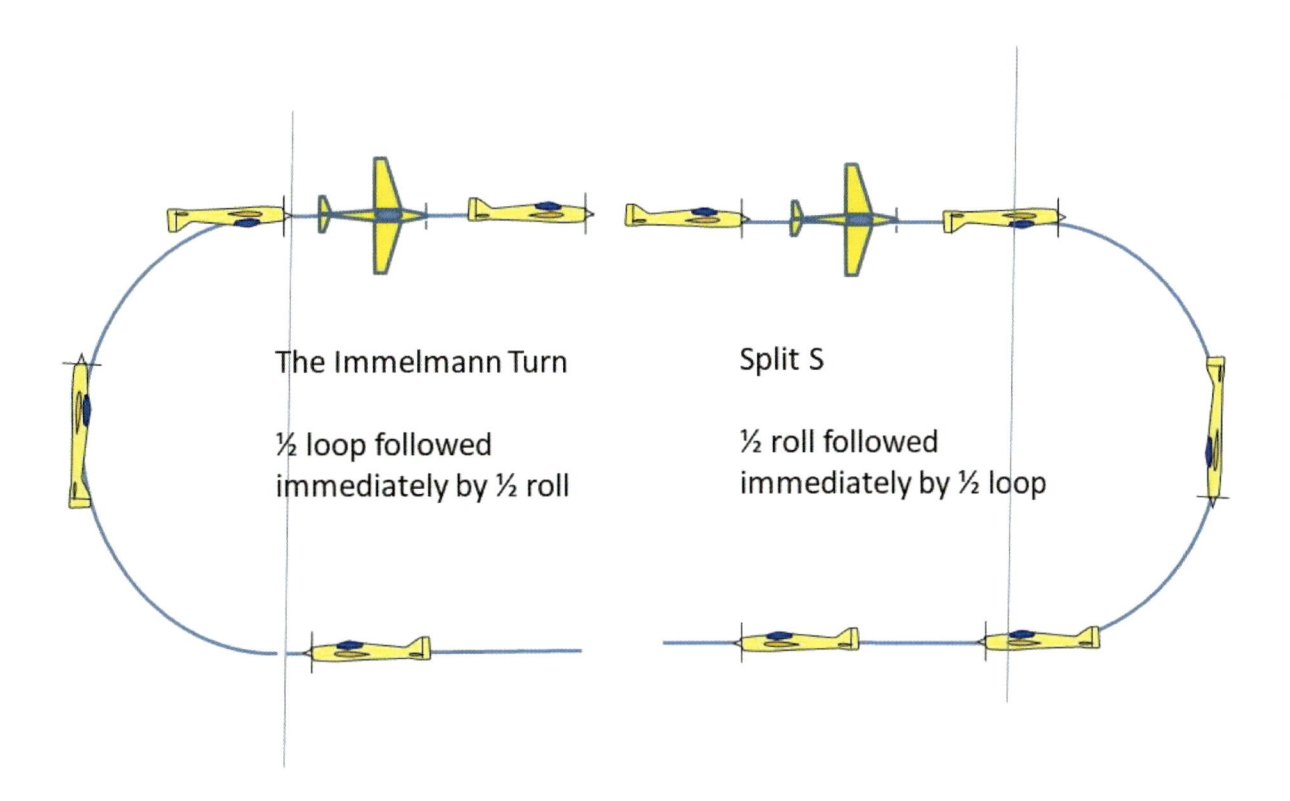

The Immelmann Turn

½ loop followed immediately by ½ roll

Split S

½ roll followed immediately by ½ loop

337. Although this is listed as a combined manoeuvre, you have the time to treat them as two separate manoeuvres but don't try using the full Box as you will make life difficult for yourself as well as scoring less well.

338. The Immelmann Turn, named after the German World War 1 fighter ace Max Immelmann, is a half loop followed by a half roll. It is important to remember that in a competition the half roll must follow **IMMEDIATELY** after the half loop has been completed. In other words, there must not be a pause or line between them.

339. Make use of the size of the Aerobatic Box by flying past centre for up to two seconds – count "one thousand two thousand". This gives you time to check and correct the aircraft's heading as well as enabling you the time and space to ensure that you establish a line before and after each manoeuvre.

340. Remember not to make the half loop too tight since you want to have space for the second part of the combination, the Split S, without worrying about running out of height! Of course, this will depend on the amount of power you have available in your aircraft so avoid making it so large that you struggle to fly a half roll at the end of the half loop. Do make sure that when you fly level after the Immelmann that you don't allow the aircraft to climb or descend as this will ruin the geometry of the manoeuvre.

341. Go back and read the comments on flying a loop (Chapter 5 para 177), especially in a crosswind, in order to make sure that your track at the top of the half loop is pointing in the desired direction.

342. Start the half roll immediately or even fractionally before the aircraft is level but not by much – it must not be obvious to the judges! A squeeze of rudder, in the same direction as you have moved the aileron stick, stops the nose of the aircraft dropping and helps to keep your roll level. Note that you can roll in either direction for this manoeuvre. You need to apply sufficient rudder to stop the nose dropping and only practice will help you to find the correct amount of rudder to use, **BUT** you **MUST** use rudder!

343. Hint: when rolling from inverted, the rudder stick goes in the same direction as the aileron stick.

344. Don't forget that you need a straight line after the completion of the manoeuvre but you can be assessing whether you are flying level and not being blown in or out. After the end of your "Line", make any corrections to make good the required ground track with the rudder while keeping the wings level. Try and avoid obvious corrections to the flight path by squeezing in rudder smoothly so that it isn't obvious otherwise those are grounds for another deduction in points. Making any corrections early, of small and really unnoticeable amounts and smoothly, will help you to score maximum points for any manoeuvre.

345. Your aircraft should now be past centre flying **level** and you are looking to start the Split S at the same distance past centre that you finished your half roll in the Immelmann Turn. Count from the end of the half roll to Centre and then backwards to zero and start the Split S half roll. The Split S is the exact reverse of the Immelmann with a half roll **IMMEDIATELY** followed by a half loop.

346. Something that you must be alert to is either over or under rolling in the first half roll. This will put your aircraft's wings at an angle so that as you fly the following half loop the aircraft will either track towards you or

C-07 Humpty Bump (Pull, Half Roll, Pull, Pull) (K = 2)

347.   Fly past centre on the baseline, pull up through a ¼ loop into a vertical up line. Half way through this line half roll. At the top of the vertical up line pull through a half inside loop into a vertical down line. At the bottom of the down line, pull through a ¼ loop to exit upright on the baseline

348.   Judging notes:

- *Half roll centre of the line*

- *Constant radius*

- *Must remain in the Box to avoid deductions*

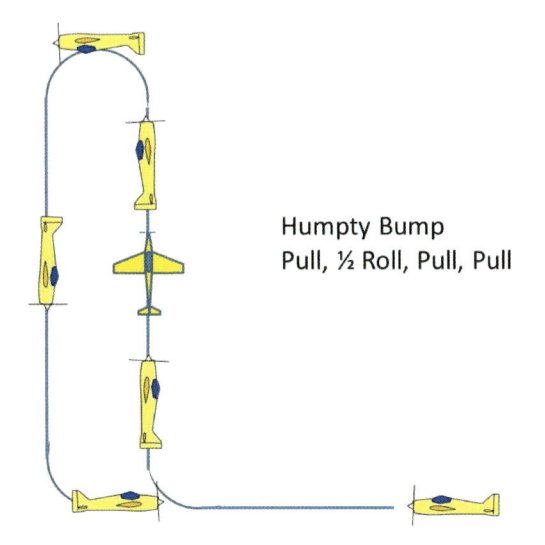

Humpty Bump
Pull, ½ Roll, Pull, Pull

349.   I have been unable to determine the origin of the name Humpty Bump but it definitely came from full size aerobatics! To carry out this manoeuvre, you need a either a model with a powerful engine or you need to build up speed so that your aircraft can climb vertically, carry out a half roll and then a half loop. The more power you have the larger you can make the manoeuvre and the less rushed it looks.

350.   Having said that, there is no reason why you cannot do a perfectly acceptable Humpty Bump with a less powerful model provided you have built up your speed beforehand. In this case, you have a long time from the

end of the Split S to track right across the manoeuvre area until you are approaching the other end. You need to time your pull up into a vertical climb so that you have just sufficient space to perform the second half of the manoeuvre while remaining in the Aerobatic Box. You should aim to use timing to help with this manoeuvre. So, on the upline, count one thousand, two thousand, half roll, one thousand, two thousand, half loop. Don't forget your throttle management as you approach the top of the half loop aiming for the fully closed throttle at, in this case, the 10 o'clock position.

351. Once again, the matter of constant radius comes into play. Each ¼ and ½ loop must have the same radius. If your aircraft cannot maintain a constant speed vertically then you have to compensate by not pulling so hard for the ½ loop at the top of the Humpty as you do for the two ¼ loops at the bottom. Depending on the speed your aircraft flies on the downline, introduce a count up to "five thousand" to start the final ¼ loop to arrive at your desired height for the next manoeuvre. It is **not** necessary to have the same entry and exit heights for a turn round manoeuvre.

352. The half roll on the way up has to be positioned in the middle of the upline. With a constant speed, you can just count off seconds with the same number before and after the ½ roll. If you are losing speed going upwards then you will need to leave a very short line before the ½ roll and hold on for a bit longer after that to get a line of the same length and still have enough speed to fly a ½ loop over the top with the same radius as the entry ¼ loop.

353. The vertical up and down lines will need attention depending on the strength of headwind. In the diagram below, you will see what you need to do with the aeroplane to counter the headwind on the way up and then down. Obviously, the stronger the headwind the more pronounced you need to make these attitude changes.

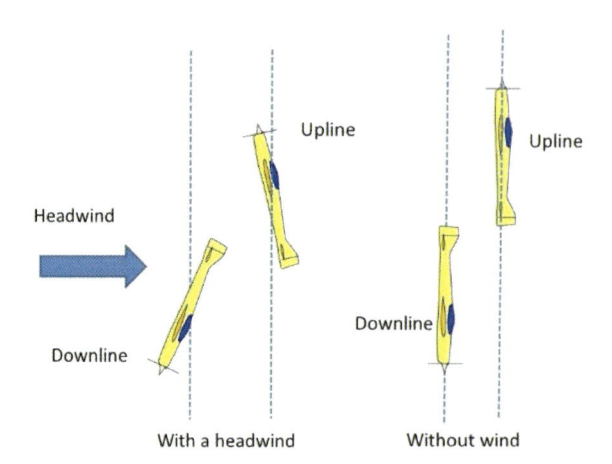

354. If you have a crosswind as well, then you will have used the rudder to alter the heading of the aircraft so the nose points to windward of the desired ground track. Say the crosswind is from right of track. As you pull up to the vertical from this position:

- You need to roll the wings gently (in the direction of the crosswind – right in this case) so that the plane of the wing is parallel to the plane of the Aerobatic Box

- When you carry out the ½ roll, make sure you do not have any rudder or elevator in use as otherwise the aircraft will fly a corkscrew!

- As you pull over the ½ loop at the top you need once again to maintain the plane of the wings and you do this by rolling in the opposite direction of the crosswind – left in this case

355. In effect, the aircraft will then fly round the outside of a cylinder and the direction in which the nose is pointing at the end of the half loop will be automatically correct. Try this with your stick plane to see how keeping the plane of the wing parallel with the plane of the cylinder surface automatically ends up with the nose pointing into wind on the downline. You may need to fine tune the amount of heading off track to counter any change in crosswind strength with height.

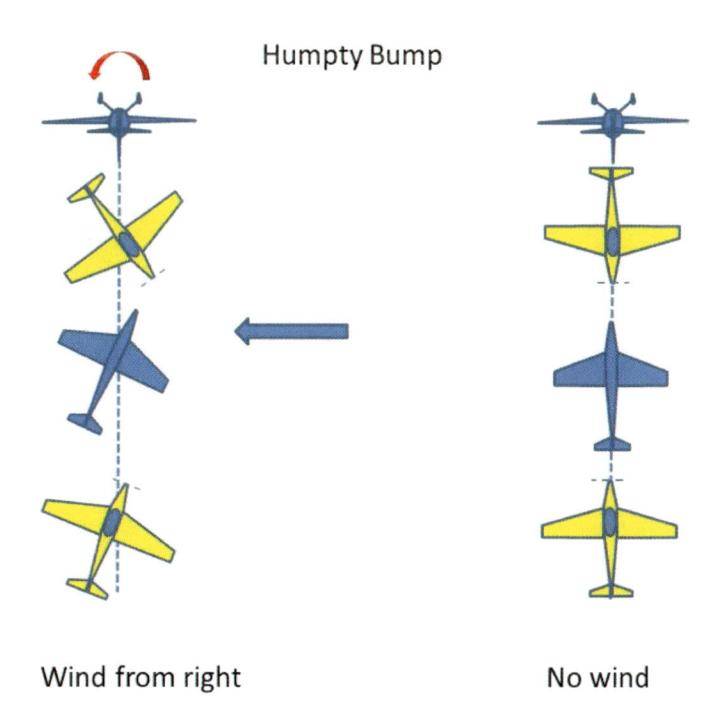

Humpty Bump

Wind from right   No wind

356. The diagram below shows the aircraft flying around a cylinder with the plane of the wing in the same plane as the surface of the cylinder. Note how the aircraft nose continues to point into the crosswind after the half loop has been completed. The crosswind is constantly pushing the aircraft back so it remains on the dotted black line above the ground.

Aircraft rolled to the left

Cross Wind direction

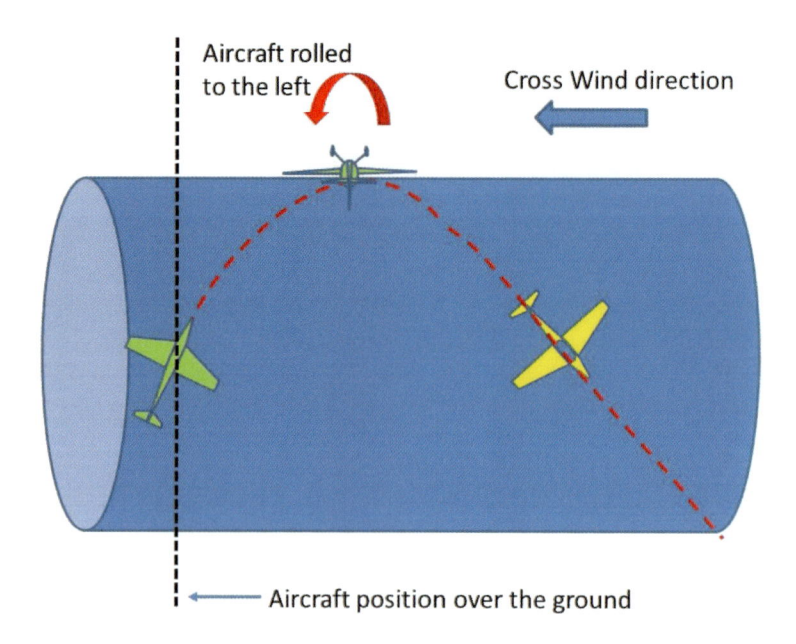

Aircraft position over the ground

C-08 HALF ROLL, INVERTED FLIGHT, HALF ROLL (K = 2)

357.   Before centre half roll to inverted, fly through centre, half roll to upright.

358.   Judging notes:

- *Half rolls should be the same distance each side of centre*
- *Rolls rates consistent*
- *Height consistent: 1 point downgrade per 15°*

359.   If you have made use of the mini schedules in Chapter 6, you should be reasonably comfortable in flying inverted. There is really no option in precision aerobatics other than to get comfortable in flying inverted since as you progress you will end up spending roughly half the time in a schedule flying inverted.

360.   Apart from the inverted flying part of this manoeuvre, the key point is to make sure that when you roll you use both rudder and elevator to make sure the ½ roll entry does not end up with the nose dropping. Think of this as an interrupted full roll. Height control is, of course, an important consideration during the whole manoeuvre so you need to be thoroughly familiar with how much down elevator is needed for the inverted flight section so you are not left hunting for the right amount all the time the aircraft is inverted. Aim for the inverted section of flight to be at least two seconds long.

361. The manoeuvre must be centred so there is a lot to keep track of while flying this manoeuvre although it seems very simple! Again, practice is vital if you are to ensure that you are ticking the key judging points that are set out above. Some pilots use full aileron stick allied to a rate that gives a comfortable roll rate. That way, you can be sure that at least the roll rate is constant provided you have moved the aileron stick to the limit.

C-09 STALL TURN (K = 3)

362. From upright on the baseline pull through a ¼ loop into a vertical up line, followed by a stall turn into a vertical down line. Pull through a ¼ loop to exit upright.

363. Judging notes:

- *Aircraft must come to a stop before pivoting around the CG*

- *If the stall turn radius is between half and 1 wingspan then downgrade 1 point*

- *If the stall turn radius is between 1 wingspan and 1.5 wingspans then downgrade 2-3 points*

- *If the stall turn radius is between 1.5 wingspans and 2 wingspans then downgrade 4-5 points*

- *If the stall turn radius is greater than 2 wingspans the score shall be zero*

- *If the aircraft exhibits a pendulum effect after exiting the stall turn then deduct 1 point*

- *Must remain in the Box to avoid deductions*

364. Review the section on Stall Turns in Chapter 5 para 203. This is another deceptively simple manoeuvre which turns out to have a sting in the tail! The requirement is for the model to be pulled to a vertical flight path, stop and then turn through 180°, dive vertically, and recover into level flight.

365. You need to have the aircraft on its desired track and with its heading keeping you away from infringing the Box edge. As you pull up for the vertical climb, you need to assess the amount of wind correction, along and cross track. As this is flown as an end manoeuvre, your entry and exit heights do not need to be the same.

366. As you can see, there is a lot to think about for a seemingly simple manoeuvre! Get it right and it looks wonderful!

C-10 Half Roll, Outside Loop, Half Roll (K = 3)

367. From upright on the baseline roll inverted, on centre push through one outside loop to exit inverted on the baseline, roll upright.

   (Note: there should be a pause between the half rolls and the start/finish of the loop)

368. Judging notes:

   - *Constant radius*
   - *Entry and exit should be same height*
   - *Loop should be on the centre line*
   - *Rolls rates consistent and line length same before and after*

½ roll, outside loop, ½ roll

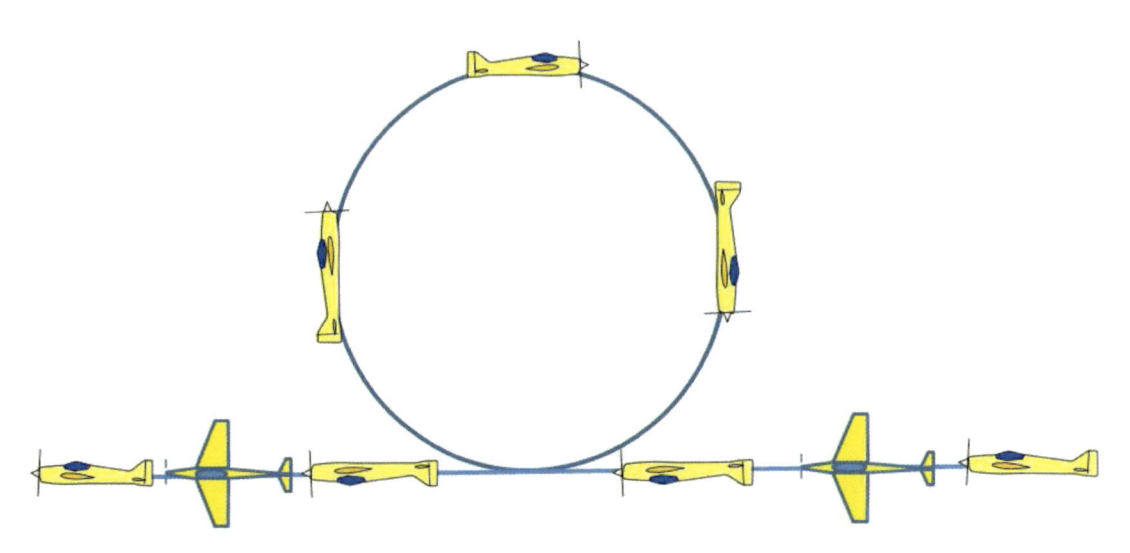

369. The next manoeuvre is the Outside Loop. The manoeuvre is begun and ended with a ½ roll. Again, you must use rudder and elevator when rolling to both keep the flight path level and on track. The judging notes tell you that you need a short pause between the ½ roll and starting the outside loop and the same after completing the outside loop. As regards the size of the outside loop, try and make it the same as your loop. This is a centre manoeuvre so begins and ends as the aircraft crosses the centre line.

370. If you have not trimmed your aircraft correctly, this manoeuvre will show up the problem most usually by screwing out of the outside loop. This can be caused by warps, elevators not aligned or engine side thrust not sorted out. The other factor that makes life more complicated is that it appears to you as if the rudder now acts in the opposite direction as your aircraft is, in effect, upside down. So, remember the tips on which way to move the rudder to keep the aircraft tracking round the outside loop accurately – see para 255.

371. Throttle control is also critical in this manoeuvre. With an IC engine, you will need to anticipate when you apply power. With a lower powered aircraft, you may have to be at full power before you begin the ½ roll. At the top of the outside loop, do not snap the throttle closed but ease it closed from the 10 o'clock to the 2 o'clock position and start opening it again at the 4 o'clock position. For those with more powerful motors you will need the same amount of power you use for entering looping manoeuvres. If you are flying in the opposite direction than adjust the o'clock positions accordingly.

372. The application of engine power at the beginning of the outside loop will increase the airflow over the elevators making them more effective so be prepared not to apply too much elevator at the beginning of the outside loop otherwise you will end up flying a tighter loop than you wanted. Clearly, with lower powered aircraft, as the speed decays on the climbing part of the Outside Loop, you need to manage the elevator position to maintain the nice round shape that is required. What you are aiming for is a perfectly round outside loop. As you get more practiced at this, you will be able to see the potential for errors and correct for them before the error becomes too visible to others.

373. You are aiming to arrive at the same height as the entry point to the outside loop with wings level, fuselage level and your throttle should be back smoothly to your normal cruise power setting. This is much easier for an IC powered aircraft than an electric powered aircraft due to the lack of noise with the latter. In that respect, if your Tx has a stick alert feature it is very helpful to set the throttle stick position for normal cruise power to give you an aural indication.

374. I won't repeat the issues about correcting for the wind speed and direction again. Please go back to the Looping description for that (Chapter 5 para 177). Note that this can be a more difficult manoeuvre to get right than the loop if for no other reason than, as you are not in the aircraft, you are dealing with what feels like reversed controls with regard to elevator and rudder! However, the ailerons operate in exactly the same way so left stick will roll the aircraft left and vice versa. Don't worry! As you get more practiced the demons fade away and confidence in your, and your model's, ability to do this sort of thing grows.

C-11 Humpty Bump – (Pull, Pull, Half Roll, Pull)

375. *Pull up through a ¼ loop into a vertical up line. At the top of the vertical up line pull through a half loop into a vertical down line. Half-way through this line, perform a half roll. At the bottom of the down line, pull through a ¼ loop to exit upright on the baseline.*

376. *Judging notes:*

- *Half roll centre of the line*

- *Constant radius*

- *Must remain in the Box to avoid deductions*

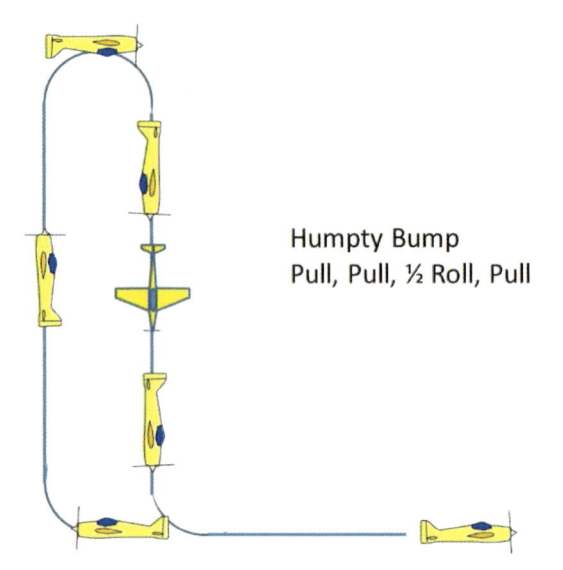

Humpty Bump
Pull, Pull, ½ Roll, Pull

377. Refer back to the first Humpty Bump (C-07) and you will see that all that has changed is ½ roll has moved to the down line. All the points I made in the first Humpty Bump section apply here with the exception that with the ½ roll in the downline, you must have a long enough upline to allow time and space for the required line before, ½ roll, line after and then pull through the ¼ loop to horizontal.

378. Note also that you can begin this manoeuvre almost at the end of the Aerobatic Box as you will be carrying out a ½ loop to come into the Box at the top of the first vertical.

379. You should aim for the identical geometry as the first Humpty Bump and remember that your entry and exit heights do not have to be identical as this is an end manoeuvre.

C-12 Cuban Eight – With Half Roll, Half Roll

380.   From upright on the baseline fly past centre and pull through 5/8 of an inside loop into a 45° down line. Perform a half roll then pull through ¾ of an inside loop into a 45° down line, perform a half roll then pull through a 1/8 loop to exit upright on the baseline.

381.   Judging notes:

- *All radii equal*

- *Entry and exit should be same height*

- *Rolls in centre of 45° down lines and must cross over on the centre line*

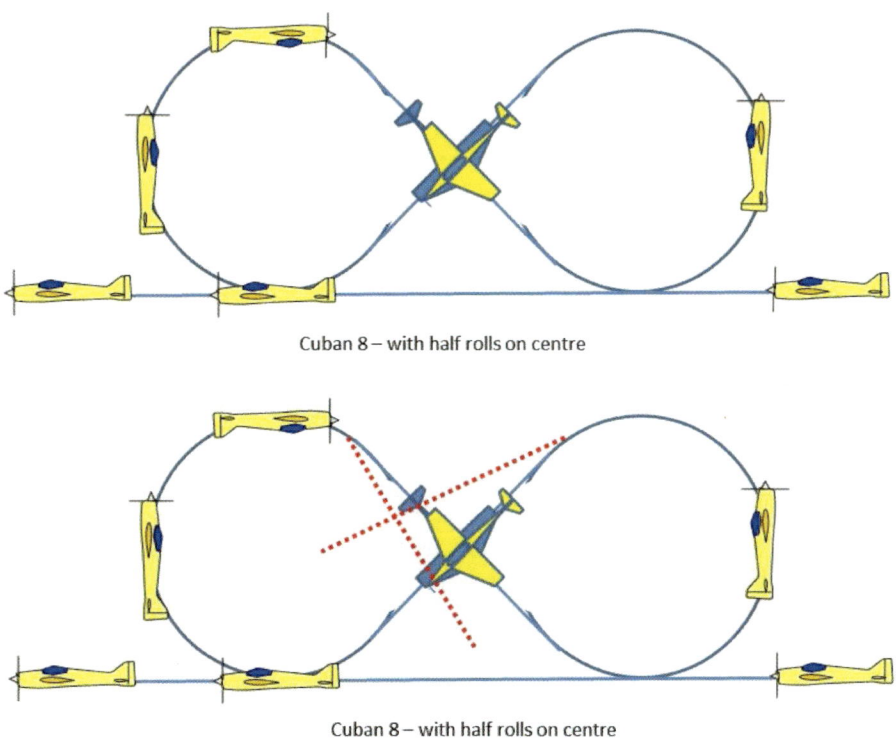

Cuban 8 – with half rolls on centre

Cuban 8 – with half rolls on centre
Dotted red line shows angle to fly in strong headwinds

382.   As you exit the Humpty Bump, you have time to check whether your aircraft is on track or you need to take corrective action to get it back onto the desired track. You do not need to start the Cuban Eight until you have flown past centre and travelled a bit more than the radius of the loop you will need to fly – see diagram. Review the guidance on how to compensate for looping with a tail wind and possible crosswind. Try not to make

the loop too tight. However, if you have a low powered aircraft, you should use the run from the end of the Humpty Bump to build up your aircraft's speed so enable you to fly a decent size first loop.

383.   The reason for a decent size first 5/8 loop is so that you have the space to fly a 45° downline with a half roll that will need a line before and line after it. You should be ready to push some down elevator once you are on the downline to maintain the 45° angle that the CG needs to follow. The half roll should be positioned such that the aircraft's wings are vertical as it passes the centre line. To avoid the nose dropping you must use rudder while you carry out the half roll and remove any down elevator you have had to use. For a low powered aircraft that may have lost a lot of speed over the top of the 5/8 loop, only reduce the throttle for a short period of time before selecting full power no later than the centre line. For adequately powered aircraft you should make sure you reduce the power to under half as you pass the top of the loop and start adding power as you begin the second 3/4 loop. Once again, you need to take action to compensate for the headwind and any side wind. Don't forget to be careful how you apply up elevator with the power raised to avoid pulling too tight a second loop. Both loops must be the same size.

384.   Now, if you have a strong headwind you will need to make the aircraft perform a shallower than 45° dive after the 5/8 loop as the wind will reduce your ground speed and appear to steepen this part of the flight bringing the aircraft to a true 45° downline. You have to judge this on each occasion as wind speeds will vary with each flight. The converse is true of the return 45° dive after the ¾ loop which you will need to make steeper than 45° as the wind will increase your ground speed and making the aircraft appear to descend less steeply thus resulting in a true 45° downline. Remember, it's not the aircraft attitude that is being judged but the flight path. Recap my comments on the loop with headwind compensation (Chapter 5 para 182).

385.   If you also have a crosswind to deal with, recap the comments I made on managing the loop in a crosswind (Chapter 5 para183). The diagram above shows the aircraft attitude you should aim for when dealing with a headwind. The stronger the wind the shallower the descent after the first loop and the steeper the descent for the second loop.

386.   The usual error with this manoeuvre is that the first looping part is started late so the first crossover is displaced downwind and then your second looping element is allowed to be blown further downwind so that your cross over point is nowhere near centre. So, make sure you get a feel for how far downwind you can fly to get the starting loop element to be completed in the right place to give the cross over point on centre and make due allowance for the headwind in positioning the second looping element crossover also on centre. You can always use **more or maximum power to fly forwards as you come round the top of first looping element** and **as you pull up in to the second looping element**. Don't be put off by the aircraft slowing down in this part of the manoeuvre. You are not being judged on the ground speed of the aircraft but on the shape of the manoeuvre so look at the shape your aircraft is tracing out in the sky. If it appears to be going slowly even with full power just remember you are looking at ground speed and allow the aircraft to continue the nice round path. **PATIENCE** is the watch

word. Don't fall into the trap of pulling the nose down too early as that ruins the round shape of the loop and you will miss the cross over point being in front of you. Just wait patiently while the aircraft chugs its way round the first loop to put you in the position you want.

C-13 HALF SQUARE LOOP, HALF ROLL ON UPLINE

387. *From upright on the baseline pull through a ¼ loop into a vertical up line. Half roll in the centre of the line. Push through a ¼ loop to exit up right on the top line.*

388. *Judging notes:*

- *All radii equal*

- *Roll to be centre of the upline*

- *Must remain in the Box to avoid deductions*

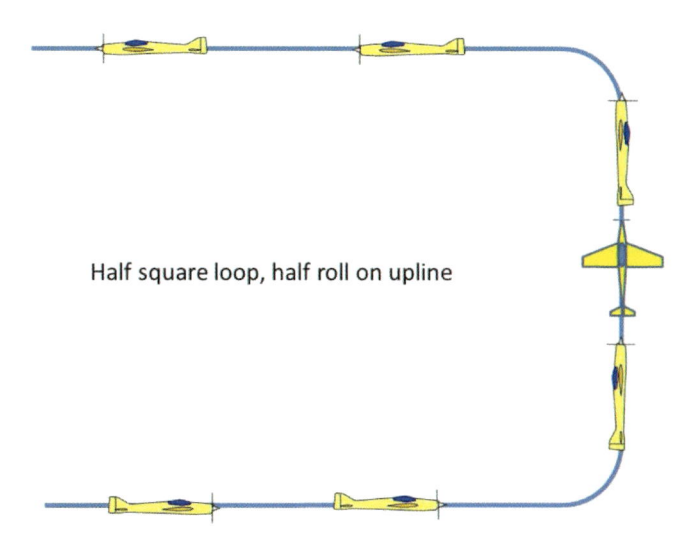

Half square loop, half roll on upline

389. As you complete the Cuban Eight, you need to assess whether you are on the right track and, if not, you need to use your rudder to get back on track. Remember to include a short line after you have pulled level from the Cuban Eight and remember to keep wings and flight path level while you push the aircraft back on the correct track.

390. Position this manoeuvre so that, on the vertical upline, you are on the edge of the Aerobatic Box. This gives you the time to decelerate the aircraft for your next manoeuvre, the three-turn spin. Bear in mind which

way the wind will be pushing you and be ready to correct. So, start by checking your wings are level before your ¼ loop to the vertical. Make this a radius similar to a loop – don't pull too hard! If you have a crosswind and have corrected for this with the aircraft tracking into the wind direction, you must correct for this as you pull to the vertical by gently banking the aircraft towards the direction of the wind. This will keep your wings at 90° to the line you are flying.

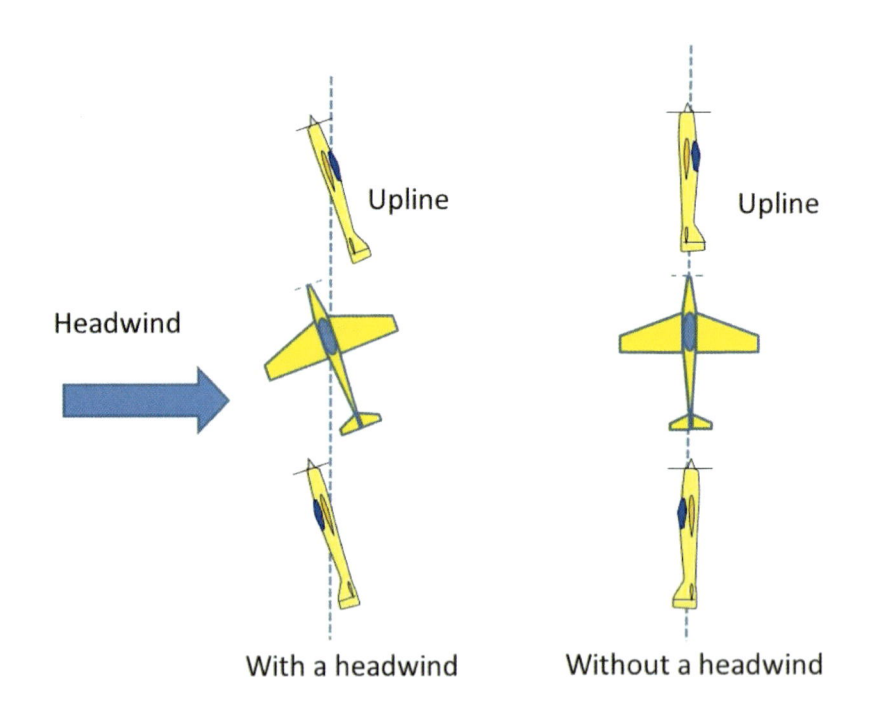

With a headwind   Without a headwind

391. Once you are established in the vertical, to cater for the wind blowing you downwind so you may need to over rotate on your entry ¼ loop so you hold position over the ground against the wind. Next, apply any additional rudder in the direction of any crosswind so that again the flight path is truly vertical. Remember that as you climb, the wind, both cross and head, will increase so you need to make sure you are alert to correct for this. You also need to decide how high you need to climb in order to give yourself the space for the next manoeuvre, the three-turn spin. This judgement comes with practice.

392. Then, after a count of two seconds, more if you consider it necessary, carry out a half roll. Make sure that you are not holding any rudder or elevator as you roll otherwise the aircraft will be yawed or pitched off line. Then after another count of two seconds you should push an outside loop of the same radius as the entry quarter loop. If the aircraft is losing speed on the upline, remember to leave a little bit more time after the half roll to centralise it on the upline before starting the ¼ loop and then be gentle with down elevator to ensure that the radius of the second ¼ loop is the same as for the first one. If you are compensating for a crosswind, remember to roll the wings

to keep them in the correct plane. **This time, as you will be flying a negative g manoeuvre, roll the wings away from the wind direction.**

393.   Since this is a half square loop, you need to fly a straight portion equal to half the vertical distance you have just flown before your start to make any change of power to slow down the aircraft for the spin.

C-14 THREE TURN SPIN

394.   From upright on the top line, on the centre line of the Box perform three consecutive spins followed by a vertical down line. At the bottom of the vertical down line, pull through a ¼ loop followed by a well-defined, straight line to exit upright on the baseline.

395.   Judging notes:

- *Climbing on entry into spin, downgrade 1 point per 15 degrees*
- *Yawing before entry into spin, downgrade 1 point per 15 degrees*
- *Snap-roll entry, zero points*
- *Forced entry, severe downgrade.*
- *Exit direction incorrect – 1 point per each 15°*
- *No vertical line*

396.   So, as soon as you have flown your aircraft half the distance of the vertical upline you have just flown and so completed the half square loop, you can reduce the power to idle to slow up the aircraft for the three-turn spin that you must perform on the centre line. As you will also want full elevator and rudder for the spin, now is the time to select your spin condition.

397.   Re-read the Spinning section in Chapter 5 Para 237. It is easier to slow down early and then add a touch of power to keep you going until you are almost at centre – this is where a Caller is very helpful. Going slowly helps you to avoid overshooting centre. It is an easy way to lose another point to go steaming past centre and then there's the temptation to climb the aircraft to slow as soon as possible. Worse still will be the temptation to commence the spin from a snap entry which will lose you all your points on this manoeuvre!

398.   It is also worth re-reading the section on weathercocking in Chapter 5 para 223. You will lose points if the aircraft turns off its heading as you slow it down. This apparent Weathercocking is caused by the aircraft's wing

being slightly banked. As soon as you start to see the aircraft turning, just bank slightly away from the direction of the turn until the turn stops. You now have wings level.

399. As you reach centre, to which your Caller should count you down, the aircraft speed should have dropped to stalling speed smoothly bring the elevator stick fully back but make sure the aircraft is not going to rear up as you do that. Rearing up is a sure indication that you are trying to stall the aircraft before its speed has dropped to stalling speed. What you want to see is the attitude of the aircraft show a smooth pitch up without the flight path following. The stall will now show itself with the wings losing lift and the nose pitching down.

400. As soon as the nose pitches down, check to see if the aircraft is yawing left or right. If it does yaw at this point, that is the direction in which to select full rudder. Forcing an aircraft to spin away from its initial direction will lose you points. If there is no yaw or wing drop at the point of stall, you can choose which way to spin. You should now have full up elevator and full rudder in the direction of the spin. At the appropriate time, which you will have identified by now, centralise the rudder and elevator and the aircraft should exit the spin with the nose pointing along the desired track. **Do not just let go of the sticks but return them to centre while you hold them!** This means you remain fully in control of the aircraft. It may be that you need to add a short pulse of opposite rudder to nail your spin recovery direction and keeping hold of the sticks allows you to make use of this refinement.

401. Once the spin has stopped, don't be in a rush to start the pull out. You need to fly a vertical (wind corrected of course!) dive that is held for a finite time, 1-2 secs ideally, and then start the ¼ loop recovery. If you used high rates for the spin, you can use the recovery dive to select low rates so you don't have a tight ¼ loop. Finally, remember to fly your line straight and level to mark the end of the manoeuvre.

C-15 RACETRACK LANDING SEQUENCE

402. *On completion of the previous manoeuvre a short straight and level flight should be flown. At reduced power the model turns 180 degrees into a level or descending downwind leg and then executes a second 180 degree turn upwind for the final descending approach to the runway, touching down inside the landing zone.*

403. *Landing is complete after the model has rolled 10 metres or has come to rest inside the landing zone. The landing zone is an area described by a circle of 50 metres radius or lines across a standard runway spaced 100 metres apart where the runway is 10 metres wide.*

404. Judging notes:

- *Model does not follow landing sequence: zero points*

- *Landing gear retracts or wheels come off on landing: zero points*

- *Model lands outside the zone: zero points*

- *180 degree turns not 180 degrees: 1-2 points*

- *Wings not level in downwind and upwind legs: 1 point per 15 degrees*

- *Model does not track on runway after touchdown: 1-2 points*

- *Model bounces on touchdown: 1-2 points*

- *Model climbs and dives on downwind leg or final approach to runway: 1-2 points*

- *Model changes heading left or right on approach to runway: 1-2 points*

405. The landing will **not** be downgraded if:

- *The pilot elects sideslip to land due to crosswind conditions, in which case the upwind wing will be low*

- *Wing dips due to crosswind turbulence and is corrected IMMEDIATELY*

406. Well, you've completed your spin, stopped exactly on three rotations, done a brilliant recovery to level flight and now all you have to do is land! Well, it all sounds simple, but it's very easy to relax and make some silly errors and since the landing, like take off, is marked, has a K factor of 1 so why throw away 10 easy points unnecessarily?

407. So, your first decision is which way to turn downwind after flying the line that ends the spin manoeuvre. Well, it depends… on the aircraft's position and the crosswind direction. If you are a bit too close in, then always turn outwards to join the downwind leg of the landing circuit. If, on the other hand, there is a strong crosswind blowing you outwards, then turn into wind to join the circuit. Also, if you are too far out at the end of the spin, consider a shallow turn inwards to position the aircraft at the correct distance out for the downwind leg. If the wind is blowing you inwards, obviously, you should turn outwards. Consider all these actions before you get airborne and reassess while you are flying that line after the spin before committing to turn onto the downwind leg.

408. All I'll say about landing is that you should remember that elevator controls speed while power controls the rate of sink, or climb for that matter. One of the challenges in flying in competition is that you don't get to fly before your competitive flight. So, you need to make a thorough assessment of how the wind and any turbulence might affect your flight path, again, before you get airborne. Also, watch everyone else and see how the wind is affecting them and what they are doing to counter it.

409. As in most things in life, if you fail to plan, plan to fail. Practicing the right things some of the time is a lot better than practicing the wrong things much more often. Where possible, always seek help from someone who appears to fly accurately and smoothly and rarely has an incident of any note. They probably know things that you could usefully learn.

410. As with the take-off, there is no taxiing the aircraft back after landing. You should brief your Helper or Caller to go and collect the aircraft and recover it back to the pits safely.

411. If you have the chance to talk to the judges at the end of your flight, then that is the best time to get feedback. Leaving it till the end of the morning will mean that unless you were really good (or really bad) they won't be able to remember why they gave you that score! Your next move is to get hold of your score sheet to see how you were scored

THE ROLE OF THE CALLER

412. Almost everyone uses a Caller in competition flying. However, relatively few do so in general flying and in practice. However, it is well worth finding a club mate who will act as your Caller and stick with that partnership. It can be very helpful if you are both interested in improving your aerobatics and you can call for each other. Why? Because you will be able to provide better long-term guidance having seen each other improve or deteriorate and you/they will have a better feel for what is being flown.

413. As I mentioned above, it is your Caller's role to take your aircraft out for take-off and recover it after landing. There is no taxiing in and out in a competition!

414. Apart from telling you what your next manoeuvre will be, your Caller can help with guiding you to use the full width of the Aerobatic Box, telling you that your aircraft is flying in or out of the desired flight path, calling "centre" when you cross the centre line on your manoeuvre e.g. loops, spin entry and giving you a cue on when to start a manoeuvre that is begun off centre but needs to be centred e.g. a square loop. I find it helpful if my Caller counts down to the centre along the lines of "3, 2, 1, centre" or just "2, 1, centre".

415. Your Caller should stand immediately behind you. You need to agree a set of points that provide you with a visible centre and end markers. It doesn't matter hugely if your 60° line is slightly off provided you get into the habit of having your Caller warn that you should start the manoeuvre as you are approaching the end of the Box. If he holds out his arm, so you can see it as well, to point to the end marker that will help both of you to judge that point.

416. Flying in or out of the desired line can be quite difficult to detect early on so having some help to point this out to you is invaluable. Also, if you are flying a vertical downline at Box edge prior to pulling to level flight it is very important to have the wings in the correct position. As you pull out, if the aircraft is rolled too much to the left of

datum as you pull out the flight path will be towards or away from you and you then have to correct the flight direction. Getting the correct aspect of the aircraft fixed in your mind is very helpful and your Caller can help here. Bear in mind that you will want to use the effect of flying in or out to combat the crosswind of the day, so your Caller might say "squeeze in some left/right rudder" so you get the correction right.

417.   Where you have to start a manoeuvre off-centre, such as a 45° climb with or without a manoeuvre, it is helpful for your Caller to count you down to the pull up point, then call "centre" and then call "end" when you should be complete.

418.   Of course, an experienced aerobatic pilot acting as your Caller can give you much more input than someone who is learning at the same time as yourself. Make sure though that the more experienced aerobatic pilot is experienced in precision aerobatics and not just 3D otherwise you could end up practising the wrong manoeuvre.

JUDGING

419.   These conventions are drawn from the current FAI Sporting Code which contains specific descriptions of all the aerobatic manoeuvres used in international competition. The code is updated at 2 yearly intervals. The code can be found and downloaded from the GBRCAA Website or from the FAI website[19]. The Sporting Code defines the schedules used in International Competitions and these are flown in the GBRCAA's competitions as well. There is a section in the code called the Manoeuvre Execution Guide and this is where the FAI sets out how each manoeuvre is to be judged.

420.   10 points are awarded for a perfect manoeuvre that meets all the judging criteria. So, the judge starts with 10 in his/her mind and then proceeds to deduct anything from 0.5 point for a minor infringement to 5 points for a major infringement. A wrong manoeuvre or a really major error (e.g. flopping over in a stall turn) results in a 0 score.

421.   Finally, F3A judging is carried out using 4 criteria:

- Geometric accuracy – how accurately is the figure flown?

- Constant flying speed – this is within each manoeuvre and not across the whole Schedule

- Correct positioning in the manoeuvre zone – is the manoeuvre properly centred for centre manoeuvres and remains within the limits of the Aerobatic Box?

---

[19] FAI Sporting Code link https://www.fai.org/page/ciam-code

- Size matching to the manoeuvre zone – is full use made of the Aerobatic Box and are all manoeuvres approximately the same size?

422. It follows from this that judging aerobatics is subjective and judges may well award different marks for the same manoeuvre. In general, these marks should not differ by more than 1 point as otherwise you have judges who are not using the same criteria for deducting points during a manoeuvre. In reality, as the experience of each judge will vary, you might see up to 2 or even more points difference. For inexperienced judges there can be a lot of factors to be considered not the least of which is "which is the next manoeuvre I'm judging!" It is not an easy task to carry out but without any judges there would be no competitions! So, if you do feel aggrieved at the score you have been awarded by one judge versus another just remember that the one who scored you low might have correctly assessed your performance with the other having missed some of your errors!

423. These days, the GBRCAA is short of judges so we are increasingly turning to pilot judges i.e. you can be flying in the competition you are judging. Sometimes, this might mean that you are actually judging the schedule you are flying and will be judged in turn by another direct competitor.

424. Learning how to judge is very useful not just to help in competition events but also to you the pilot as you will begin to be aware of what you are to be judged against. That allows you to focus on the areas of your weakness which otherwise you might not have picked up.

425. The GBRCAA website has a Judging Tab[20] which contains a lot of useful information, including the latest FAI Manoeuvre Execution Guide (MEG) presentation that helps to explain the words of the MEG in the Sporting Code. There is also a link to a judging exam that the Australian Precision Aerobatics group has developed. To become a judge for the GBRCAA, you need to pass this exam. However, it is also an excellent way to learn about all the intricacies of the manoeuvres that you are trying to fly!

---

[20] GBRCAA Judging Tab - http://www.gbrcaa.org/?page_id=1027

CHAPTER 8.   HOW TO START FLYING IN COMPETITIONS

426.   Many Club pilots are put off by the thought of flying in competition. While everyone gets nervous when flying in competition, you will find that other pilots, even your direct competitors, are always ready to help and encourage you. Unlike the leg pulling you might endure at your Club if you do something wrong, in Competition you will always find that other pilots are quick to offer to help you to remedy the problems you are having.

427.   For the past couple of years, holding a BMFA B Certificate to enter aerobatic competition was not required, at least to enter the Clubman or Intermediate Schedules. It is still worth taking the B Certificate Test as it's easier to fly than the Clubman as the B Test is not flown as a schedule.

428.   Flying in Competition is rather like being a member of a very helpful and knowledgeable Club.

INTRODUCTION TO AEROBATICS EVENTS

429.   You have to start somewhere though. There is now a number of Introduction to Aerobatics events held by the GBRCAA at the BMFA National Centre at Buckminister Lodge[21]. Details on these events are posted on the GBRCAA Forum page[22]. There is also a description of these days on the GBRCAA website[23].

430.   These events are fully described on the GBRCAA Forum so suffice to say that any pilot with an A Certificate can attend. They will get tuition and coaching on aircraft set up, radio setup and how to fly basic aerobatics. The coaching is provided by pilots who currently fly in GBRCAA competitions and some even fly in the GB Aerobatic Team so can provide some very advanced training.

NEW PILOT OPEN DAYS (NPOD)

431.   Once again, the GBRCAA Forum[24] is a good place to start.

432.   NPODs vary in how frequently and where they are run. Essentially, they are events that help pilots new to aerobatics, and competition for that matter, to be coached by experienced aerobatic pilots. Generally, they are tailored to the individual pilots' requirements but this can include flying the full or partial Clubman Schedule.

---

[21] Website for the BMFA National Centre https://nationalcentre.bmfa.org/
[22] GBRCAA Forum page - http://www.gbrcaa.org/smf/index.php?board=45.0
[23] Description of Introduction to Aerobatics Days - http://www.gbrcaa.org/?page_id=1064
[24] GBRCAA Forum – NPOD thread http://www.gbrcaa.org/smf/index.php?board=26.0

433. From my own experience of running a number of NPODs, pilots who attend are nervous but rapidly realise that they are being helped by some very experienced pilots to improve their flying in a helpful and supportive manner. To enter the NPOD you needed an A certificate although a few BMFA B Certificate holders also came.

434. For my NPODs, I used to get one of the mentors to fly the Clubman Schedule to show the standard that is required. During lunch, some would also fly the FAI schedules used for preliminary and final rounds. As in my case when I first saw these schedules flown, the NPOD attendees are usually astonished and ask how these manoeuvres are flown as it is something that normal club pilots never see.

435. By the end of the day, all those who attended these events were absolutely bursting with pride at how much their flying had improved and keen to try out a full competition in the realisation that they would learn a lot without being humiliated if their flying was not as good as everyone else's.

436. While NPOD formats may vary, the ones that I ran followed the process set out below:

- Entrants limited to 12 pilots so with four mentors you were in a group of three

- Attendees were encouraged to arrive by 8.15ish to check in and get their aircraft rigged.

- We started at 9 am with a briefing on the site rules, what the day was about and who would be flying when.

- Each pilot was able to fly four times during the day and we only flew one at a time

- We ran three rounds where pilots could ask for help on any manoeuvre or fly the Clubman or parts of the Clubman

- The fourth round was flown as a low-key competition and while some were reluctant to fly this in the end all pilots flew in the competition round. The mentors acted as Callers for this round although many were guiding the pilots around the Clubman as well.

- We explained how judging worked and every pilot had a go at scribing for the judges

- After the fourth round was flown, the scores were totted up and the results announced.

- The day finished around 4.30-5 pm.

437. I don't recall anyone crashing during one of these NPODs although there were a few near misses!

WHAT TO EXPECT AT YOUR FIRST COMPETITION

438.   You might be wondering what happens at a GBRCAA Aerobatic Competition – at least, I hope you might!

439.   The procedures are very similar to those I have described above for the NPOD except that you don't get a mentor unless you arrange, either beforehand or on the day, for this assistance. There is no reason why your Caller cannot give you all the advice concerning positioning, stretching the bottom of a loop, making due allowance for the crosswind and so on.

440.   Competitions are announced on the GBRCAA forum under the Competition News tab[25] where you will also find the annual Competition Calendar. You are allowed to enter one competition without being a member of the GBRCAA. Membership cost is modest while under-18s get free membership. The main GBRCAA website has a tab marked "The GBRCAA" and select the "Join the GBRCAA" tab. This takes you to an electronic form where you can fill in your personal details and pay either electronically (using PayPal) or by cheque.

441.   Entering a Competition is also carried out via the Website. Follow the "Contests & Events" tab and select "Competition Entry Form". The entry fees are listed for all schedules. You must pay this even if you are entering your first competition as a non-member.

442.   Each Competition is administered by the Contest Director (CD) and their name, together with the name of the Contest, appears on the Competition Calendar. It is important to pick the right date, contest name and CD name when you enter the competition. The CD opens a thread in the Competition News section of the Forum and gives full details of the contest and competitors who have entered. You must pay your competition entry fee before you are listed as competing on that thread. All communication with the CD is via the thread. The details of how to find the site and any entry procedures are all posted well before hand on the competition thread usually with a contact mobile number for the day. Please make a note of the contact telephone number as it's useful to be able to update the CD on the day if you are running late or are unable to attend at the last minute. The current rules state that provided you cancel your entry 14 days before the competition date you will get a refund. That is done again via the competition thread.

443.   On the day, the process is as follows:

- Arrive in good time to assemble and check your model, meet the CD and be ready for the briefing that normally occurs between 08:45 and 09:00. The CD will cover any site-specific issues and identify the flying order as well as any scribing duties.

---

[25] GBRCAA Competition News http://www.gbrcaa.org/smf/index.php?board=12.0

- The flight order usually starts with FAI, then Masters, Intermediate and Clubman.

- It's always worth volunteering to scribe early as that will give you a front row seat (literally) to watch the action and you can quiz the judge on what he's looking for when he marks manoeuvres.

- Always use your time at a competition to watch others fly especially your fellow competitors as you can learn a lot. Everyone is usually quite open about what they find difficult and how they are trying out different approaches.

- Normally 16 entries are permitted before a reserve list is opened. There are three rounds flown with the best two flights counting. With 48 flights, it takes until around 4 pm to get through the list.

- Once you have flown your last flight, it's OK to de-rig your model but you should stay for the announcement of the results. You never know, you might have won!

- If it is possible to fly after the competition flying has finished then do take the opportunity to fly your schedule again, preferably with one of the FAI pilots with you to give advice on how you could improve.

444.   You will be pleasantly surprised at how much you learn from your first competition. Most pilots can't wait to get to the next competition to put all they have learned into practice.

Your checklist for heading off to a competition should include as a minimum:

- All the bits of your aircraft! Both wings, wing joiner, spare wing bolts, canopy. Also any stands you need to help you to assemble or start the aircraft if it's IC powered.

- Large ground sheet to cover your aircraft and support equipment, should it rain.

- Sufficient fuel, glow starts, spare glow plugs and props. Or for electric, at least one more flight pack than you are expecting to fly. You can charge of course but most club sites do not have electric power so you need to take either a generator or leisure battery.

- Food, drink, a chair and don't forget your anti sun equipment – sunglasses, sun hat, skin cream, etc.

CHAPTER 9.   AEROBATIC AIRCRAFT CHARACTERISTICS

WHAT SORT OF MODEL MAKES A GOOD AEROBATIC STEED?

445.   If you are interested in aerobatics, you may probably already have an aerobatic aircraft. There are a number of good club aerobatic aircraft that are capable of being competitive in Clubman and Intermediate. Indeed, a young competitor took a Black Horse Super Air right up to Masters before he bought a specialist aerobatic airframe.

446.   So, what sort of aircraft makes a good aerobatic airframe? In brief:

- An aircraft that has a good power to weight ratio that allows large manoeuvres to be flown relatively easily. Ideally you want something with unlimited vertical performance but something a bit less is fine to start with.

- Allied to the above will be a light but strong airframe construction. We want an aircraft that is designed to fly and not designed to survive high speed impacts with the ground! That's what your trainer and early low winger were meant to teach you.

- A design with a long tail moment arm. That is the distance from the wing to the tail plane is between 2.5 and 3 times the tail plane chord. Short tail moment arms make the aircraft less easy to fix its attitude accurately.

- A colour scheme that is easy to see in both dull and bright light and with an underside pattern that is easily differentiated from the top.

447.   You should remember that most new designs of F3A aircraft are driven by the top pilots who design airframes to meet the challenges that are posed by either the new schedules or the expected weather at the site of the next World Championships. Almost all F3A specific airframes will be suitable as a first specialist aerobatic aircraft for a beginner since you are unlikely to have the developed the skills to differentiate between one such airframe and another. However, look at what other pilots are flying and ask them for their opinions and see if you can cadge a flight to see what it's like. Remember though that the way they have set up their aircraft and transmitter may not suit the way you fly.

SPECIFIC DESIGN FEATURES OF F3A AEROBATIC MODELS

448.   When designing for F3A aerobatics, the critical design case is either the current, or about to be released, schedule. This will identify the extent to which knife edge and snap or flick manoeuvres are going to feature. Some design points though will be there all the time.

449.   For example, when you apply rudder in say a Wot 4, the aircraft has a strong roll almost immediately. That is what you don't want in an F3A design. The reason for this is that almost the entire rudder is above the fuselage centre line which is taken as the motor centre line. That is relatively easy to resolve at the design stage as you will see in the diagrams below.

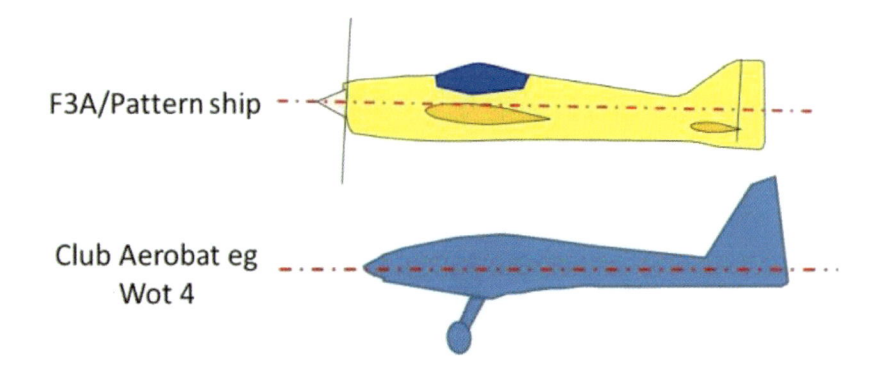

F3A/Pattern ship

Club Aerobat eg
Wot 4

450.   You can get rid of this unwanted feature by mixing opposite aileron to the rudder. However, it's much better not to have the problem in the first place.

451.   These days, most wings are tapered and there are two reasons for that. First, the wing is lighter especially at the tip and so it is easier to stop a roll than with a heavier wing. Second, the increased use of snaps in the schedule gives a tapered wing an advantage over a constant chord wing. Some wings now have a second taper about one chord length in from the tip. This is supposed to provide a more rapid entry and exit from the snap.

452.   The international 2 m size airframe is required to fit into a 2 m x 2 m Box. However, most, but not all, designs tend to have spans of around 1.8 m with the fuselage at 2 m. Chord length at the root will be larger in order to keep the wing loading low. The maximum weight of the airframe is 5,000 g with a 1% tolerance. For electric power, the flight pack is included in this weight while for IC powered aircraft it is with the tank empty.

453.   To meet these specifications, the airframe construction aims for both lightness and strength but these airframes are intolerant of any abuse in the way they are landed.

454.   Most F3A airframes today are of the ARTF type (though some are ARTC or Almost Ready to Cover) since many come with sandwich balsa and fibreglass construction, of at least the fuselage, requiring the use of moulds.

There are still some pilots who continue the tradition of designing and building their own 2 m airframe but for the majority of pilots the time, space and skill needed to undertake this is beyond them.

455. Some 2 m designs are also produced in smaller sizes e.g. 120. 110, 70 or 50 size.

456. The one area in which all F3A airframes are relatively weak is in the undercarriage attachment – some more so than others. While you are expected to be able to land an aircraft accurately and gently when you fly F3A there can be the occasional mishap where a heavy landing results in damage to the undercarriage attachment to the fuselage. Many pilots beef up the area around the undercarriage fixing with carbon fibre cloth but be careful not to add too much weight.

EXAMPLES OF AEROBATIC AIRFRAMES

457. The following pictures show examples of a typical club aerobat (Wot 4) and a specialist F3A design (Fantasista 70). As you can see, the Fantasista has a much longer tail moment arm compared with the Wot 4. Note the very much deeper fuselage of the Fantasista that can easily fly a knife edge loop.

458. I fitted a throttle pipe to the Irvine 53 in the Wot 4 and that gave a very useful boost to power providing the ability to fly much bigger loops than hitherto. A throttle pipe is a relatively cheap way of boosting the power of an existing engine. The next photo shows the installation.

459. Another interesting comparison is with an F3A type designed in 1996, the Loaded Dice in its 2 m form and another 2 m design from 2000 called the Majestic designed by Christophe Paysant Le Roux, who by 2019 was the nine times World Champion!

460. The Loaded Dice has retracts and a very slim fuselage. When it was designed, knife edge manoeuvres did not have as much emphasis in the schedule. The Majestic has a fixed undercarriage and a larger fuselage cross section as the aim is now to increase drag to help to achieve the constant airspeed through the schedule. Although the Majestic is much better at knife edge than the Loaded Dice, it's certainly not as good as current airframes which have much deeper fuselages.

461.   This particular Loaded Dice has had the IC engine replaced with an electric motor driven by a 10 cell LiPo pack. The Majestic has a 35 cc 2 stroke petrol engine instead of the more usual and more powerful YS140 four stroke glow engine.

462.   Compare the long tail moment arm of the Loaded Dice and Majestic with an example of an aircraft with a short tail moment arm, the Sbach 342, which is a scale version of the full-size aerobatic aircraft. This one is a combined 3D and Precision Aerobatics airframe. For F3A aerobatics the amount of elevator movement is minute! However, aircraft such as these are generally cheaper to buy as they have a bigger market than pure F3A airframes.

463.   Cheaper still is the Black Horse Super Air that is still available and which is capable, adequately powered of course, of taking you comfortably up to Intermediate. If you want to build your own aircraft, the same applies to the Gangster 63 lite. Both are still available by the way.

Chapter 9 – Aerobatic Aircraft Characteristics   Model Aircraft Precision Aerobatics

464. Contrast the designs above with one from 1967 below by the then World Champion Phil Kraft, called the Kwik Fli III:

465. Back then, the limit for engine size was 10 cc or 0.6 cu in. You can find plans for similar aircraft, sometimes with short kits, so you could build your own specialist aerobat. These aircraft will be perfectly able to fly the Clubman. They might also be fine with the Intermediate but you might need to boost engine performance to have a reserve for flying large manoeuvres.

466. Here is an example of a biplane, the Citrin, and a monoplane, the Agenda, which has a deep fuselage, an all-flying tail plane and a canalyser. Both perform very well but represent the design status of around nine years ago for the Citrin and six years ago for the Agenda. Both designs are for electric power only.

467. The next two photos show the Element, a development of the Agenda and the latest design the Epilogue. The casual observer would be hard pushed to tell the difference between the three monoplanes but there is much tweaking of the basic design to extract small gains. For example, the Element design is slightly superior to the Agenda in being able to sustain knife edge without any mixing of aileron and elevator provided the CG is at a specific point. The Element wing has been moved up closer to the motor thrust line compared with the Agenda while in the case of the Epilogue the wing has been moved down again.

IC or Electric Power

468. Electric power has taken around 90% of the market. However, the 8 times World Champion, Christophe Paysant Le Roux, has flown the YS 4 stroke glow engine in all his competitions. The YS is a supercharged and fuel injected engine and is very powerful, but also quite quiet using the canister silencers that are readily available.

469. There is no doubt that the convenience and significantly less noise from an electric setup has considerable advantages these days. You must factor into the overall costs purchasing all the charging equipment to feed 10S LiPo packs versus the cost for high nitro content glow fuel.

470. Overall though, it will be down to personal preference and also the fact that you can now buy a lot of second-hand IC F3A models at very attractive prices. Operating a YS engine, and they are the only option for IC these days, requires you to develop the knack of starting and adjusting them to run properly. They also require soft mounting to keep the worst of the vibration away from the airframe. On the other hand, a YS sounds superb in the air although an electric contra drive can sound pretty good as well!

471. In-runner based electric motors tend to use epicyclic reduction gearboxes and some contra rotating gearboxes are also based on the same principle. In-runners and gearboxes required good cooling arrangements otherwise their life is limited! These epicyclic gearboxes require cleaning and lubricating every 50 flights or so. This isn't a difficult task but does require the motor and gearbox to be removed from the aircraft. Gear and belt drive contra gearboxes are now available that are virtually maintenance free thus overcoming the gearbox maintenance greasing issue.

Advice on Purchasing F3A Equipment

472. There are relatively few F3A specific suppliers in the UK. One is run by current competitors in the GBRCAA and can provide advice and guidance as well as supply of new equipment. They are Bondaero[26]. Take a look at their website or contact them directly to discuss your requirements –they are all practising aerobatic pilots. They also appear under the Commercial section of the GBRCAA forum.

473. Internationally, there are suppliers in most European, Asian and North American countries that a search of the internet will bring up.

474. Going the second-hand route can yield major savings but there could be pit falls. The best advice I can offer is to take a look at the GBRCAA Forum in the For Sale and Wanted section. Buying from within the GBRCAA community gives you some peace of mind in that it is a very small world and almost all sellers are practicing

---

[26] Bondaero website - https://www.bondaero.co.uk/

competition pilots who would not wish to sell you a pup! If there is nothing listed for sale, try putting in a wanted advert.

CHAPTER 10. CONCLUSIONS

475.   If you have reached this Chapter, you are clearly keen on learning about precision aerobatics! I hope you will have found the information understandable and that you have been able to use the information contained to set up your aircraft and have a go at flying a few of the tasks. It is a good way to see if you might like to take this new skill set further.

476.   Many club pilots don't really want to get involved in flying in competitions. This is a pity as the popular view of a competitions being full of very competitive and elite and "stand offish" group of people is just not true. Everyone is always very welcoming especially if you are attending your first competition. It's rather like joining a very nice Club full of nice people who share your passion. You will be surprised at how much you learn at your first competition and every subsequent one as well! No amount of practice is as valuable as flying in competition. At the same time though, there is no substitute for practice, practice and more practice. Again, remember the Alex Scott quote:

"Hard work always beats talent when talent doesn't work hard"

477.   You don't need to spend vast amounts of money to get a competitive aircraft. In the first instance, you could use a standard club aerobat like I did when I used a Wot 4 to fly in my first competition. As far as the GBRCAA is concerned, you don't even need to join the Association to take part in your first competition so the only outlay will be the Competition fee and travelling to the event. At least give it a go and then decide if F3A competition is for you. You are also welcome to visit a competition just to see what goes on without entering but do contact the CD first to let him know you'd like to attend. You can do this by posting a message on the GBRCAA Forum in the relevant competition thread.

478.   If you get the chance to attend an NPOD or another aerobatic introductory course, do take it. You will learn a good deal on how to improve your flying so that you will be better placed if you go on to compete. You could even ask one of the mentors to test fly your model to check on its setup and advise how you could improve it. You will also get coaching on how to improve your flying from current competition pilots. This is gold dust – unless you are lucky enough to have such a beast in your club!

479.   Be warned though! Once you have been bitten by the F3A bug, you are well and truly hooked. It is a great sport and one in which you are forever learning new techniques. Your standard of flying will push you to the top of your club, unless it's already full of F3A competitors!

480.   Good luck with your endeavours and I hope to see some of you at a competition if you are flying in Great Britain.

ANNEX A. MORE DETAILS ON SETUP AND TRIMMING

INTRODUCTION

481.   This Annex expands on Chapter 3 – Setup and Trimming, by giving more information on how to achieve the changes required. Some information duplicates what's in Chapter 3 for completeness.

SERVO SETUP

482.   The best way to ensure that you are making full use of the power and resolution of your servos is to spend a little time on setting them up correctly.

483.   Start by looking at what you want to produce in the way of movement on your control surface. If you are intending to fly traditional, or precision, aerobatics then you do not need vast amounts of throw. Most beginners to aerobatics are always surprised at what low control surface movement is required. Ailerons and elevators are usually set for around 10° each way with the rudder around 25° each way or there about. For spinning you need to increase rates to allow more movement for the elevator and rudder but more on this later.

484.   **Neutral Position**. When you mounted your servos did you set the sub-trim to 0 on your Transmitter and then place the servo arm on so that you get the servo arm as close to 90° to the servo centreline? (Incidentally, Futaba servos come with a 4-arm horn that allows you to adjust the arm position by four slightly different positions by placing the arm on one of the four positions on the servo output splines – see below.) Then, and only then, use the sub-trim for fine adjustments. This prevents problems of having a lot of sub trim wound in to get the servo arm centred which will cause difficulty with non-linear movement of servo travel either side of neutral. This you would feel when you fly an F3A aerobatic aircraft.

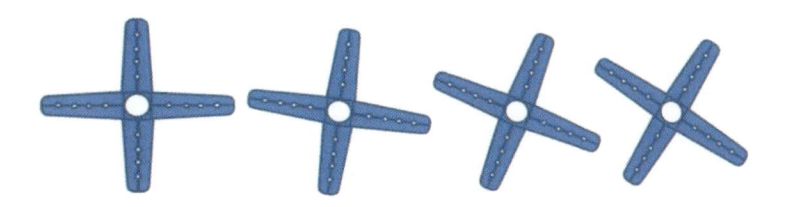

485.   **Torque and Resolution**. Servos generate a torque or moment using a rotary motion. This force is expressed, in SI units, as a Newton metre (N.m), the Newton being the measure of force. (A Newton is defined as the SI unit of force. It is equal to the force that would give a mass of one kilogram an acceleration of one metre per second per second.) However, you will rarely see that nomenclature used in servo specifications as you see either Kg cm (European) or ounce inch (US or Imperial). (Note: this is not kg(or N)/cm it is X Kg at Y cm expressed as Kg(N) cm.) The closer in to the servo shaft you connect your pushrod, the greater the servo's torque and the

smaller the movement you get. In the diagram below, with a pushrod in the 1 cm hole of the servo arm the servo would generate a force of 5 N but double that if connected to the 0.5 cm hole in the servo arm. Connecting the other end of the pushrod to the control horn at the same distance out as the servo arm hole would make the same torque available to move the flying surface. It may require some adjustment to which hole to use in the control horn to provide the desired maximum control movement. Always start with 100%, or even the full 120%, of servo movement to make maximum use of the servo resolution and to produce your desired control surface movement. What this also does is to minimise the effect of any backlash in servo gears, and maximises the servo's power. **Only use the Transmitter ATV to fine tune your set up. You should aim to get to the exact setup required using mechanical means and only use the Tx electronics when the mechanical setup has reached its limit of adjustability.** This will avoid any non-linearity in the movement of your control surfaces.

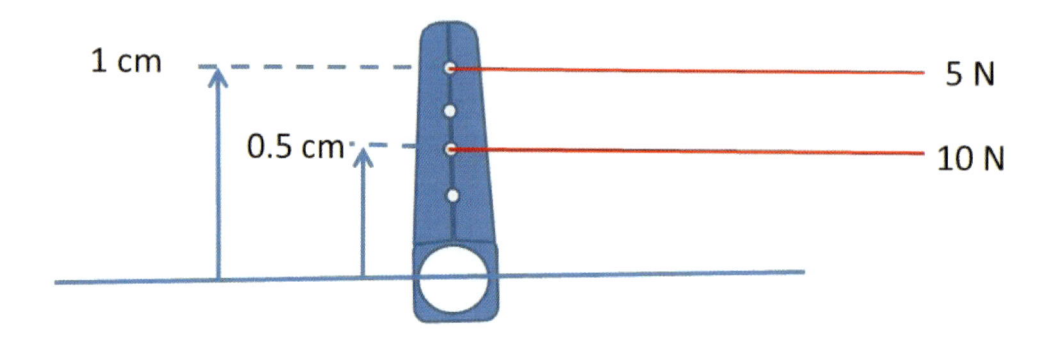

486. **Pushrod Connectors**. You also do not want to have oversize holes for your pushrod to rattle around in as you are introducing control linkage slop into the control run. The question of using Z bends is a thorny one! Some expert pilots use them! However, they must be a tight fit. If you cannot achieve a tight fit avoid Z bends. The alternative is either a simple 90° bend with a swing keeper or else use the correct size quick link or ball links to ensure a solid slop free linkage. If having done all this, your setup still has backlash, it may be the servo you are using is the cause. Some makes of servo can have excessive play in the gear train which you see as the servo arm moving slightly when the servo is powered on and you gently move the control surface up and down and get movement. It is worth changing the servo for either another one of the same sort, or if the problem is still there, replacing it with another more expensive make but check first that the backlash is minimal.

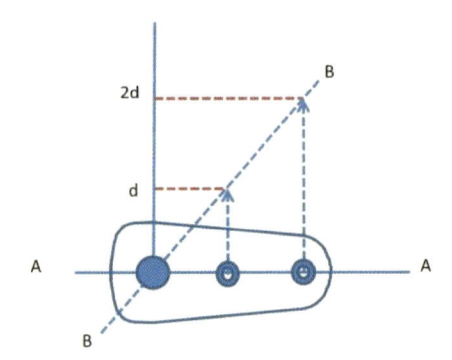

487. The diagram above shows a servo arm with two holes, one is twice as far from the centre as the other. The lines AA and BB show some greatly exaggerated slop in the servo gear train to illustrate my point. With a pushrod mounted in the hole closer to the centre the slop is "d" but at twice the distance it is "2d". It is clear from the diagram that slop is greater the further out on the servo arm you go.

488. On the other hand, if you now think of this as the control surface horn, you can have twice as much slop for the same resolution of the control surface if you connect your pushrod to the outer hole of the control surface horn.

489. So, using the innermost hole on the servo arm and the outermost hole on the control horn gives you the best way of reducing the slop in the servo being felt as slop in the control surface. Clearly, you may not get the required movement for the control surface in which case move the pushrod connection inwards on the control surface horn until you do.

Twin Servo Setup

490. Many 2 m class aircraft use two mini servos to power the elevators. Always use servos of the same make and, even then, do check that they move together over the whole range of movement. A way to do this is to securely attach two pencils with sharp points to each elevator half with the points aligned with each other. Then move the elevator stick and see if the pencil points remain together over the whole range of movement.

491. The chances are that the servos will not operate in exactly the same way and that the pencil points will indicate where there are different deflections of the elevator for the same stick movement. This is an undesirable situation as elevators deflecting with slightly different movements will cause the aircraft to roll slightly. This might be enough to cause you problems with maintaining wings level during pitching manoeuvres.

492. Some Txs have the ability to use one servo as the master and slave the other one to it. It is then a case of using the Tx facilities to get the slave servo to follow the master as closely as possible. If your Tx does not have this facility then mixing one elevator servo to the other is another option. You can then adjust the mix to achieve equal movement of the two servos over their range. I say equal, but, in practice, you may find that there are minor variations in places between the two servo positions. However, you will have done your best to eliminate variation in servo movement on the two elevators.

Servo Centring

493. The ability of a servo to centre accurately is essential if you are to be able to trim the aircraft accurately. As an example, early in my aerobatic life, I used servos that were moderately expensive but which came back to slightly different positions after pulling the stick one way and returning to centre and then going the other way and returning to centre. On the elevator, this translated to the aircraft being pulled out of a dive and then climbing slightly or pushed out of a climb and then diving slightly. Early on in my aerobatic life, I asked an experienced pilot to fly my aircraft and tell me what he thought of its setup. He commented that the aircraft was untrimmable as the servo centre varied. With electrically powered aircraft, servos lead a much easier life than when being subjected to the vibration from say a YS four stroke. As such, servos with plastic gear trains allow a tighter clearance to be achieved than metal geared servos. Some F3A servos are sold with either metal or plastic gears so the option is there if you prefer metal gears. It used to be that only Futaba or JR servos were used in F3A but, today, the choices are now wider so look around and ask what others are using. This is where using the GBRCAA Forum is so helpful.

Control Throws

494. For most precision aerobatic manoeuvres, you'll find that 10° to 15° control surface movement is all you'll need. That's not much movement but it's enough when you have the CG in the right place. So the rule is, mount your pushrod as close in to the servo shaft as possible and position the pushrod in the appropriate hole on the control surface horn to give you the desired movement. Why use degrees and not mm or inches of movement? Depends on how long your control surface is (measured along the direction of flight not spanwise – if you see what I mean) how much movement you need to measure at its end. Measured in degrees it's the same for long or short surfaces. OK, but how to convert the degrees into movement at the trailing edge of the control surface? If we call the control surface length L and the movement we want M, and the angle is A degrees, then the movement we want is:

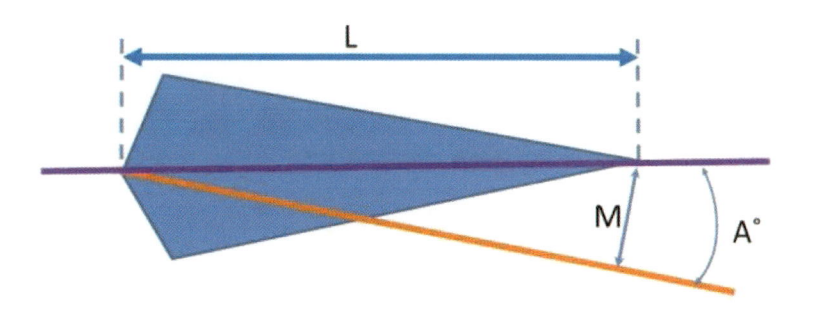

M = L x SinA (where A is in degrees)

Sin 10° = 0.17; Sin 15° = 0.26; Sin 20° = 0.34

So for 10° and L = 25 mm -------- M = 25 x 0.17 = 4.25 mm

495. Alternatively, you can use one of these angular measurement devices that you can buy commercially.

496. You could also make one for yourself out of a large clothes peg, a ply plate marked in degrees, a weighted pointer with a decent bearing and a nut and bolt to hold the whole thing together. You clip the device to you control surface, and align the movable ply scale to show 0° for the pointer. Then as you move the control surface the pointer shows you the deflection in degrees. It's very simple to use. For the Rudder, simply turn the airframe on its side and you can measure the rudder deflection.

497. It's not much movement, is it! Spins and flick manoeuvres will require more so set that for high rates and this for low rates. You can also use exponential to give you the same effect over, say, half the stick movement for both rate settings so the aircraft doesn't suddenly become twitchy when you change rates.

498. What is the **maximum** movement you need?

- For elevator, it must be sufficient to be able to stall the aircraft and keep it in a spin. The rest of the time somewhere around 10° up and down – set using your rates

- For the aileron, it is less critical but sufficient to allow control for landing in gusty conditions. Later, you will want to revisit this for setting the snap, or flick, roll. For low rates around 10° each way – as a starting point.

- For rudder, you are aiming for sufficient to keep the aircraft spinning and around 25°-30° for low rates.

HINGES

499.   OK, we've got our servos sorted out and the pushrods connected up and the next area to examine is the hinging. The key issue with hinging control surfaces is that it is accurately done.

500.   First, not all ARTF[27]'s have the hinge slots in the middle of the wing/tail plane/rudder and the control surface. It's worth checking this by dry fitting the hinges and control surfaces and seeing if the surface is not displaced from centre. If it is, then take the time to correct the hinge slots or holes.

501.   Second, ensure that the gap between, say the wing and aileron, is as small as possible but that the control surface movement is not inhibited. If you have got a gap and do not want to cut off the hinges and start again, you can always seal the gap with either some spare covering material or something else like Blenderm Tape (available from Chemists). Finally, make sure that the hinge is free moving (especially if you have sealed the gap) so that your servo is not constantly trying to overcome mechanical stiffness as well as the air loads.

502.   Third, the pushrod holes in the control horn must line up with the middle of the hinge line when the surface is at neutral – see diagram below. Otherwise, you will get some non-linear movement introduced – i.e. more up than down or vice versa – and that will make accurate flying more difficult.

---

[27] ARTF is an Almost Ready to Fly aircraft kit. Some assembly is required but all the major components are built and covered at the factory. Most ARTF kits come with suitable hardware such as undercarriages, hinges etc but generally not engines or radio equipment in the larger size of model aircraft. Smaller aircraft constructed of expanded foam can sometimes come fully equipped with servos, motor, speed controller receiver and transmitter and just need batteries to be ready for flight.

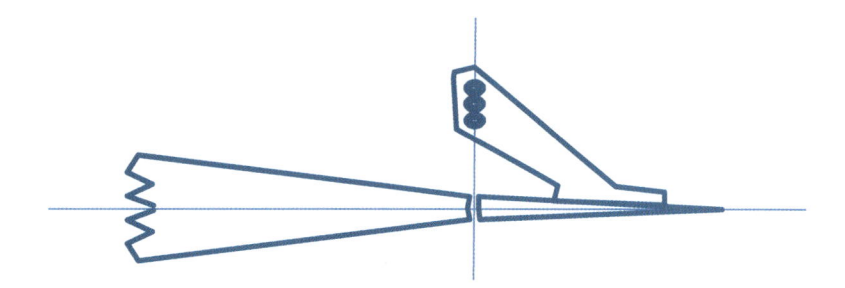

CONDITION SWITCHES

503. Some high-end Txs provide Condition Switches also sometimes called Flight Modes. These switches enable you to group together functions that fulfil a range of actions. For example, a condition switch enables you to group Rudder, Elevator and Aileron rates on one switch. Once you have reached the correct mix of rates for you primary flying controls, you only need one switch to control all actions. So, for example, I use the Condition/Flight Mode Switch in position "0" for Spinning, position "1" for landing and position "2" for all other aerobatic manoeuvres.

504. You can also add functions such as a mix of down elevator triggered by fully closed throttle for the vertical downline. What you don't want is for this mix to come in when you flare for landing! So, you can designate one of your conditions to aerobatics and one to landing and the down elevator mix will only be live when you have the aerobatic condition selected. This avoids an unintended pitch down just as you are about to land and close the throttle!

505. For the Spin condition, you can allow full elevator, full rudder and make live a function to allow a rudder to aileron mix if your aircraft needs aileron to spin. This can be further enhanced by using the stick switch function on the Rudder to trigger one mix to aileron for upright spinning and one for inverted spinning. Remember, that when inverted the rudder moves to the right to spin left as it is under the aircraft but you still want left aileron to help with the spin.

506. As you can see, condition switches make your life easier once you are airborne but they do need a good deal of thought on the ground in setting them up.

507. ALWAYS check the correct functioning of all your conditions and mixes before you get airborne!

Trimming for Straight and Level Flight and Fine Trimming the CG

508. OK, the CG is in the mid position, the control throws are set and we have some lower rates set as well. Typical low rates are:

- Aileron - 10° up and down
- Elevator - 10° up and down
- Rudder - 25° left and right.

509. To avoid repeating what I've already written, please see Chapter 4 para 136 onwards before reading further.

510. Adjust the position of your battery pack to achieve the change in CG or else use sticky lead weights mounted on the extreme tail of the aircraft – but not on the flying surfaces! This will give you the greatest effect for least weight added. If using sticky lead weights make sure you have 5g and 10g weights.

511. Once you have the CG right you will find that you may have to adjust your elevator trim as well. If you've had to use any trim to achieve level flight at your selected cruise power, you should adjust the linkage rod so that the surface is in the trimmed position with the servo at neutral. A turnbuckle linkage allows this to be done very easily by just turning the rod to either lengthen or shorten the pushrod. By doing this, you will have an equal amount of control movement around your chosen straight and level position.

512. Some specialist aerobatic aircraft have adjustable incidences for the wing and tail plane. If you have such an aircraft, then to adjust the wing incidences the first thing is to find the datum for the aircraft and set up the fuselage to be at 0° that will then allow you to adjust the wing to the recommended incidence. Once you have flown the aircraft, if you have had to use aileron trim to achieve straight and level flight, you should aim to alter the individual wing incidence so that the aileron trim returns to 0. If you had to use left aileron trim, as the aircraft was rolling to the right, you would need to increase the incidence on the right wing and vice versa. This might take a few flights to get right.

513. Similarly, if you have had to use some elevator trim then adjust the tail plane incidence so that the elevator trim can be returned to 0 as well. If you had to use some up elevator trim then you need to lower the leading edge of the tail plane and vice versa. Keep going with the adjustment till you achieve a zero-elevator angle to the tail plane and zero trim on the Tx. This is an excellent check on whether the aircraft's trim has changed due to structural changes – heat, humidity etc.

514. If your aircraft does not have any incidence adjustment, then use the clevis rod to adjust the elevator or aileron accordingly while reducing the Tx trim to 0.

515. It's worth spending time on getting your trim set up correctly as it can make a huge difference to the way an aircraft feels. Your aircraft should feel stable and rock steady and in no way twitchy. You may think you need a lot of stick movement to get the aircraft to roll quickly but that's the point of precision aerobatics – you have precise control over what the aircraft is doing at all times. If you have never experienced this then it comes as a real eye opener as to what trimming can do for the way your aircraft flies.

516. As an aside, a club mate who flew my Wot 4 after I had finished trimming it could not believe how much better it flew than his Wot 4. He said it was like flying a completely different aircraft. After setting his aircraft up properly his flew as well as mine! So, it really is worth doing this even on "ordinary" Club aircraft and getting it right before your move on to the next step.

OTHER TRIMMING METHODS

517. There are quite a few trimming methods. The ones you might hear most frequently are:

- "Zero Gravity" trimming

- Triangulation trimming.

"Zero Gravity" Trimming

518. This system has nothing to do with altering gravity by the way! Briefly, this is to do with trimming the aircraft to go vertically downwards (in still air conditions) hands off. This means that for level upright and inverted flight you will need to hold the same amount of up and down elevator. The upline is adjusted by changing the engine/motor side and up thrust so that the model flies hands-off vertically upwards (in still air conditions). All the other trimming I have described above remains to be carried out after setting this condition. You must be comfortable flying an aircraft with this setup as you can never just leave the aircraft to fly itself for a brief moment of relaxation between manoeuvres. The other snag is that you might not notice a minor trim change should one happen whereas if trimmed to fly hands off upright, any out of trim is usually immediately obvious.

519. The reason for using this technique is that in aerobatics you tend to spend as much time upright as inverted and so an aircraft that is trimmed for the so called Zero Gravity condition, will feel the same to the pilot. Normally, you will need to push more down elevator to do the same size outside loop as a loop when you trim the aircraft to fly hands off upright.

Triangulation Trimming

520. This trimming method has been developed by Bryan Hebert. He has a website[28] in which he sets out the whole process although you will need to buy the specific details of what to do for fine tuning your trim from him. His process is quite different from most others but he does have a lot of top pilots who use his system with excellent results. Rather than steal his thunder and describe the process here, please visit his website and read the full article there. You will need to buy the guide that gives you all the detailed information. That is also on his website. Note that he warns you that his system only works where you can easily alter wing, engine/motor and tailplane incidence.

---

[28] Brian Hebert's Website for Triangulation Trimming https://www.ckaero.net/pages/triangulation-trimming

ANNEX B. SOME AERODYNAMIC ISSUES

Canalyser

521. You may have heard the term Canalyser or Tcan. These can be fitted to some monoplanes and can vary in size. They are usually to be found mounted on or just aft of the canopy and if you look carefully this is usually the thickest part of the fuselage. The Canalyser acts to speed up the airflow down the fuselage and also over the wing just aft of the thickest part of the wing section. Speeding up the airflow will be a very useful function for a laminar flow boundary layer and persuade it to remain attached for longer than it was planning to do so! So, the effect will be to improve the flow over the wing, rudder and tail plane/elevator. Most noticeably though is that the rudder suddenly becomes very powerful, particularly with today's very tall fuselages making flying knife edge and doing knife edge loops very easy.

522. The ultimate Canalyser is when it becomes so big it's called a biplane!

Monoplane vs Biplane

523. As you will have seen from the photos earlier in the book, there are monoplane and biplane F3A models. Which is better I hear you ask? Well, it depends. Here are some issues:

- Biplanes have a larger wing area than monoplanes so have a lower wing loading, tend to fly more slowly and have more drag which helps to achieve a constant speed flight more easily.

- Because they fly more slowly, biplanes are more affected by crosswinds and have to hold a heading more into wind than monoplanes.

- With two wings it takes longer to rig and de-rig a biplane than a monoplane.

- With two wings there are twice as many wing incidence checks to be made.

- Twice as many wing bags are needed to protect the wings.

- With two wings to manufacture biplanes can be more expensive than a monoplane.

- Some monoplanes use a canalyser that adds to the cost of manufacture and the setup issues.

524. At the end of the day, you will be swayed by how successful a particular model has been but remember that most of this is down to the top pilot performing better than most others and would probably have won with either a monoplane or biplane. So, don't spend too long deciding on which type will do better. Go for the one

THE ISSUE OF WEATHERCOCKING

525. In Chapter 5, I discussed weathercocking. In this Annex, I will give an explanation of what is actually happening as the aircraft reduces speed to enter a spin in a crosswind. To do this, I'm using a construct called the Triangle of Velocities. Full size pilots will be familiar with this as it is an integral part of calculating an aircraft's heading to fly to reach a destination when dealing with a crosswind. In the full-size pilot's case, he is interested in his ground speed along the track to his destination so he can calculate when he will get there.

526. What is the triangle of velocities? In brief, it is a scale graphical representation of the two velocity vectors[29]: the wind speed and direction and the aircraft's speed and direction.

If we draw a line to represent the wind speed and direction, the length of the line will be the speed and the orientation of the line will be its direction as shown here. The blue line is called the wind vector as it gives the speed and direction of the wind.	
Next, we use a line of the length to represent the aircraft's speed and direction. The green line is called the aircraft's vector.	
Now connect the arrow end of the aircraft's vector with the tail end of the wind vector and then draw a red line from the tail of the aircraft's vector to the arrow of the wind's vector and we get our triangle of velocities that gives us our ground track direction and speed.	

---

[29] The arrows in the diagram above represent both the speed, by their length, and the direction in which that force is acting. We call this a vector since that covers both force and direction.

Since we are only concerned with the direction of the aircraft's ground track, we just adjust the aircraft heading so that the ground track sits on the line we are trying to follow on the ground which is at 150 m away from you – or a lesser figure depending on the size of your aircraft.	
Now, as you reduce the aircraft's speed but leave the heading unchanged, as you slow down towards the stall (green line) you will see this picture since the wind vector (blue line) remains unchanged. So the track vector has now changed both direction and speed. The aircraft heading is unchanged while the aircraft tracks downwind at a reduced speed.	

527. With wings level, the aircraft heading remains the same in both cases but the aircraft will be seen to move, or translate, sideways. Again, this is relative motion since the aircraft is still travelling through the air in the same direction. It's just the block of air speed and direction is having a different effect on the ground track of the aircraft as it slows down.

528. It is important to remember this point. In flight, when you slow the aircraft speed it will NOT *WEATHERCOCK into any crosswind. To believe this is to misunderstand the Laws of Physics. Do not be misled!* **However, if the wings aren't level, then the aircraft will turn in the direction of bank.**

ANNEX C. EXPLANATION OF ARESTI SYMBOLS

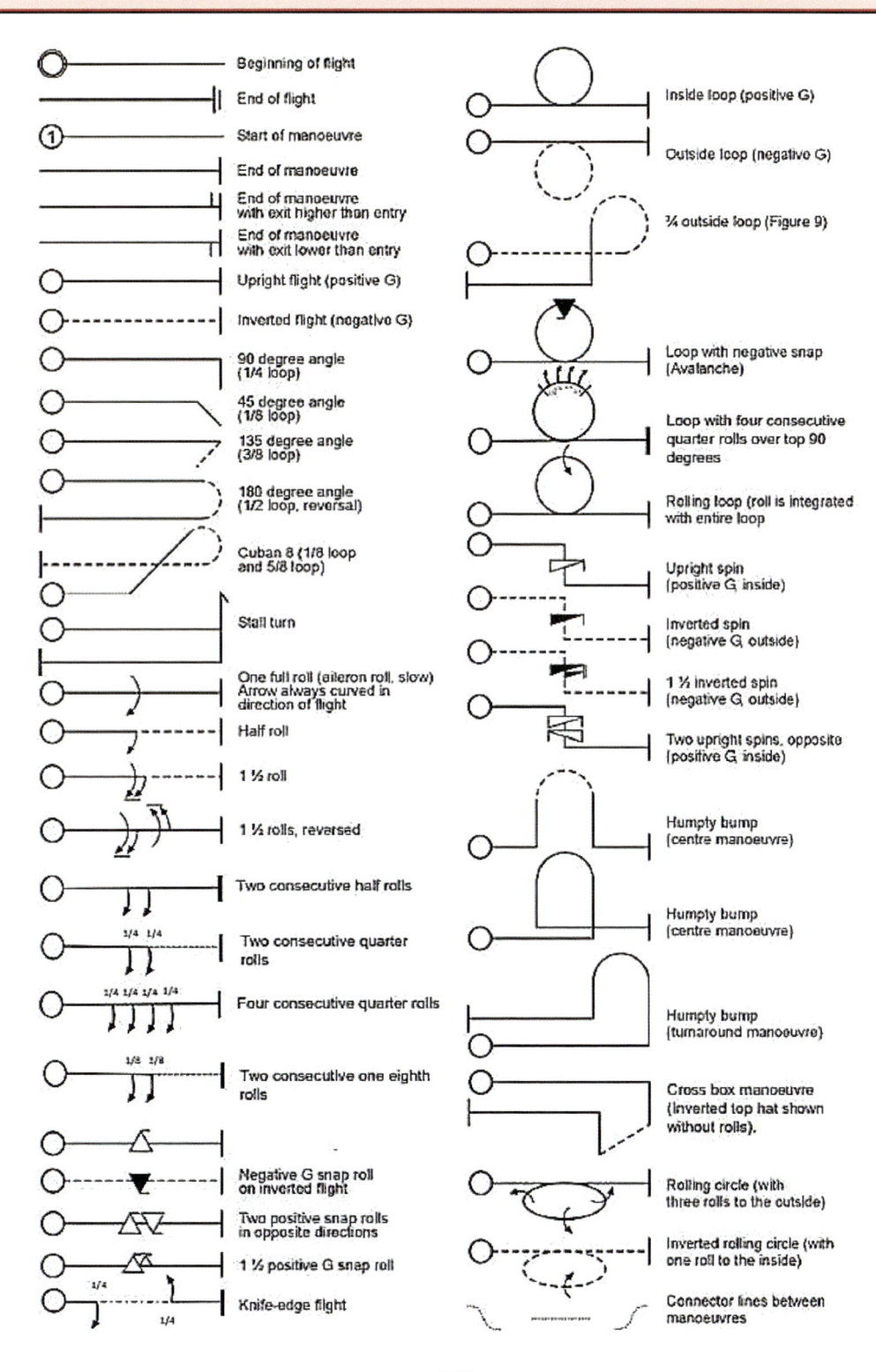

○————	Beginning of flight
————||	End of flight
①————	Start of manoeuvre
————	End of manoeuvre
————||	End of manoeuvre with exit higher than entry
————||	End of manoeuvre with exit lower than entry
○————	Upright flight (positive G)
○- - - -	Inverted flight (negative G)
○———⌐	90 degree angle (1/4 loop)
○———╲	45 degree angle (1/8 loop)
○———╲	135 degree angle (3/8 loop)
○———⌒	180 degree angle (1/2 loop, reversal)
	Cuban 8 (1/8 loop and 5/8 loop)
○——⊓——	Stall turn
○—↷——	One full roll (aileron roll, slow) Arrow always curved in direction of flight
○—↷- - -	Half roll
○—↷——	1 ½ roll
○—↷↶——	1 ½ rolls, reversed
○—↷↷——	Two consecutive half rolls
○—¼ ¼——	Two consecutive quarter rolls
○—¼ ¼ ¼ ¼——	Four consecutive quarter rolls
○—⅛ ⅛——	Two consecutive one eighth rolls
○—△——	Negative G snap roll on inverted flight
○- - -▼- - -	
○—△▽——	Two positive snap rolls in opposite directions
○—△▽——	1 ½ positive G snap roll
○—¼ ¼——	Knife-edge flight

	Inside loop (positive G)
	Outside loop (negative G)
	¾ outside loop (Figure 9)
	Loop with negative snap (Avalanche)
	Loop with four consecutive quarter rolls over top 90 degrees
	Rolling loop (roll is integrated with entire loop)
	Upright spin (positive G, inside)
	Inverted spin (negative G, outside)
	1 ½ inverted spin (negative G, outside)
	Two upright spins, opposite (positive G, inside)
	Humpty bump (centre manoeuvre)
	Humpty bump (centre manoeuvre)
	Humpty bump (turnaround manoeuvre)
	Cross box manoeuvre (Inverted top hat shown without rolls).
	Rolling circle (with three rolls to the outside)
	Inverted rolling circle (with one roll to the inside)
	Connector lines between manoeuvres

ANNEX D.   MINI SCHEDULE CALLING CARDS

1ST MINI SCHEDULE

No	Mini Schedule 1
1	Take-off Sequence
2	Loop on Centre
3	Half Loop
4	Inverted Flight
5	Loop on Centre (downwards)
6	Half Loop
7	Repeat from No 2

2ND MINI SCHEDULE

No	Mini Schedule 2
1	Take-off Sequence
2	Loop on Centre
3	Half Reverse Cuban Eight
4	Four Point Roll
5	Half Cuban Eight
6	Repeat from No 2

3ʳᵈ Mini Schedule

No	Mini Schedule 3
1	Take-off Sequence
2	Immelmann
3	Slow Roll
4	Split S
5	!/2 Roll, Outside Loop, 1/2 Roll
6	Repeat from No 2

4ᵀᴴ Mini Schedule

No	Mini Schedule 4
1	Take-off Sequence
2	Loop on Centre
3	Humpty Bump, 1/2 Roll Up
4	Cuban Eight with 1/2 Rolls
5	Hjumpty Bump, 1/2 Roll Down
6	Repeat from No 2

5th Mini Schedule

No	Mini Schedule 5
1	Take-off Sequence
2	Inverted Flight
3	Humpty Bump, 1/2 Roll Down
4	Cuban Eight with 1/2 Rolls
5	Stall Turn
6	Repeat from No 2

6th Mini Schedule

No	Mini Schedule 6
1	Take-off Sequence
2	1/2 Roll, Outside Loop, 1/2 Roll
3	Humpty Bump, 1/2 Roll Up
4	Slow Roll
5	1/2 Square Loop, 1/2 Roll Up
6	3 Turn Spin
7	1/2 Reverse Cuban 8
8	45° Upline, 1/2 Roll
9	1/2 Loop
10	Repeat from No 2

ANNEX E.   GBRCAA INTERMEDIATE SCHEDULE

INTRODUCTION

529.   A number of pilots have either started in competition by going straight to the Intermediate Schedule or else have flown only one Clubman competition and then moved up to fly the Intermediate Schedule. Pilots are allowed to select which schedule they fly and to move up, or down the schedules.

530.   The Intermediate Schedule details can be found on the GBRCAA website[30]. I have reproduced the Intermediate Schedule Calling Card and Ribbon Diagram below:

No	GBR/CAA **Intermediate** Schedule	K
1	Take-off Sequence	1
2	Triangular Loop (Base at the bottom)	3
3	Stall Turn, Full Roll Up	3
4	Four Point Roll	3
5	Immelman Turn with Half Roll	2
6	Square Loop with ½ Rolls in legs 1 and 3	4
7	Split S Full Roll, Exit Inverted	2
8	Cuban Eight with Half Rolls, Exit Inverted	3
9	Humpty Bump Push, Pull, Pull	2
10	Figure S	4
11	Figure 6, Half roll down.	3
12	Knife Edge, Exit Inverted	4
13	Half Outside Loop	1
14	Three Turn Spin	4
15	Landing Sequence	1

Max Score = 400   Advisory Promotion = 260 (65%)

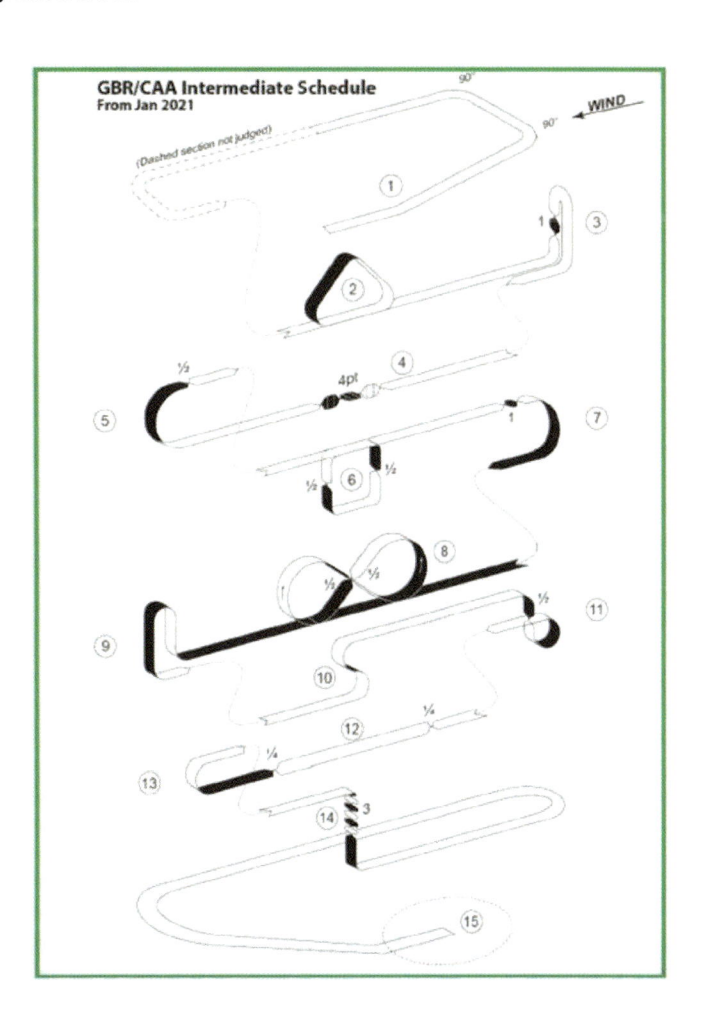

---

[30] GBRCAA Intermediate Schedule - http://www.gbrcaa.org/?page_id=99

531. I do not think an aircraft that does not have adequate power will be suitable for this schedule. Your chosen aircraft needs to be able to maintain the same speed vertically as you are flying horizontally. In rough terms, you need enough power to fly at half throttle for horizontal manoeuvres using either full or sufficient power to maintain the same speed vertically.

532. *I have placed the GBRCAA description of the manoeuvre and the judging notes in italics to differentiate them from my text.*

I-01 Racetrack Take-off Sequence (K=1)

533. *The model is placed on the take-off area, parallel to the flight line and released. The model rolls along the take-off area until flying speed is achieved, then establishes straight climbing flight parallel to the flight line. The model then turns through 180 degrees in a continuous turn and flies back over the manoeuvring area centre line. Take-off is completed once the centre line has been crossed and the model then performs a 180° turnaround of the pilot's choice, which is not scored.*

534. *Notes: Box limitations do not apply to this manoeuvre. On rough surfaces or when there is a crosswind, it is acceptable for a helper to restrain the model on the ground until take-off power is applied.*

535. *Judging notes:*

- *Model does not track straight on take-off: 1-2 points. (Disregard the effect of the take-off surface e.g. ruts and pot holes on grass sites)*

- *Wings not level after take-off: 1 point per 15 degrees*

- *Rate of climb too steep: 1-2 points above 30 degrees*

- *Model goes behind judge's line after take-off: zero points*

- *Model retouches runway after lift-off: 1 point*

- *Any part of the aircraft structure becomes detached on take-off: zero points for the whole flight*

536. As for the Clubman, I am assuming that the aircraft will take off from right to left, i.e. the wind is coming from the left of the page. Note that the Ribbon Diagram above shows the wind coming from the opposite direction. Refer to the notes in Chapter 7 para 298 since the take-off for both the Clubman and Intermediate is the same.

Model Aircraft Precision Aerobatics   Annex E – GBRCAA Intermediate Schedule

I-02 TRIANGULAR LOOP (BASE AT THE BOTTOM) (K=3)

537.   From upright on the baseline pass centre and pull through a 3/8 loop into a 45° up line. Pull through a 1/4 loop positioned on the centre line into a 45° down line. Pull through a 3/8 loop to exit upright at baseline height.

538.   Judging notes:

- *All radii equal*

- *Entry and exit should be same height*

- *Base of a 45° triangle is longer than other two lines*

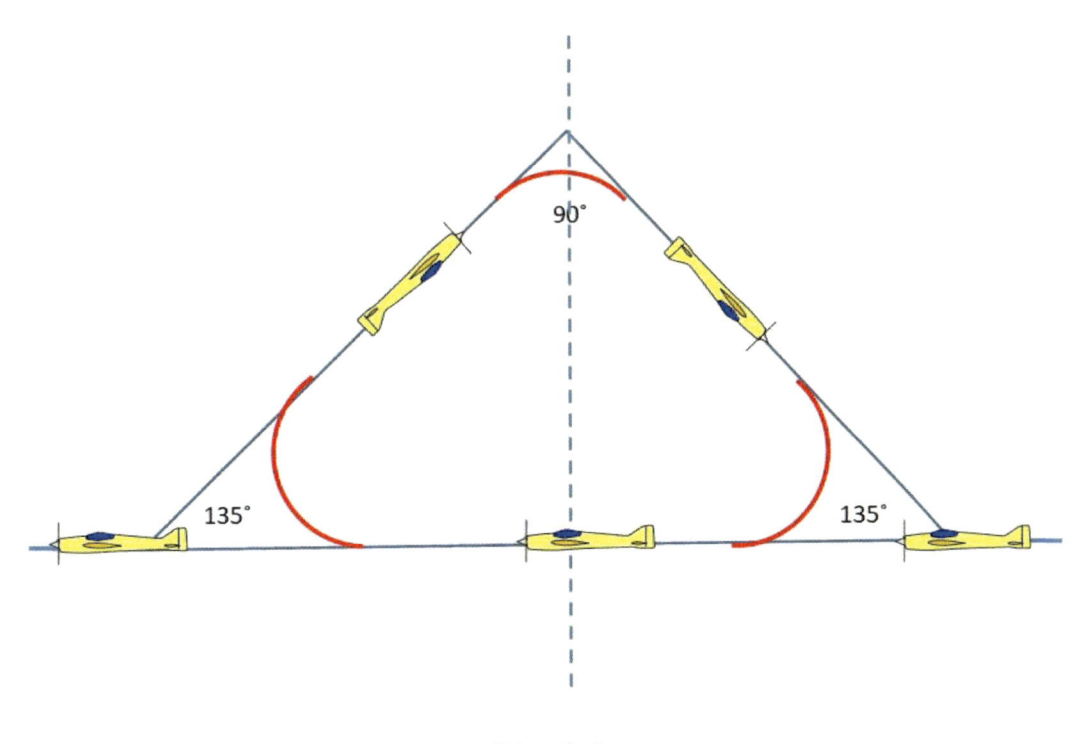

Triangle Loop

539.   The geometry for this triangle is of a 90° triangle with two 45° angles. If you remember your geometry lessons you will recognise that Pythagoras gave the relationships of 90° triangles as: "The square of the hypotenuse is the sum of the squares of the other two sides". Let's say the two sides adjacent to the 90° angle are one unit of length. That means we can say that the length of the long side (hypotenuse) is the square root of two or roughly 1.4. **A good way to visualise this is to use a 45° setsquare and place the long side parallel with the horizon.** That

will give you the idea of how steep the two 45° lines should appear and the relative lengths of each leg. In fact, you can ask a helper to hold the setsquare up to the sky while you are flying and tell you to commence your part loop just before you reach each of the apexes such that the aircraft path so that each radius is as near as possible the same size with your aircraft moves smoothly from line to line as in the diagram below.

540. Try and fly a reasonably large figure. As you pass centre, aim to fly around 4-5 seconds before starting your first looping manoeuvre. I cannot stress how important it is to have your aircraft's wings level before you start the first part loop. If the aircraft is banked towards you as you start the part loop, the aircraft will appear to be yawing to the left. If the wing is banked away from you then this will appear to you that the aircraft is yawing to the right. This is caused by the aircraft looping at an angle to the vertical. You can, and should, use rudder to correct this error but the reason for the error in the aircraft's path is due to the wings not being level. The same problem makes itself felt when flying the second and third "part loops". The third "part loop" is especially important as, without level wings, the aircraft will end up either heading towards you or away from you requiring you to use the rudder to bring the aircraft back onto course, increasing your workload. You must also end the third part loop at the same height as your entry height since this is a centre manoeuvre. You will lose points if you do not achieve the same height. You must also maintain a constant height until you are past centre and the line after the manoeuvre has been completed.

541. You will see from the diagram that the top "part loop" looks smaller than the first and third "part loops" and this is just down to the larger angle you are turning the aircraft through in "part loops" one and three. The radius for all three "part loops" must be the same radius as, indeed, they are in the diagram.

542. Making the climbing and diving sides equal in length and don't forget to compensate for any wind. If there is a significant headwind, the first part loop should be less than 135° so that the aircraft appears to be at a steeper angle of climb as the wind will drift the aircraft back onto the required 135° angle. You will need to turn the aircraft more than the 90° shown on the diagram so that the aircraft appears to be at a steeper angle of dive as the wind will drift it back onto the correct angle of dive. You can get your helper to hold the set square up to the sky and let you know how closely the path of the aircraft's CG along the set square sides and adjust your angle of climb/dive accordingly.

543. The most difficult part of this manoeuvre is to decide when to start the third part loop so that the aircraft ends up at the same height as its entry height and the radius of the part loop is the same as the preceding ones. Again, your helper with the set square can help especially if they have marked the position of the start of the part loops onto the set square and tell you when to start and finish the part loops.

544. Use rudder to maintain the aircraft tracking correctly to counter any crosswind component and make sure the wings remain level at the same time.

545.   Remember to apply and remove power smoothly during the looping sections so that you maintain a constant speed around the manoeuvre.

546.   Finally, the manoeuvre starts and finishes on the centre line.

I-03 STALL TURN, FULL ROLL UP (K=3)

547.   From upright on the baseline pull through a 1⁄4 loop into a vertical up line, perform a full roll, followed by a stall turn into a vertical down line. Pull through a 1⁄4 loop to exit upright.

548.   Judging notes:

- *Full roll should be centred on vertical up line*

- *If the stall turn radius is between ½ and 1 wingspan: downgrade 1 point*

- *If the stall turn radius is between 1 and 1½ wingspans: downgrade 2-3 points*

- *If the stall turn radius is between 1½ and 2 wingspans: downgrade 4-5 points*

- *If the stall turn radius is greater than 2 wingspans: score shall be zero*

- *If the aircraft exhibits a pendulum effect after exiting the stall turn: deduct 1 point*

549.   Review the information in Chapter 5 para 223, Stall Turn. As you pass centre to complete the Triangle Loop, check the position of the aircraft and make any corrections with the rudder to get you back on track. You will have had some experience of the head and crosswind components so now is the time to make up your mind how you need to position the aircraft for the Stall Turn remembering that the next manoeuvre is the Four Point Roll for which you want as much room as possible. So, make sure that:

- As you pull to the vertical you are as close to the upwind end of the Box as you can be.

- If there is a significant crosswind that you are ready to smoothly bank the aircraft in the direction of the crosswind as you pull up for the ¼ loop, see Chapter 5 para 183. Make sure you use the first part of the climb to get the angle correct so that the aircraft is not blown back into the Box.

- Before you start the full roll, make sure that you centralise both the elevator and rudder. Rolling with either or both applied will pull the aircraft off track and lose you points. You want a nice axial roll. Don't roll so fast that you cannot stop it accurately after one revolution.

- Count the line length from the moment you finish the ¼ loop and do the same after you finish the roll. However, you must also decelerate the aircraft so that it comes to a stop before you carry out the stall turn. That means that your second count will have to be longer than the first count as the aircraft will be slowing to a stop. So, if you count to two for the first line you might want to count to three or four for the second count.

- Avoid closing the throttle completely when decelerating the aircraft. Setting 1/3 throttle in the first instance will give you a yard stick on how much you need to set to get the line length the same with the aircraft coming to a stop. Adding a bit more power as the aircraft is close to stopping will give you greater control of the actual stall turn. It's better than giving a burst of power as that can unsettle the aircraft and cause yawing due to torque effect with low airspeed.

- Remember to carry out the stall turn **towards** the direction of any crosswind by applying full rudder in that direction and closing the throttle completely as the nose drops through 90° from the vertical and to hold the aircraft's attitude with rudder to match the aircraft's yaw to the crosswind strength for the down line. **You will not be penalised if the aircraft loses position at the point of the stall turn.** Even with no crosswind, you must still use opposite rudder just before the nose reaches the vertical down line to stop any pendulum effect.

- If you have a significant headwind and have had the aircraft tilted towards the wind on the way up, as the aircraft is rotating remember to push down elevator to push the nose past the vertical and pointing back into wind.

- The final ¼ loop must be the same radius as the entry ¼ loop. Once again, you will need to check your wing orientation to ensure that as you pull out of the dive the aircraft tracks correctly and does not end up either flying in towards you or out away from you. If this happens, you then need to spend time with the rudder to get the aircraft back on track before starting your next manoeuvre increasing your workload unnecessarily.

I-04 FOUR POINT ROLL (K=3)

550. From upright, perform four consecutive 1/4 rolls, exit upright.

551. Judging notes:

- *Pauses between rolls should be short and of equal length*

- *Constant roll rate*

- *Aircraft is on centre line of Box in middle of inverted line*

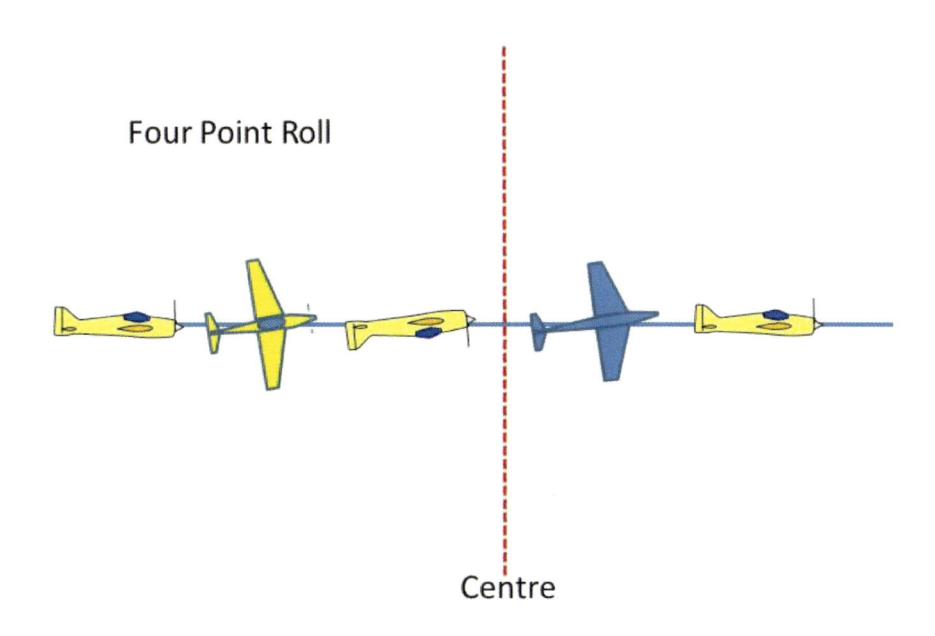

Four Point Roll

Centre

552. You will definitely need to use both rudder and elevator for the Four Point Roll, so review Chapter 5 from para 206. Remember that the roll rate must be the same for each of the four "part rolls" and that there must be a line of the same length between each "part roll". Stopping the roll exactly every 90° can be tricky and so you may find that rolling more slowly can help to improve your rolling accuracy. The diagram shows the attitude of the aircraft at each of three points, where it isn't upright, with suitable yaw and pitch attitudes so that the aircraft maintains height.

553. Remember to set the aircraft on the right heading so that it sits on the required ground track before you start the Four Point Roll. The good news is that you do not need to make any corrections for crosswinds in a horizontal rolling manoeuvre! Do remember to count, or just say "pause", to give the same length to each of the pauses between the four rolling segments.

554. Notice the description of the middle of the manoeuvre. It is the middle of the line between the beginning and end of the inverted section and not at the end of the second "part roll". Again, there is no substitute for practising in all wind conditions so that you are able to judge by eye when to start the Four Point Roll so that you hit the correct centre point.

555. Although not specifically called up in the judging points, you will be judged on maintaining a constant height for the whole manoeuvre. The usual deduction of 1 point per 15° deviation is applied.

I-05 IMMELMANN TURN WITH HALF ROLL (K=2)

556. *From upright pull into a half loop and immediately perform a half roll to exit upright.*

557. *Judging notes*

- Constant radius through half loop
- Half roll must immediately follow half loop

558. This is the same manoeuvre as in the Clubman so please review the description in Chapter 5 para 338.

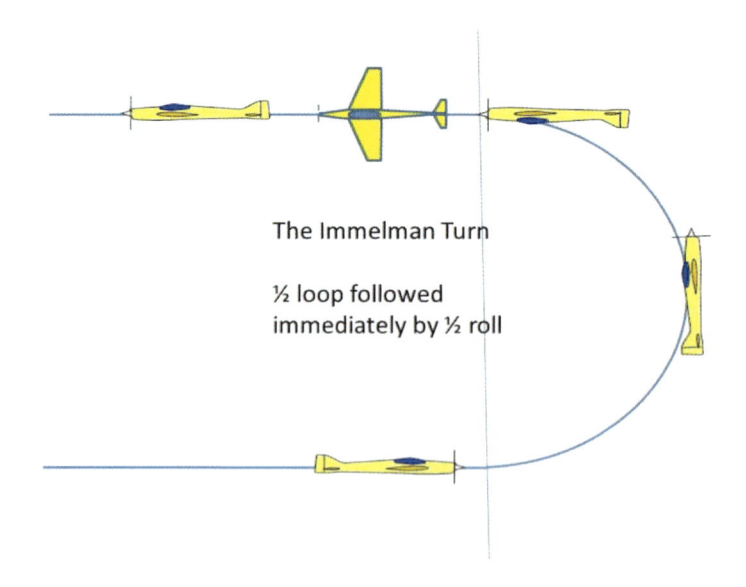

The Immelman Turn

½ loop followed immediately by ½ roll

559. The key difference between the Clubman and the Intermediate Immelmann is that here you need to fly a big manoeuvre and so you will really need an aircraft with good power to weight ratio. The reason you need to fly a big manoeuvre is to give you the vertical space you will need for your next manoeuvre, the Square Loop. A large vertical manoeuvre means that you need to really focus on keeping the wings level before you start the ½ loop using the rudder (and ailerons if necessary) to counter any crosswind component and to make sure the aircraft is tracking correctly immediately after completing the Immelmann.

560. Again, you must use rudder for the half roll otherwise the nose will drop and you will lose a point! As you are rolling from inverted, move the rudder stick in the same direction as the aileron stick.

I-06 Square Loop with 1/2 Rolls in Legs 1 and 3 (K=4)

561.   From upright on the top line pass centre and push through a 1/4 loop into a vertical down line. Perform a half roll centred on the vertical down line. Pull through a 1/4 loop to upright on the baseline and fly past centre and pull through a 1/4 loop to a vertical up line. Perform a half roll centred on the vertical up line. Push through a 1/4 loop to exit upright on the top line.

562.   Judging notes:

- All radii equal

- Manoeuvre performed on centre line

- Half rolls to be in centre of lines

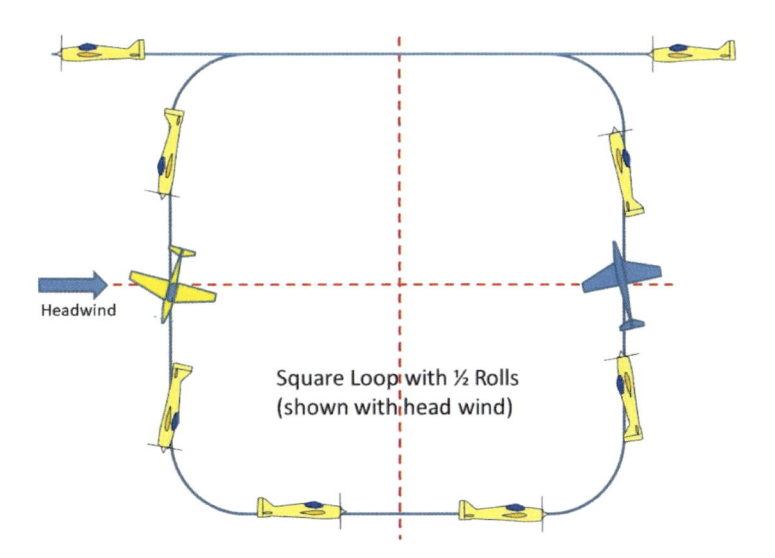

Square Loop with ½ Rolls (shown with head wind)

563.   The biggest problem with this manoeuvre is making it square! It is very easy to end up with a short top element and a longer vertical element as the vertical part has to include a half roll. You will quickly find that not entering this manoeuvre high enough will cause your vertical line to be uncomfortably close to the ground! Remember also that you cannot climb from the end of the Immelmann to the start of the Square Loop as you will lose points. You must aim to fly a big Immelmann Turn!

564.   The wind plays a major role in how well you fly this manoeuvre. On the into wind legs on windy days, the ground speed will be low but on the downwind legs the ground speed will be high and you should make due allowance for this in the way you count down to centre and the looping parts. You will also need to adjust the

aircraft attitude on the down and up legs by pointing the vertical axis of the aircraft into wind to hold your position over the ground.

565.   It is vital that you know you have hit centre for this manoeuvre. Brief your Caller to count you down to centre and out to the other side. Something like "three, two, one, centre, one, two, three". On the count of three being reached, carry out a quarter outside loop smoothly closing the throttle completely as you do so. Arrange the down line attitude to your aircraft to reflect the prevailing wind conditions including crosswinds.

566.   Count "one thousand" and initiate your half roll after which count "one thousand" and pull through a quarter loop to the horizontal selecting your cruise power setting. Brief your Caller to count down from this point to centre and then beyond. Remember, in a flat calm, you would expect your ground speed to be the same up and down wind. However, in a strong wind your Caller may only count "one, centre, one"! Remember to keep your horizontal flight path level and as soon as you hear your Caller's last number call, immediately start your second quarter loop and adjust for the prevailing wind conditions. Remember to apply the required power for the upline. It is easy to under power this part of the manoeuvre! Count "one thousand" and start your second half roll, count "one thousand" and begin your second quarter outside loop. This is an into wind quarter outside loop so don't push too much down elevator and end up lower than your entry height. If your Caller can help as regards your height, they might usefully give you guidance on how hard to push to make the entry height. Do not be surprised if the square is anything but! It takes a good deal of practice to get this right which is why this manoeuvre has a K=4 rating!

567.   Finally, note the attitude of the aircraft when flown in a headwind on both the vertical legs. If you do not make these corrections then the geometry of the Square Loop will be wrong and you will be penalised. Also, note that the radius of your last quarter loop will be used as the comparator with all the other quarter loops in order to decide whether your radii are the same and, if not, what downgrade to apply.

I-07 SPLIT S FULL ROLL, EXIT INVERTED (K=2)

568.   From upright on the top line perform a full roll immediately followed by half an outside loop to exit inverted on the baseline.

569.   Judging notes:

- *Half loop immediately follows full roll*

- *Constant radius through half outside loop*

Split S
Full roll followed immediately
by ½ outside loop

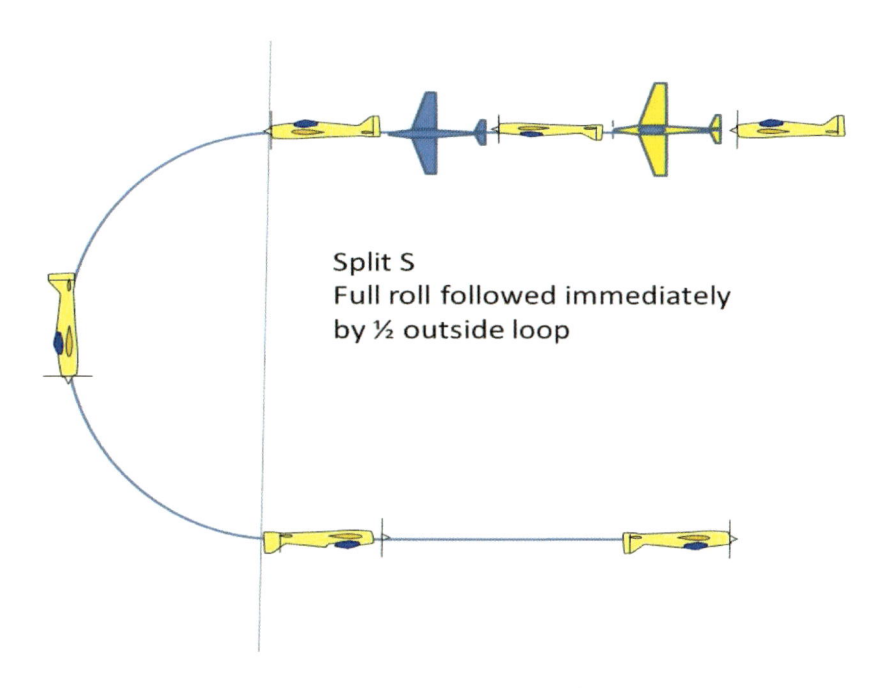

570. As you can see from the description, the Split S in the Intermediate differs by requiring a full roll followed by a ½ outside loop. **You must use rudder for the roll otherwise the aircraft's nose will drop.** If you are not used to doing an outside loop from the top, now's the time to start getting rid of any fear you may have! Once you have completed your outside loop, you must fly level inverted for some distance past centre for the next manoeuvre, the Cuban Eight.

571. As usual, you will need to assess the head and crosswind components of the wind and make the usual corrections. Remember that as the aircraft is performing a negative g manoeuvre, the hint is to roll away from the direction from which the crosswind is coming. In this example, with the crosswind coming from the left of the aircraft, you will need to roll to the right to maintain the wings in the correct plane for the outside loop. If you do this correctly, you should not need to correct the aircraft's heading too much at the bottom of the outside loop.

I-08 CUBAN EIGHT WITH HALF ROLLS, EXIT INVERTED (K=3)

572. From inverted on the baseline fly past centre and push through 5/8 of an outside loop into a 45° down line. Perform a half roll in the centre of the 45° down line. Push through 3/4 of an outside loop into a 45° down line. Perform a half roll in the centre of the 45° down line. Push through a 1/8 loop to exit inverted on the baseline.

573. Judging notes:

- *Half rolls performed on centre line of Box, and in middle of 45°line*

- *All radii equal*

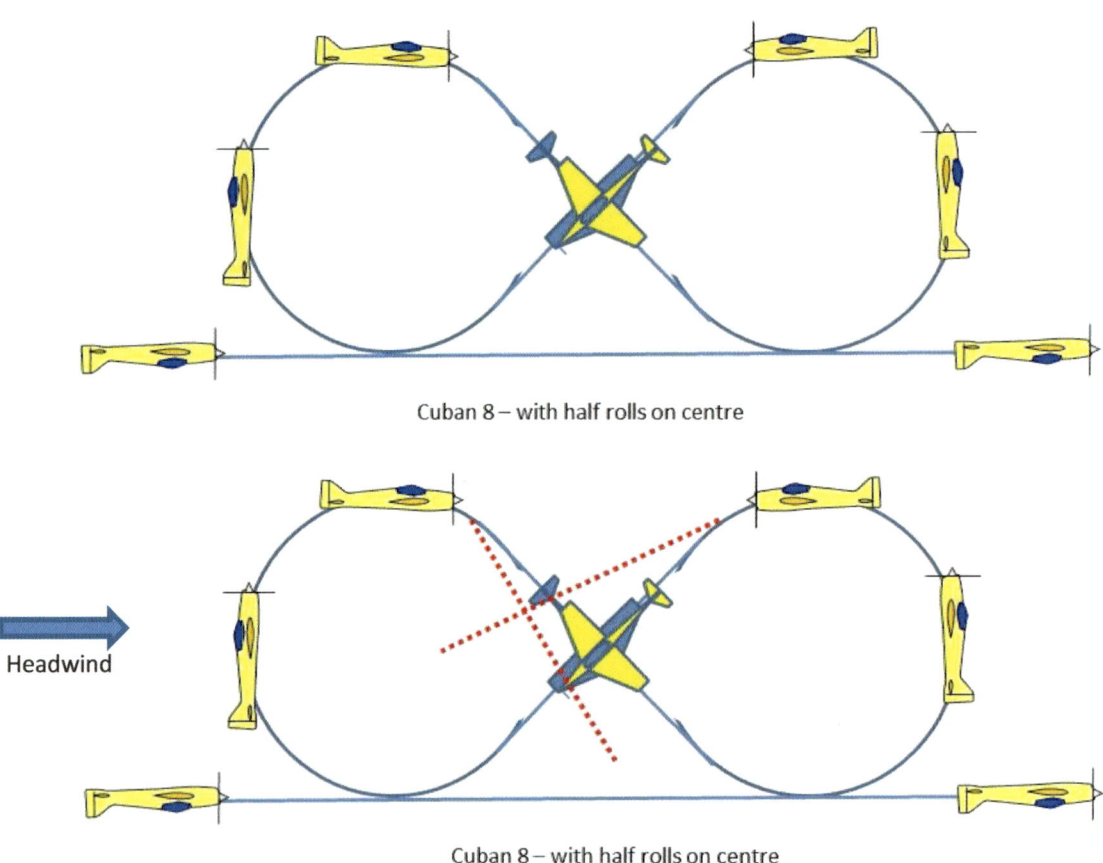

Cuban 8 – with half rolls on centre

Headwind →

Cuban 8 – with half rolls on centre
Dotted red line shows angle to fly in strong headwinds

574. Again, this Cuban Eight is a challenge compared with the Clubman version as you enter and depart the manoeuvre inverted on the bottom line. As you exit the Split S, you have to fly past centre inverted maintaining a level flight path corrected to remain on the desired track. Maintaining direction while inverted and using the rudder can be confusing. In this instance, the easiest way to get the rudder correction correct is to use the hint of looking at the wingtip nearest you. Use your rudder stick to move the wingtip forward or back. In this case, with the aircraft flying from left to right, to move wingtip forward, or to the right, move the rudder stick to the right and vice versa. See Chapter 5 para 256.

575. As per the Clubman version, deciding where to start the push for the first part of the Cuban Eight will vary with wind conditions. The best advice I can offer is to fly as often as you can in as many different wind conditions that you can to give you a feel for when to start the first outside loop for this Cuban Eight.

576. Review the guidance on flying loops in a head and crosswind, see Chapter 5 para 182 and 183. Remember this is a negative g manoeuvre but starting from inverted so as you start the outside loop, you need to roll the wings in the same direction from which the crosswind is blowing. So, if the wind is blowing from the left of the aircraft, you will need to roll the wings to the left to keep them in the correct plane.

I-09 Humpty Bump Push, Pull, Pull (K=2)

577. *From inverted on the baseline push through a 1⁄4 loop into a vertical up line. At the top of the vertical up line pull through a half inside loop into a vertical down line. At the bottom of the down line, pull through a 1⁄4 loop to exit upright on the baseline.*

578. Judging notes:

- *All radii equal*

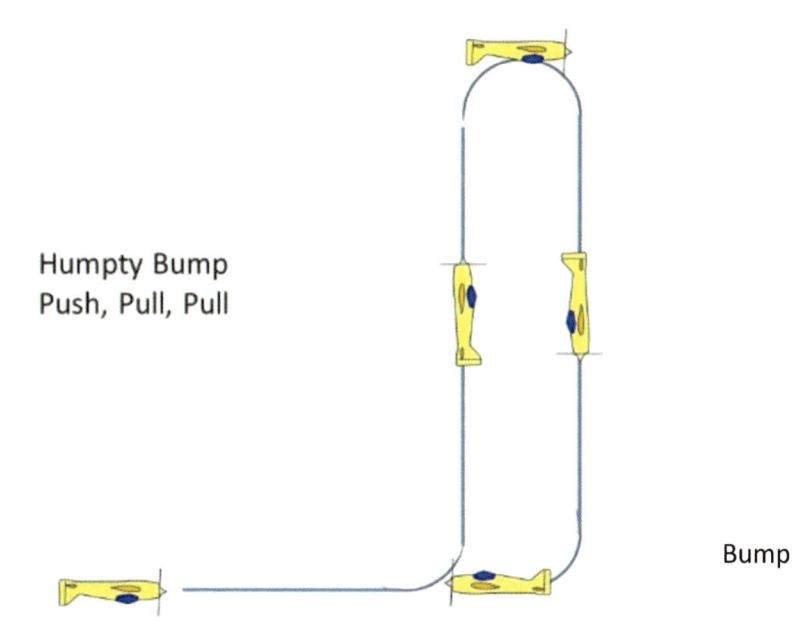

579. In comparison with the Clubman Schedule, the Humpty in the Intermediate Schedule appears less complicated. However, the entry to the Humpty Bump is inverted and there isn't much time between exiting the Cuban Eight and entering the Humpty Bump as otherwise the aircraft stands a chance of exiting the Box boundary.

580. Since there are no half rolls in this manoeuvre, it is not necessary to go particularly high but making the manoeuvre too small will earn you a lower score so you need to keep the relationship between this manoeuvre and all the other manoeuvres approximately constant. So, it is worth going at least as high as you did with the Cuban Eight.

581. Remember to keep the aircraft attitude such that you counter any impact from head and crosswinds. Correct rudder control is essential if the aircraft is not to jink around and lose you points. The hint here is to use the rudder stick while looking at the back end of the aircraft. The rudder stick will move the aircraft tail in the

direction in which the rudder stick is pushed. Perfecting that technique will allow you to fly a straight, long upline without using the rudder stick in the wrong way!

I-10 FIGURE S (K=4)

582.   *From upright on the baseline on centre pull through half an inside loop and immediately push into half an outside loop to exit upright on the top line.*

583.   *Judging notes:*

- *All radii equal*

- *There should be no line between half loops*

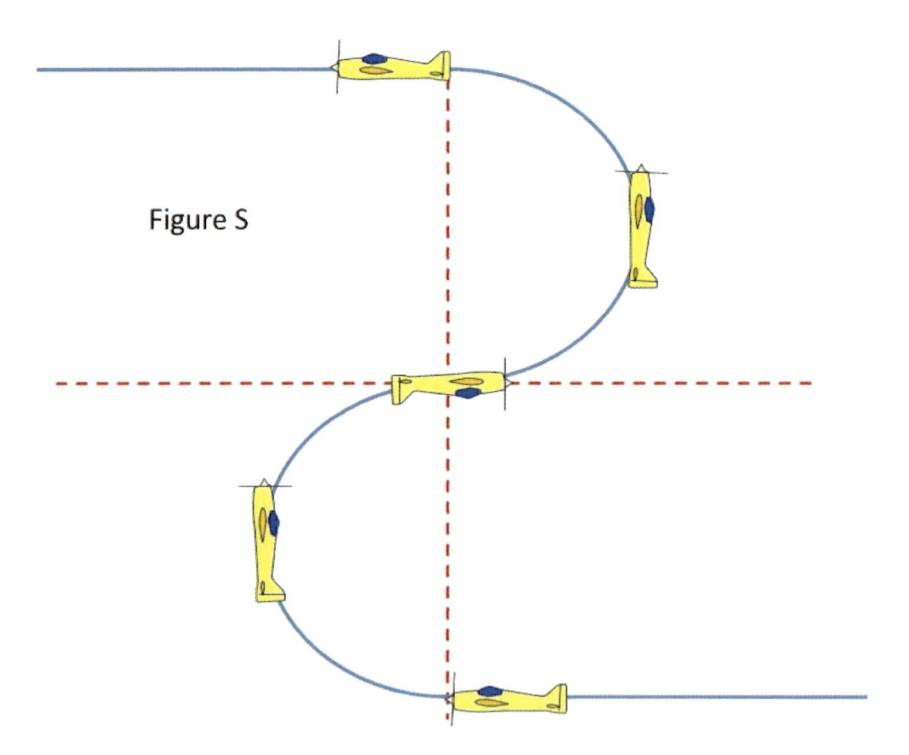

Figure S

584.   The first thing to notice about this manoeuvre is that it has a K=4 rating. That means it's not as simple as it looks! Position, shape and size are what this manoeuvre is all about. The first half loop must be started and completed exactly on centre. The half loop must be round and at the point the aircraft is at the top of the half loop it must also be right on the centre line. As usual, you must make the necessary corrections for head and crosswinds.

585. The second part of the manoeuvre is an outside loop of the same size and starting exactly on centre and ending exactly on centre. Now you need to make the half outside loop the same size as the first half loop.

586. The most common error is not having the aircraft level inverted on centre before starting the outside loop. It is a very easily seen error and so you will be docked marks. Sometimes, it's likely that you will both miss centre and not have the aircraft level before you start the outside loop. If it looks like you will not have perfect geometry you must assess which of the two factors you are more likely to make and go for that one. So, if you are going to miss centre but you could get the aircraft level before starting the outside loop, or vice versa, then at least meet one of these two critical judging points.

I-11 FIGURE 6, HALF ROLL DOWN (K=3)

587. From upright on the top line, push into a vertical down line. Perform a half roll centred on the vertical down line. At the bottom of the down line, push through 3/4 of an outside loop to exit upright at mid height.

588. Judging notes:

- *All radii equal*

- *Roll must be in middle of down line*

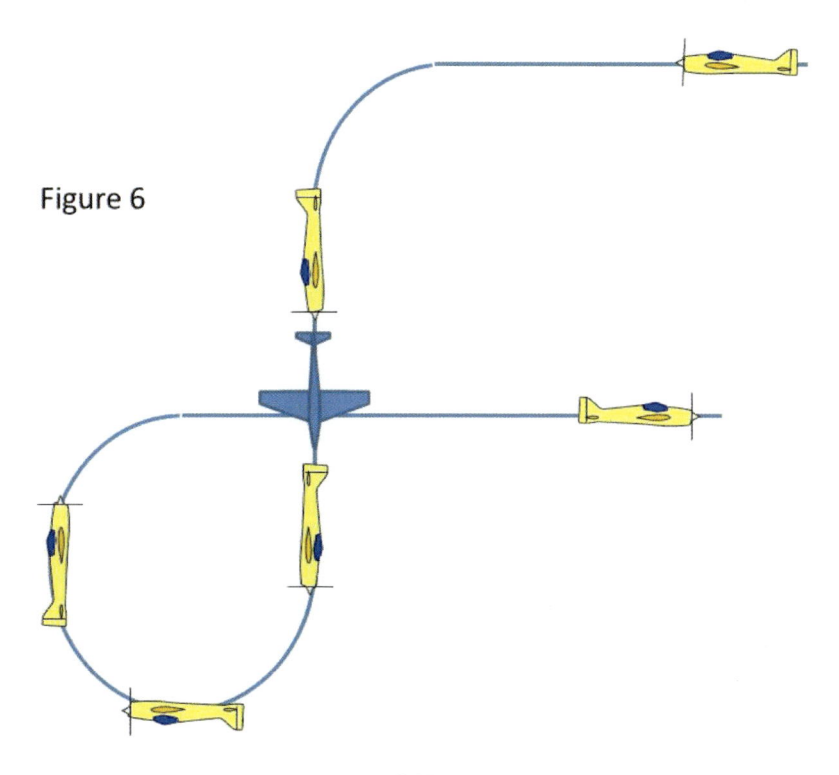

Figure 6

589. As soon as you have exited the Figure S, check heading and attitude and prepare for this manoeuvre. You need to ensure that the ¾ outside loop will be close to the edge of the Box. Make your initial quarter outside loop smooth and of a tighter radius than you used for the Figure S. Incidentally, regardless of which way you fly the loop at the bottom of the Figure 6 it is always called a Figure 6 even though, in this case, it is back to front!

590. The half roll must be centred on the downline so back to counting "one thousand etc", perform the half roll and count to the same as the line before. As soon as you reach the end of the count, smoothly commence the ¾ outside loop adding power to maintain a constant speed around the loop and reducing power as you approach the top of the looping segment. The point at which you cross the downline you flew is immaterial since all you were judged on for the downline was that the half loop was properly centred.

591. It is easy to rush the half roll as the aircraft heads vertically downwards. However, you should know by now that this is just another aerobatic manoeuvre, you know how to fly an outside loop and the aircraft has the ability to follow your commands. So, don't panic! Keep things smooth and make sure the radius of the two looping segments is the same. Remember that you need to exit this manoeuvre at mid height. So, when planning the manoeuvre, you must address that issue. If you are too high, then your spin entry will be too high which is not too much of an issue but if your spin entry is too low, then that might compromise your spin recovery. Practice is your friend.

I-12 KNIFE EDGE, EXIT INVERTED (K=4)

592. *From upright at mid height before centre perform a 1⁄4 roll (either direction) into knife edge. Past centre perform a 1⁄4 roll to exit inverted at mid height.*

593. Judging notes:

- *Knife edge should be held long enough to demonstrate controlled, sustained knife- edge flight (3 to 5 seconds as a guide).*

- *Whole manoeuvre should be centred*

Knife Edge Flight

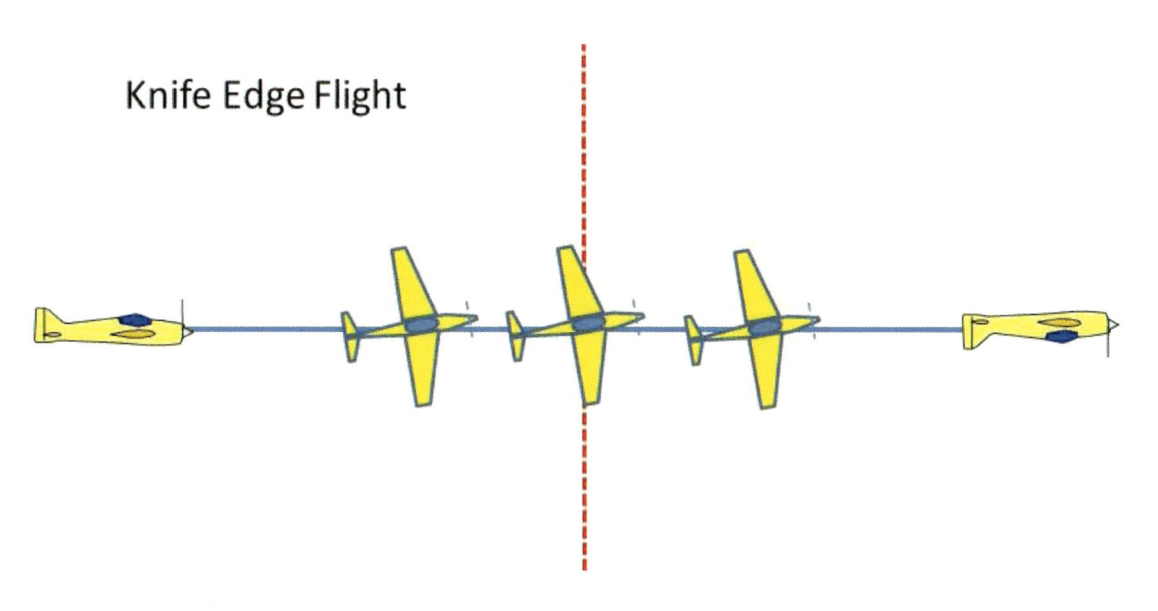

594. This is another K=4 manoeuvre. So, it's not as simple as it looks! The issues are that the Knife Edge flight must be centred and must be held for three to five seconds. This manoeuvre will show if you have managed to trim your aircraft to fly Knife Edge with minimum input from you needed. What the judges will be looking for during Knife Edge flight is the wing at exactly 90° and the height and heading remain constant. Remember to end the Knife Edge by rolling to inverted! The judges will be looking for the same rate of roll into and out of Knife Edge and no variation in height or heading while rolling.

I-13 HALF OUTSIDE LOOP (K=1)

595. *From inverted at mid height, push through half an outside loop to exit upright on the top line.*

596. *Judging notes:*

- *Radius must be constant*

Half Outside Loop

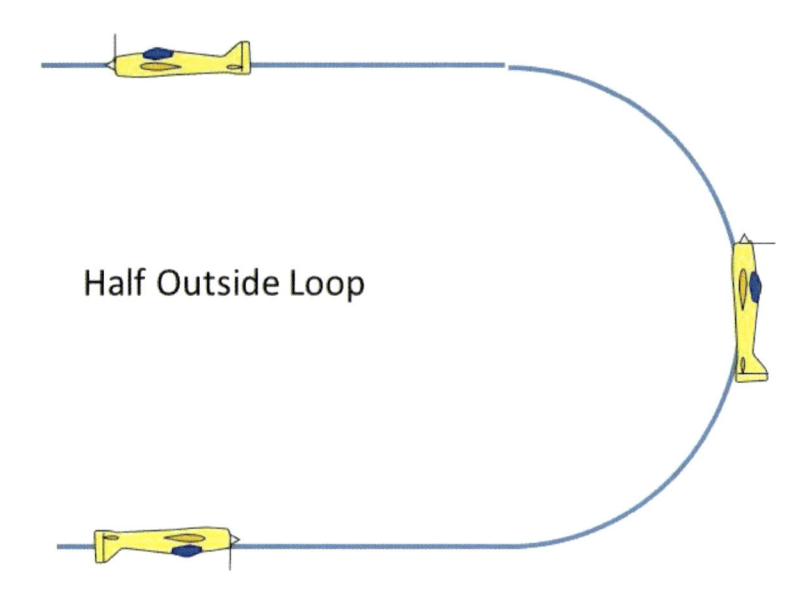

597. The point to focus on is making the half outside loop look smooth and to maintain heading and loop shape. This is a K=1 manoeuvre but you shouldn't relax as a moment's inattention can lose you a lot of easy points! Make sure you perform the outside loop as close to the Box edge as possible. This will give you the time to bleed off speed for an unhurried spin entry.

I-14 THREE TURN SPIN (K=4)

598. *From upright on the top line, on the centre line of the Box perform three consecutive spins followed by a vertical down line. At bottom of vertical down line, pull through a 1/4 loop followed by a well-defined, straight line to exit upright on the baseline.*

599. Judging notes:

- *Climbing on entry into spin: downgrade 1 point per 15 degrees*

- *Yawing before entry into spin: downgrade 1 point per 15 degrees*

- *Snap-roll entry: zero points*

- *Forced entry: severe downgrade*

- *Spin under or over rotation: downgrade 1 point per 15 degrees*

600. Speed control is the secret to being able to enter the spin in a controlled manner and on the centre line. So, as soon as you have completed the line after the Half Outside Loop, reduce the throttle, or even close it, to slow the aircraft down. Remember that the approach to the spin should be with the aircraft flying level although with an increasingly nose high attitude. This is a good time to select your Spin condition. If you have a Caller, ask them to count you down to the centre, something along the lines of "three, two, one, centre". If it looks like your aircraft is going to stall before it reaches centre, add a touch of power to keep it moving. What you want is for the aircraft to be in a position where your Caller says "one" the throttle should be closed and the aircraft's speed bled off so that at the call of "centre" the aircraft's nose drops indicating the stall. At that point, and not before, apply full up elevator, if you have not already reached it, and full rudder in the direction in which the aircraft has started to yaw. If the aircraft remains wings level as the nose drops then you have the choice of which way to spin. If given the choice, pick the direction of spin that gives you the greatest chance of stopping the spin at exactly the right point.

601. In the approach to centre, as you slow down the aircraft, you may find that the aircraft starts turning one way or the other. This is not due to weathercocking but to the fact that you have not got the aircraft's wings level. See Chapter 5 para 243 and Annex A para 525. To stop this turn, roll gently away from the turn until the turn stops. You now have your wings level so the aircraft stops turning.

602. If there is a crosswind and the aircraft heading is to windward of the required ground track, you will not be penalised for this as it is a natural consequence of correcting for the crosswind. You will not be penalised for drifting off track as you slow the aircraft either. The heading must stay constant and deviation from heading is what the judges will penalise.

603. Use the appropriate spin recovery technique you have developed to ensure that the spin stops with the aircraft's nose exactly ON TRACK. There is no requirement to spin exactly three turns and end up with the nose off track. All the drift while the aircraft is stalled and spinning is not penalised but stopping with the nose off track is penalised, as in the judging notes, at 1 point per 15 degrees off course. Hence, you almost always lose 1 point unless you are spot on!

604. The down line must be flown as wind corrected for both head and crosswinds. You should by now have a pretty good feel for the conditions during your flight and should have built up the mental picture that helps you to get the aircraft's attitude right in pitch and yaw to provide the necessary wind corrected down line. I would aim for a down line of at least two seconds so count "one thousand, two thousand". If your spin entry was high, then you could usefully fly a longer down line before the final quarter loop. While flying the down line is a good time to deselect the spin condition!

605. Don't rush the quarter loop recovery to level flight. Make it both smooth and accurate and don't forget to fly the line after the manoeuvre before you do anything else!

I-15 Racetrack Landing Sequence (K=1)

606.　On completion of the previous manoeuvre a short straight and level flight should be flown. At reduced power the model turns 180 degrees into a level or descending downwind leg and then executes a second 180 degree turn upwind for the final descending approach to the runway, touching down inside the landing zone.

607.　Landing is complete after the model has rolled 10 metres or has come to rest inside the landing zone. The landing zone is an area described by a circle of 50 metres radius or lines across a standard runway spaced 100 metres apart where the runway is 10 metres wide.

608.　Judging notes

- Model does not follow landing sequence: zero points

- Landing gear retracts or wheels come off on landing: zero points

- Model lands outside the zone: zero points

- 90 or 180 degree turns not 90 or 180 degrees: 1-2 points

- Wings not level in downwind and upwind legs: 1 point per 15 degrees

- Model does not track on runway after touchdown: 1-2 points

- Model bounces on touchdown: 1-2 points

- Model climbs and dives on downwind leg or final approach to runway: 1-2 points

- Model changes heading left or right on approach to runway: 1-2 points

609.　The landing will **not** be downgraded if:

- The pilot elects sideslip to land due to crosswind conditions, in which case the upwind wing will be low

- Wing dips due to crosswind turbulence and is corrected IMMEDIATELY

610.　The judging notes tell you all you need to know about what to focus on during the landing phase. The only issue not covered is which way to turn at the completion of the Spin. As I said in the Clubman section, consider the wind speed and direction and plan accordingly.

611. There are 10 points available for landing and you should aim to try and gain all of them! These are easy points to gain so it's worth concentrating on flying a perfect landing procedure.

612. I have yet to see a landing area marked out in competition but aim to land about 10-15 ft out from yourself and touch down close to the centre line. No judge is going to take issue with that! However, if you are finding it difficult to land in virtually the same place consistently, you need more PRACTICE!

613. Finally, as your Helper collects your model, ask the judges for any comments on your flight. It is tough enough remembering all the points they saw you get wrong straight after your flight so leaving it till later means you will never get good feedback. Do not think this is a lack of interest from the judges. They have a lot of information to sift in order to decide whether and how much to down grade each manoeuvre before it's on to the next manoeuvre. They will probably be better placed to give an overall assessment of your flight but some, no names, seem to have photographic memories!

INDEX

1ST MINI SCHEDULE 87, 155
2ND MINI SCHEDULE 88, 155
3D 11, 43, 123, 133
3RD MINI SCHEDULE 89, 156
45° SETSQUARE 162
4TH MINI SCHEDULE 90, 156
5TH MINI SCHEDULE 157
5TH MINI-SCHEDULE 91
6TH MINI SCHEDULE 91, 157
AEROBATICS 1, 9, *10*, *11*, *13*, *15*, *32*, *124*, *125*, *133*
AGENDA *134*, *135*
AILERON *19*, *20*, *21*, *22*, *53*, *66*, *67*, *68*, *69*, *70*, *71*, *72*, *77*, *83*, *96*, *102*, *106*, *130*, *135*, *146*, *147*, *148*
AILERON *53*, *147*, *148*
AILERON DIFFERENTIAL 53, 54
ANGULAR MEASUREMENT DEVICES 145
ARESTI 12, 95, 154
BASIC TRIMMING AND SETUP 15
BIPLANE 41, 152
BLACK HORSE SUPER AIR *129*, *133*
BMFA 9, 11, 13, 31, 75, 96, 125, 126
BMFA A CERTIFICATE 11
BMFA B CERTIFICATE 9
BONDAERO 136
BOUNDARY LAYER 151
BOX 12, 14, 25, 26, 27, 28, 29, 56, 57, 63, 73, 76, 79, 80, 87, 88, 89, 90, 91, 92, 93, 96, 97, 98, 100, 101, 103, 104, 105, 106, 107, 108, 109, 111, 114, 117, 118, 119, 122, 123, 124, 130, 160, 163, 165, 170, 172, 174, 176, 177
BRITISH MODEL FLYING ASSOCIATION 9, 13
BRYAN HEBERT 43, 47, 53, 150
CALLER 96, 97, 119, 120, 122, 123, *127*, 168, 177
CANALYSER 40, 134, 151
CANALYSER *25*, 40, 151
CD *127*, *128*, *139*
CENTRE OF GRAVITY 46
CG *15*, *16*, *36*, *43*, *45*, *46*, *49*, *50*, *53*, *72*, *73*, *74*, *76*, *77*, *80*, *135*, *144*, *148*

CHRISTOPHE PAYSANT LE ROUX *132*, *136*
CITRIN *134*
CLUB AEROBATIC AIRCRAFT *129*
CLUBMAN SCHEDULE 9, 93, 95, 126
CONDITION SWITCHES *147*
CONSTANT FLYING SPEED *124*
CONTEST DIRECTOR *127*
CONTROL THROWS *45*, *144*
CORRECT POSITIONING IN THE MANOEUVRE ZONE *124*
CROSS WIND *32*, *35*, *38*, *61*, *72*, *73*, *75*, *79*, *88*, *99*, *103*, *106*, *116*, *118*, *121*, *123*, *127*, *152*, *153*
CROSSWIND 30, 35, 37, 57, 61, 62, 73, 75, 77, 90, 91, 92, 97, 107, 109, 110, 115, 116, 119, 121, 152, 160, 163, 164, 167, 169, 171, 177, 179
CUBAN 8 .... *86*, *87*, *88*, *89*, *90*, *91*
CUBAN EIGHT 30, 90, 91, 115, 117, 156, 157, 169, 170, 171, 172
ELEMENT *135*
ELEVATOR *17*, *18*, *19*, *20*, *21*, *22*, *23*, *33*, *41*, *45*, *46*, *47*, *52*, *59*, *61*, *64*, *67*, *68*, *69*, *70*, *71*, *72*, *73*, *74*, *75*, *76*, *77*, *80*, *81*, *83*, *89*, *113*, *121*, *133*, *135*, *141*, *144*, *146*, *147*, *148*, *149*, *151*
ELEVATOR *45*, *53*, *67*, *68*, *147*, *148*
ELEVATOR AND RUDDER ROLLS *68*
ELEVATOR ONLY ROLLING *67*
ENGINE/MOTOR THRUST LINE *50*
EPILOGUE *135*
EXPONENTIAL *82*
F3A *9*, *11*, *12*, *13*, *45*, *74*, *123*, *129*, *130*, *131*, *132*, *133*, *136*, *139*, *141*, *144*, *151*
FAI SPORTING CODE *13*, *32*, *123*
FAI WORLD CUP 9
FANTASISTA 70 .... *131*
FÉDÉRATION AÉRONAUTIQUE INTERNATIONALE 9
FIGURE 6 174
FIGURE S 172, 174
FIRST COMPETITION *127*
FLIGHT MODES *147*

FLYING THE LINE	27, 86
FOUR POINT ROLL	88, 155, 163, 165, 166
FULL ROLL	163, 169
GANGSTER 63 LITE	133
GBRCAA	9, 10, 11, 13, 43, 44, 93, 95, 96, 123, 124, 125, 127, 136, 139, 144, 159, 160
GBRCAA TRIMMING GUIDE	43
GEOMETRIC ACCURACY	123
GREAT BRITAIN RADIO CONTROL AEROBATIC ASSOCIATION	9
HALF CUBAN 8	88, 92
HALF CUBAN EIGHT	88, 101, 103, 104, 155
HALF OUTSIDE LOOP	176, 177
HALF REVERSE CUBAN EIGHT	87, 88, 89, 90, 91, 92, 98, 99, 101, 103, 104, 155
HALF ROLL	92, 103, 107, 110, 112, 114, 115, 166, 174
HALF SQUARE LOOP	92, 117
HAMMERHEAD	55, 72
HEAD WIND	60, 72, 73, 74, 75, 116
HEADWIND	30, 36, 60, 61, 99, 108, 116, 162, 164, 168
HINGES	45, 146
HUMPTY BUMP	90, 91, 92, 107, 108, 114, 115, 156, 157, 171, 172
IC OR ELECTRIC POWER	136
IMMELMAN TURN	22, 23, 106
IMMELMANN TURN	104, 106, 166, 168
INCIDENCE METER	52
INTERMEDIATE SCHEDULE	10, 12, 159, 172
INTERNATIONAL 2 MTR SIZE	130
INVERTED FLIGHT	91, 110, 155, 157
INVERTED FLYING	55, 79
INVERTED FLYING	86
IRVINE 53	131
JUDGING	32, 57, 71, 96, 97, 123, 124, 126
JUDGING	123
KNIFE EDGE	53, 82, 175
LANDING SEQUENCE	120
LATERAL BALANCE	50
LINE AFTER	28, 32, 88, 93, 98, 106, 114, 116, 117, 121, 160, 162, 177, 178
LINE BEFORE	28, 32, 90, 91, 103, 106, 108, 114, 116, 174, 178
LOADED DICE	132, 133
LOOP	20, 21, 22, 23, 24, 25, 31, 33, 36, 37, 38, 39, 40, 57, 58, 59, 61, 62, 63, 64, 75, 77, 80, 87, 88, 90, 91, 96, 98, 99, 100, 106, 113, 116, 118, 119, 120, 122, 127, 131, 149
LOOPS	55, 57, 98
MAC	46
MAJESTIC	132, 133
MIKE CHIPCHASE	43
MINI SCHEDULES	10, 85
MIXES	83
MIXING	82
NATIONAL CENTRE	125
NEGATIVE STABILITY	47
NEIL WILLIAMS	10
NEUTRAL POSITION	44, 141
NEUTRAL STABILITY	47
NORMAL SPEED ROLL	67
NPOD	125, 126, 127, 139
OUTSIDE LOOP	50, 56, 63, 89, 92, 112, 113, 118, 168, 169, 170, 171, 172, 173, 174, 175, 176
OUTSIDE LOOP	112
PETE GOLDSMITH	43
PITCH	19
POINT ROLLS	67, 71
POSITIVELY STABLE	47
PRACTICE	11, 13, 14, 27, 36, 43, 74, 88, 91, 93, 103, 106, 122, 128, 139, 152
PRACTICE ROUTINES	85
PRECISION AEROBATICS	9, 11, 13, 20, 24, 35, 43, 64, 65, 67, 68, 71, 82, 123, 139, 149
PRECISION AEROBATICS/PATTERN FLYING	11
PRE-SET MIXES	83
PUSHROD CONNECTORS	44, 142
RACETRACK LANDING SEQUENCE	178
RACETRACK TAKE-OFF SEQUENCE	160
RATES	18, 82
REVERSE CUBAN EIGHT	100
ROLL	19, 21, 22, 23, 67, 71, 72, 92, 117
ROLLS	55, 67, 68
RUDDER	17, 18, 19, 22, 23, 32, 34, 40, 41, 45, 52, 53, 62, 66, 67, 68, 69, 70, 71, 72, 73, 74, 76, 77, 80, 82, 85, 86, 87, 89, 90, 91, 92, 98, 102, 106, 113, 117, 118, 123, 130, 141, 145, 146, 147, 151
RUDDER	53, 68, 83, 145, 147, 148

SBACH 342	*133*
SERVO CENTRING	*45, 144*
SERVO MATCHING	*83*
SERVO SETUP	*44, 141*
SIZE MATCHING TO THE MANOEUVRE ZONE	124
SLOW ROLL	*67, 71, 88, 89, 101, 102, 103*
SLOW ROLL	*67*
SLOW ROLL	*89, 101, 103, 104, 156, 157*
SNAP OR FLICK ROLLS	*67*
SPIN	*71, 76, 77, 78, 79, 82, 96, 119, 120, 121, 122, 146, 147, 152*
SPINNING	*55, 76, 119*
SPLIT S	*23, 89, 104, 106, 108, 156, 169, 171*
SPRING TENSION	*82*
SQUARE LOOP	*51, 92, 157, 167, 168*
STALL	*30, 39, 72, 74, 75, 76, 77, 78, 79, 82, 86, 111, 123, 146, 153*
STALL TURN	*55, 72, 101, 111, 157, 163*
STALLING	*55, 75*
STICK ALERT	*82*
STICK MODEL	*31*
STICK POSITION SWITCHES	*82*
STICK SWITCH FUNCTION	147
TAKE OFF	97
THE AEROBATIC BOX	25, 26
THE CLUBMAN SCHEDULE	95
THE LINE	25
THE LINE	20, 26, 30, 62, 75, 85, 87, 89, 90, 91, 92
THE ROLE OF THE CALLER	*122*
THREE TURN SPIN	*92, 119, 177*
THROTTLE CURVE	*65*
THROTTLE CURVES	*83*
THROTTLE PIPE	*131*
TOP RUDDER	*69, 70*
TOP, BOTTOM AND MIDDLE LINES	*56*
TORQUE	*44, 141*
TRANSMITTER FUNCTIONS	*55, 82*
TRAY MOUNTED TRANSMITTER	*81*
TRIANGLE OF VELOCITIES	*152*
TRIANGULAR LOOP	*161*
TRIANGULATION TRIMMING	*150*
TRIM STEPS	*47*
TURNAROUND SCHEDULES	*14*
USE OF RUDDER	*55, 66*
USE OF THE THROTTLE	*55, 64*
VERTICAL DOWNLINE	43, 50, 51, 52, 123, 147
VERTICAL UPLINE	*52, 118, 119*
VOICE ALARMS	*83*
WEATHERCOCK	*78*
WEATHERCOCKING	*55, 78, 152*
WING INCIDENCE	*52*
WORLD CHAMPION	*132, 136*
WOT 4	9, 15, 43, *46*, 96, *130*, 131, *139*, 149
YAW	19
ZERO GRAVITY	*149*

Printed in Great Britain
by Amazon